THE LIGHTING BOOK

THE LIGHTING

BOOK

A Complete Guide To Lighting Your Home

Deyan Sudjic

MITCHELL BEAZLEY

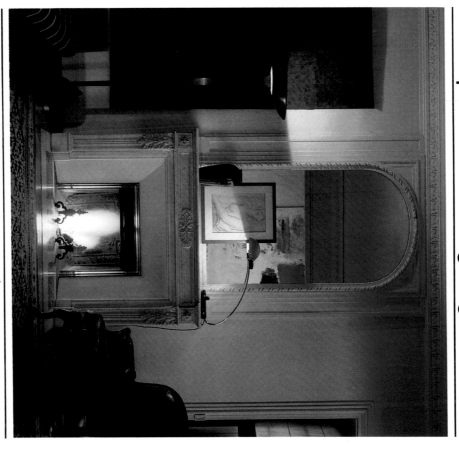

THE LIGHTING BOOK
Deyan Sudjic

Edited and designed by Mitchell Beazley International Ltd, Artists House, 14–15 Manette Street, London W1V 5LB

Executive Editor Robert Saxton
Executive Art Editor Jackie Small
Editor Carolyn Ryden
Assistant Art Editor Spencer Holbrook
Picture Research Diana Korchien
Electrical Consultant Mike Lawrence
Illustrations Mulkern and Rutherford, Trevor Lawrence and Pavel Kostal
Production Peter Phillips

ISBN 0 85533 577 7

Text filmset by Tradespools Ltd, Frome, Somerset, England
Reproduction by Gilchrist Brothers Ltd, Leeds, England
Printed in the Netherlands by Koninklijke Smeets Offset b.v., Weert

Contents

Introduction 6

Lighting Basics
The Nature of Light 8
Measuring Light 10
Light and Our Surroundings 12
Light and Our Eyes 14
Light, Form and Texture 16
Lighting Psychology 18
The History of Lighting 20
22

Sources of Light
Choosing the Light Source 26
The Tungsten Bulb 28
Tungsten-halogen Lamps 29
The Fluorescent Tube 32
Miniature Fluorescents 33
Other Lamp Types 34
35

The Hardware
Choosing the Fitting 36
Ceiling-mounted Downlighters 38
Spotlights 48
Pendants 52
Fluorescent Fittings 58
Wall Lights 66
Table Lights and Task Lights 68
Floor Lights 76
Oddities 86
Exterior Lights 94
96

The Art of Lighting
Task Lighting 100
Background Lighting 102
104

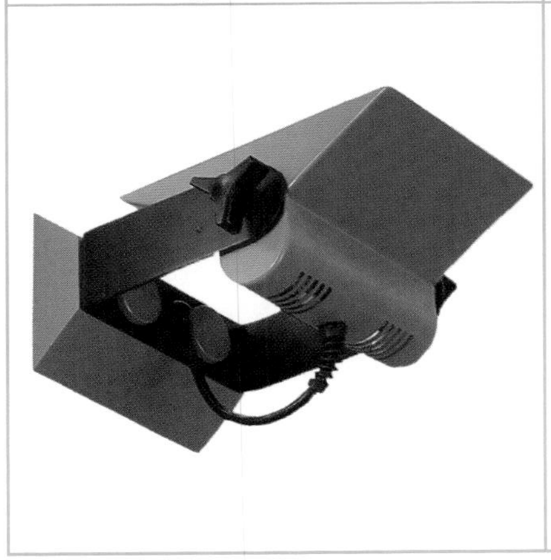

The Decorative Approach 106
Highlighting Walls 108
Creating a Style 110
Display Lighting 112
Lighting for Plants and Flowers 116
Fittings as Furniture 118
Planning a Scheme 120
Making Do 124

Room by Room
Entrances and Passageways 126
The Kitchen 128
The Bathroom 132
Living Rooms 138
Bedrooms 142
The Dining Room 148
Children's Rooms 154
Studies and Libraries 160
Gardens, Patios and Pools 162
164

Practicalities
Electricity in the Home 168
Materials and Techniques 170
Plug-in Lighting 172
Fixed Lighting 174
Cleaning and Maintenance 176
Employing Others 182
Glossary 182
Common Lamp Types 183
Useful Addresses 185
187

Index 189

Acknowledgments 192

Introduction

Lighting has long been the most neglected aspect of home design. Despite the increasing attention given to furniture, colour, fabrics and finishes, and the way they set the style and mood of an interior, lighting has continued to be dominated by the despotism of the single pendant light dangling right in the middle of each room. This unsatisfactory arrangement has its origins in the earliest installations of electric lighting at the turn of the century. Today, there is no excuse for such an inflexible approach. The baleful presence of that single pendant can undo any amount of care lavished on interior design. On the other hand, a thoughtful, sensitive lighting scheme can supply the warmth and mood that turn an anonymous interior into a real home.

Until recently, lighting has remained a highly specialized skill, with a dense thicket of technical jargon to repulse the outsider. Many of the most exciting fittings have been available only from specialist outlets. But now, the situation is beginning to change. The public is becoming more informed, and retailers are stocking an ever expanding range. I hope this book will accelerate the trend.

Lighting is a technical subject that progresses in tandem with the development of new kinds of light source. However, this is only part of the picture. It is important not to lose sight of the fact that lighting is also an art, and that to master it properly we need to apply a range of creative skills with taste and discrimination. *The Lighting Book* brings the technical and aesthetic sides of the subject together for the first time, offering new ways of looking at the way we light our homes.

Deyan Sudjic

Lighting Basics

To use lighting in the home to best advantage, it helps to understand something of the elementary physics of light. Taking this as its main theme, the first section of the book looks at the wavelength composition of light, explains how we see colour and goes on to show how different light sources vary in their colour qualities. The importance of shadows for revealing form and texture is also discussed, and some thought-provoking ideas are offered on the psychological aspects of lighting. The section concludes with a brief historical survey of artificial light sources.

Our perceptions of what the world is like depend, for the most part, upon light. When the sources of light change, the way our surroundings appear to us changes with them. Daylight filtering into a room through a window fluctuates constantly, varying in its intensity, its direction, and the way in which it renders colours throughout the day. For example, from the plain white light of midday, daylight may modulate to the lurid yellow cast of a stormy afternoon, and then by imperceptible degrees to the monochrome gloom of twilight.

Similarly, the qualities of artificial light vary widely in character, depending on the type of bulb that is used. Some kinds, such as the familiar domestic tungsten-filament bulb, produce a light that is close to daylight, although yellower. Others, such as sodium streetlights, exhibit an unnatural-looking yellow tinge that would be quite unsuitable in a domestic interior.

To understand these variations in the quality of light, it helps to know something about light's fundamental nature. Briefly defined, light is the visible part of the spectrum of electro-magnetic radiation that all things emit or reflect, to a greater or lesser extent. In other words, light, like heat, is a form of energy. The sun, which is the primary source of our light, pours out energy all the time in invisible waves. A tiny fraction of this energy is reflected off objects and decoded by the human eye as light, which makes the objects "visible". Waves of light may vary in intensity, producing stronger or weaker vibrations: these variations are perceived as differences in "brightness".

Light and colour
Each colour in the visible spectrum corresponds with light of a particular wavelength – a term denoting the distance between successive vibrations in each wave of light. Average midday sunlight is a balanced mixture of all these wavelengths, combining all colours of the spectrum (from red through orange, yellow, green, blue and indigo to violet) to make "white light". We see the colour of an object when light of mixed wavelengths is reflected selectively into the eye from the object's surface. Depending on the

THE ELECTROMAGNETIC SPECTRUM

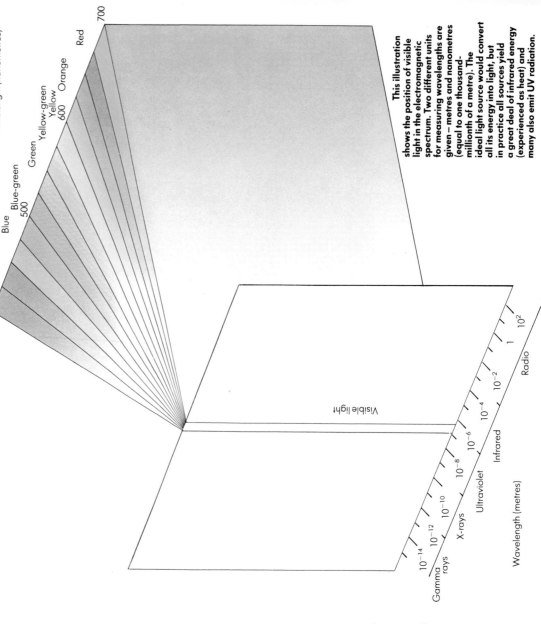

This illustration shows the position of visible light in the electromagnetic spectrum. Two different units for measuring wavelengths are given – metres and nanometres (equal to one thousand-millionth of a metre). The ideal light source would convert all its energy into light, but in practice all sources yield a great deal of infrared energy (experienced as heat) and many also emit UV radiation.

Wavelength (nanometres)

Red — 700
Orange
Yellow — 600
Yellow-green
Green
Blue-green — 500
Blue
Violet — 400

Gamma rays — 10⁻¹⁴
10⁻¹²
X-rays — 10⁻¹⁰
10⁻⁸
Ultraviolet — 10⁻⁶
Visible light
Infrared — 10⁻⁴
10⁻²
Radio — 1 — 10²

Wavelength (metres)

HOW WE SEE COLOURS
The retina of the eye contains three kinds of light sensors, which detect different ranges of light frequencies, roughly corresponding to the red, green and blue parts of the spectrum. All other colours can be produced by combining light of these three "primary" colours in various amounts. All three primary colours combine to give white light.

A white porcelain bowl looks white because it reflects all the wavelengths from all parts of the spectrum – reds, greens and blues. This mixture, reaching the eye, looks white. A red armchair looks red because it absorbs most of the light waves reaching it (the greens and blues), but reflects those in the red part of the spectrum. If daylight were substituted for the tungsten domestic light, the whites would look cooler and the reds less intense. However, such discrepancies are not always apparent to the eye.

composition of that surface, some colours of the spectrum may be absorbed, others reflected. A red object is one whose surface reflects wavelengths in the red part of the spectrum but absorbs wavelengths of other colours.

Artificial light sources emit electromagnetic radiation (both visible and invisible), just as the sun does. Some sources, such as gas lamps, do this by combustion, giving off both heat and light. In modern times the more usual way to create light is to pass electrical current through the filament of a lamp or to electrically excite the atoms in a gas- or vapour-filled envelope. However, unless the radiation emitted approximates to that of the sun, the light produced will have a different mix of wavelengths from daylight. And if this difference is especially marked, the light may appear unnatural or even uncomfortable—an effect that lighting designers seek to avoid when their aim is to create a homely environment.

The importance of ultraviolet

The ultraviolet part of the spectrum is also of great significance in lighting technology, as it is the key to an understanding of how fluorescent tubes work. Fluorescence is a property possessed by phosphors, enabling them to change the wavelength of invisible UV radiation to those of visible radiation. When an electric discharge is passed through the fluorescent lamp, the UV rays emitted excite a phosphor coating inside the glass tube, causing it to glow with a bright, uniform light.

REFRACTION
When light falls on a transparent object, most of the rays are bent or "refracted" through that object. This is the principle of the prism, which is used to demonstrate the composition of white light. Different wavelengths of light reaching the prism are refracted at different angles, so that the light is broken down into its basic components—the colours of the spectrum. The glass droplets of a chandelier similarly refract the light passing through them, which is why chandeliers often seem fringed with colour.

In a specific location, we can describe the light in either of two ways: by quantity or by quality. Being mathematically measurable, quantity receives its full share of attention from engineers, although it is by no means adequate on its own as a way of assessing a lighting scheme.

Quantity

The intensity of a light source is measured in candelas (Latin for "candles"). However, for practical design purposes, we often need to assess the amount of light falling upon a particular surface. This is known as illuminance, and varies according to many factors – for example, the number of lamps used, their total wattage, their distance from the surface, and whether or not they are modified by a shade, diffuser or similar method of control. To express illuminance, we make use of a unit of light output – the lumen. For a particular kind of interior, we can say that the recommended illuminance is so many lumens per unit area. In metric units illuminance is measured in lumens per square metre, or "lux". In Imperial units (used in the USA) the measurement is in lumens per square foot, or "footcandles" (fc). The ratio of footcandles to lux is 1:10.76.

You can use an ordinary photographic light meter, or a camera with a built-in meter, to measure luminance very approximately. Set the film speed dial at ASA 100 and aim the meter at a white card positioned on the plane where you want to take the measurement (for example, a tabletop). Read off the shutter speed required for an aperture setting of f/4, and interpret this as a whole number instead of a fraction – for example, treat 1/60 as 60. This gives roughly the number of foot-candles. Multiply by 10 to convert to lux.

The colour of lighting

We have already noted that different light sources have different characteristics, which may or may not be obvious to the eye. These differences need to be considered in two distinct ways. First, there is the "colour appearance" of a light source – whether it looks warm or cool, yellowish or white to the observer. Second, there is "colour rendering" – the effect of a light source on the colours of an object it illuminates. These terms are not interchangeable, but relate to quite separate concepts, which are often confused. (Colour rendering is described in detail on pages 14–15.)

The sun, oil lamps, gas lamps, candles and tungsten-filament light bulbs are alike in being incandescent: they emit light as a by-product of heat. All incandescent light sources can be graded according to their "colour temperature" (rated in kelvins), which affects their colour appearance. To grasp the basic idea, it helps to think of an iron bar, which will change colour as it is heated. At fairly low temperatures the bar will glow red; then, with more heat, it will change to orange, through yellow, to white. This process of visible change corresponds to a rise in colour temperature. The colour temperature of a light source rises as the proportion of blue wavelenths in the light increases. Thus, the warm, yellow glow of a candle flame will probably have a rating of about 1,900 kelvins; while the illumination in a daylit room out of the direct sun may be provided solely by blue light from the sky, which can give a

SAME ROOM, DIFFERENT LIGHT
The three kitchen views here show how light sources have widely varying colour characteristics. Daylight from a cloudy sky filtering down through a skylight looks decidedly bluish (1). Switching on a tungsten light creates a golden hue (2). But now add fluorescent lighting from under the cupboard, and the lighting colour changes again, cancelling most of the tungsten yellow to create a much cooler effect (3).

We tend to be more aware of the warm tones of tungsten lighting when daylight is also present in the room as a comparison. For example, in this picture of an understair area (right), the yellowish patches of light from tungsten downlighters contrast strikingly with the afternoon light outside the window.

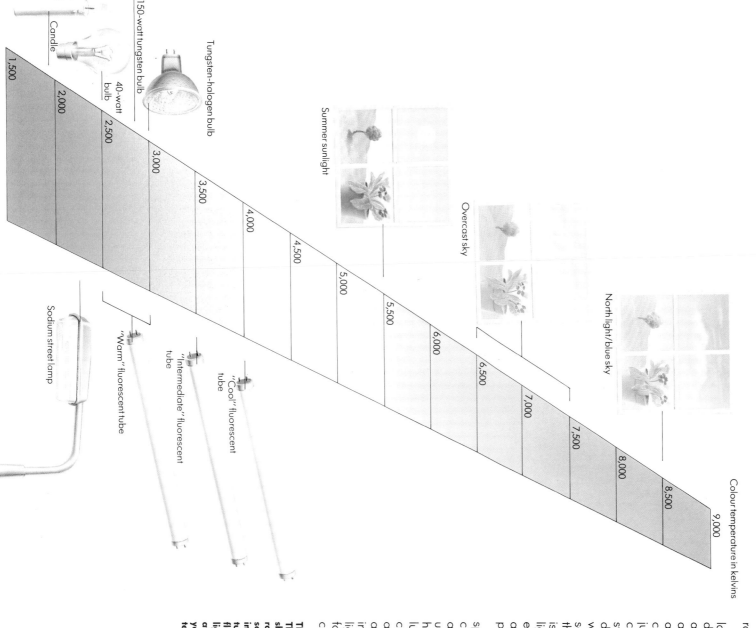

Candle

150-watt tungsten bulb

40-watt bulb

Tungsten-halogen bulb

Summer sunlight

Overcast sky

North light/blue sky

Sodium street lamp

"Warm" fluorescent tube

"Intermediate" fluorescent tube

"Cool" fluorescent tube

1,500
2,000
2,500
3,000
3,500
4,000
4,500
5,000
5,500
6,000
6,500
7,000
7,500
8,000
8,500
9,000

Colour temperature in kelvins

rating of 9,000 kelvins or higher.

Tungsten-filament lighting, having a lower colour temperature than daylight, is warmer and yellower. When a room is lit by tungsten-filament bulbs at night, the yellowish glow may not be apparent, because the eye tends to compensate for colour differences, judging a wide range of lighting conditions as "normal". However, try switching on a tungsten table lamp in daylight: a pool of localized yellow light will become apparent around the light source, emphasized by contrast with the cooler daylight. As a general rule, it is inadvisable to mix warm and cool light sources in this way. In a living environment, such conflicts of colour appearance look unsettling to most people.

Fluorescent tubes have their own special properties that rather complicate the picture. We generally associate fluorescents with a cold unflattering light, which looks dull and harsh at low levels of illuminance (300 lux or lower). However, colour-corrected fluorescents are also available. These offer a warmer light, and are particularly useful for installations that supplement natural light with artificial light for daytime use – for example, to dispel gloom in dark corners.

THE COLOURS OF LIGHT
This colour-temperature chart shows kelvin ratings for a range of different light sources – natural, incandescent (candles and tungsten-filament bulbs), fluorescent and sodium. The light given off has a bluish cast at high colour temperatures, a yellowish cast at low colour temperatures.

The colour-rendering capacity of a light source – the way a light affects the look of colours in a room – depends on the composition of the spectrum of light emitted. Tungsten-filament lamps are biased towards the red end of the spectrum, and thus bring out red tones but suppress greens and blues. This is somewhat different from the way daylight renders colours. However, there are other kinds of artificial light that differ even more markedly from daylight in their colour-rendering capacity. The extreme cases all occur outside the home. Street lights are the most obvious example. The main aim here is to throw maximum light onto the road or pavement surface for minimum

cost. This requirement is satisfied by the low-pressure sodium lamp, which emits only yellow light, making yellow objects appear yellow, but showing everything else as black or shades of grey. Sodium lamps do their job on the road, but would obviously be totally unsuitable for an interior.

Considerations of colour rendering can be of critical importance to all designers of interiors, however modest a scale they are working on. To put the matter plainly, things look different under different lighting types. A furnishing fabric or a wallpaper examined under the fluorescent lights of a department store may look significantly different from the same material seen under tungsten lighting

at home. Colours that seem to match each other in daylight may look uncomfortable together in artificial light. It is hard to predict these effects exactly, so if possible you should experiment with colour swatches or offcuts before committing yourself to a choice of furnishing or coverings for the home. It is too much to expect colours to look exactly the same by night and by day, but certainly they should look equally acceptable.

Fluorescent lights in the home are the ones most likely to cause colour shock. However, manufacturers or stockists of fluorescents will provide useful guidance on the colour-rendering properties of different tube types. "Artificial Daylight" tubes give

the closest approximation to daylight. Research of this kind is particularly important when planning fluorescent lighting for kitchens. A misguided choice of tube for kitchen work surfaces could lead to some singularly unappetizing-looking dishes.

Light distribution

There is another important aspect of the way lighting and interior design interact with each other, and this is to do with how light reflects off surfaces, affecting the total distribution of light within a room. Walls and ceilings reflect varying amounts of the light that falls on them according to whether they are light-toned or dark-toned. The proportion of light that is

1 In a scheme that relies on concealed, indirect lighting, it is essential to choose the wall and ceiling finishes with particular care. Here, a high-reflectance ceiling works with pale-coloured walls to create a high level of overall illumination.

2 Apple-green walls in this traditional-style living room reflect only a small proportion of light from shaded table fittings. Paler walls would have thrown back more light, but with some sacrifice in the atmosphere, which here is pleasantly mellow and intimate.

The principle of reflectance

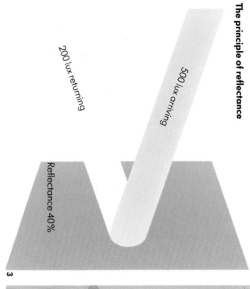

500 lux arriving

200 lux returning

Reflectance 40%

3

5

reflected off a particular surface is known to specialists as its "reflectance", normally expressed as a percentage. Whatever we think of all-white rooms, there is no doubt that they spread the light around evenly and efficiently. A white-painted surface typically has a reflectance of about 70 percent, compared with 60 percent for a cream surface. In large rooms the walls have less importance than the ceiling, which to provide a good overall lighting level must effectively reflect light downward into the middle of the room; this means giving the ceiling a high-reflectance finish. A dark-toned ceiling in a large room will soak up light like blotting paper. However, in a small room pale walls will often be sufficient to maintain an adequate distribution of light, so a dark ceiling may be chosen.

In the planning of a colour scheme, daylight should also enter into the calculations. If the sunlight comes into the room solely from side windows, a dark ceiling may cause the room to look gloomy. Normally, a pale floor covering is desirable to reflect window light entering a room obliquely. For sunny climates and high-rise buildings, there are special considerations. For example, white walls may tend to create an uncomfortable brightness, while a dark-coloured window wall may present too glaring a contrast with the sunlight outside.

A comparative sequence of pictures that illustrate the varying colour-rendering characteristics of different light sources.

3 Daylight: the reference point by which we judge the naturalness of colour rendering.

4 Tungsten lighting: the usual way to light a living room. White surfaces look much yellower than in daylight, while the reds of the flowers and the yellow of the cushion fabric are noticeably enriched.

5 "Cool" fluorescent lighting: the colours have acquired a cold, bluish tinge that most people find unattractive.

Some understanding of how our eyes react to different levels of illumination is essential when planning a lighting scheme for the home. Using this knowledge, you can avoid the pitfalls of intense contrast and glare – two of the most troublesome problems of interior lighting.

Our eyes can function within enormous variations of illumination, from the 100,000 lux of bright sunshine to the 0.5 lux of moonlight. However, they need time to adapt to extreme changes in brightness – a few moments to adjust from generally light to fairly dark conditions, and rather longer to adapt when moving from intense sunlight to a dark interior. Lighting in the home should be arranged so that the eye does not have to cope with too great a change in lighting levels in too brief a time. For example, where you have two neighbouring areas with very different levels of illumination (such as a brightly lit living room and a dark corridor), you may need to create a "buffer zone" of transitional lighting in which the eye can adjust gradually from one level to the other.

Another danger is that of monotony. We are all accustomed to the constant fluctuations of natural daylight, and to its patterns of light and shade. Artificial lighting schemes should also be variable if they are not to feel oppressive and monotonous. A room with a calculated arrangement of different lighting levels not only looks more interesting, but also allows the eyes to relax by glancing periodically from brighter to darker areas –

provided, of course, that the contrast is carefully controlled. And if, like daylight, the lighting is flexible, with a wide range of permutations to suit varying needs and moods, then you can be sure that the room will never pall.

Glare

Glare occurs when the eye has to cope with a light source that is much brighter than the overall lighting in a room. There are two kinds of glare, defined according to the physiological effect. "Discomfort glare" causes eyestrain. Glare so strong that it actually prevents us from performing a specific task because of impaired vision is called "disability glare".

There are various lighting situations that can lead to discomfort glare. One area of a room may be much brighter than others, so that the eye has to cope with two lighting levels simultaneously. Eyestrain can also occur when a bright light is positioned against a dark background, or when a naked bulb of medium to high wattage is used in a room. Often the strain put upon the eye by working in such circumstances

1 Glare from reflections in a shiny tabletop is a common difficulty in dining areas. Here, the view from the head of the marble table includes a distracting mirror image of windows. Similar effects can occur with tables of polished wood. The offending light source can be either a window or a pendant above the table.

2 In this city apartment, the lighting has been carefully planned to prevent accidental glimpses of naked light sources from normal viewing angles – and also to eliminate reflected lights on the glass picture covers.

3

becomes evident only after prolonged exposure. It varies from one individual to another, and also changes with age.

Disability glare usually occurs when an area close to your line of vision is of much higher luminance than the object you are looking at. The eye obeys what is known as "phototropic" impulse: it is drawn instinctively to the brighter light, adapting to it so that the less bright object is no longer discernible in detail. For example, sunlight streaming through a window may prevent us from picking out detail in a picture near the window on the same wall.

One way to avoid glare is to reduce the strength of the potentially troublesome light source. The optimum wattage will vary according to the background colour of the room. The darker the background, the lower the bulb strength demanded. As a general rule, lamps above 25 watts will be too bright to be viewed directly by the eye. When ample light is required, one or two very bright lamps will usually give a less pleasing result than more lamps of lower wattage.

There are several other ways to combat glare. For example, you can use a shade to diffuse a lamp, or you can change the lamp's position so that an object you want to be able to see clearly receives the light indirectly—for example, reflected from a pale-coloured wall or ceiling. When planning a lighting scheme, pay particular attention to the effect of glass or metal, or areas with a high-gloss finish, as these surfaces often cause glare by reflecting a bright light source.

3 Bare bulbs are not always glaring, but can sometimes add a touch of sparkle to an interior. The secret is to choose low-wattage lamps, as in the ceiling canopy of this bedroom. Had this been a house in the country, the reflection of the bulbs and television in the window might have been unfortunate. However, in this situation the reflections blend in perfectly well with the panoramic view of city lights.

17

Aside from its colour qualities, the property of light that has the most direct relevance to interior design is its capacity to show off form and texture. Properly used, a light source can emphasize the three-dimensional character of, for example, an area of traditional-style plasterwork moulding or a statuette or bust. Conversely, light can also be used to give things a two-dimensional appearance. The key to these effects is the way we interpret shadows. We understand a thing's shape and texture by the interplay of light and shadow on and around it. An object or relief surface without shadows will look flat.

To create well-defined shadows and highlights, a light source needs to be direct and fairly strong. The brighter and more concentrated the beam, the more dramatic the effect will be. We need to bear this idea in mind when

planning how to light a sculpted object. A narrow spotlight beam will create deep, sharp-edged shadows for eye-catching theatricality and an emphatic sense of form. On the other hand, we may prefer a more diffused light source (bounced from the ceiling perhaps) that will throw a softer, more natural light. Lighting direction may also be a factor in determining whether an effect is theatrical or understated.

Different surfaces, materials and textures are enhanced by different lighting strategies. For example, sidelighting accentuates the smooth surface and shine of polished metals, and may also suit certain high-relief surfaces, such as a stone chimney breast. Glass objects can appear dramatically luminous when lit from above or below. When shape is the distinctive feature of an object, consider backlighting to create a silhouette.

1 Upward light from a table lamp gives soft modelling to the delicate plasterwork on the walls above. In the same room, a well-placed mini spotlight (also on the corner table) exploits shadows in a more obvious way – by casting a shadow pattern of the metalwork sculpture onto the wall over the fireplace.

2 This globe light emphasizes both the volume and texture of a vaulted ceiling. Without the deep shadow on the left, we would lose the strong sense of structure.

LIGHTING A 3D OBJECT

To demonstrate some of the options for lighting a sculptural object, the same bust was illuminated by six different lighting setups, as shown in the diagram (left). The results are illustrated below. Note how both the concentration and direction of the lighting influence the effect. Another factor is distance: the farther the lamp, the softer the shadows.

As a rule, the lighting direction we find most natural is diagonally from one side, at around 15°–45° to the horizontal: this corresponds to our experience of daylight through a window. Decidedly unnatural effects can be obtained by using vertical or deeply angled downlighting or uplighting – a technique that may be more appropriate for an abstract sculpture than a figurative one.

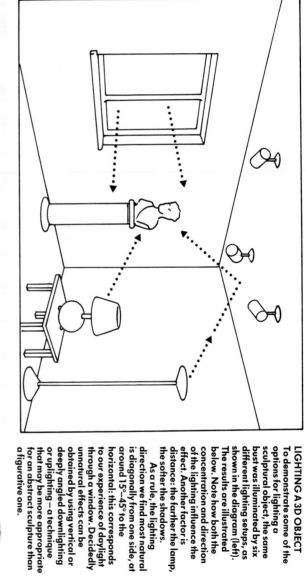

Daylight from window

Spotlight above and in front

Indirect light from uplighter

Spotlight above and at right

Diffused light from table lamp

Spotlight above and behind

Lighting satisfies emotional as well as physical needs. We still see light as a source and sign of life, with deep connotations of security, comfort and warmth, as underlined by the sight of lights in an empty night landscape, indicating a dwelling or settlement. This atavistic attitude toward light has scarcely diminished with our increasing sophistication and ability to manipulate light in our surroundings. Deep down, fear of the dark remains one of the most widespread human anxieties. At night, children, and many adults too, appreciate knowing that there is a light switch close to hand. It is as well to keep such emotional aspects in mind when thinking about lighting for the home.

The exterior appearance of a house at night conveys both psychological and practical meanings. On the practical side, a brightly lit exterior makes it more difficult for intruders to break in unobserved, and lights the way for more welcome visitors to find the door. No less importantly, a warm glow pouring out through windows plays a large part in creating first impressions for a nighttime visitor. Even when the expected guest is prevented from seeing inside by drawn curtains or blinds, the effect is always inviting. A light in the porch or lobby reinforces the friendly impact, acting as a sign of welcome, a statement of place and home. Conversely, a house without lights at night often looks empty and forbidding, as if there were no life inside.

Indoors, too, the emotional dimension should never be overlooked. Lighting is of central importance in establishing mood. Just as sunny days can create a feeling of elation, similarly an attractive indoor lighting scheme, rich in contrasts and points of interest,

can have a stimulating effect. Gloom, on the other hand, whether indoors or out, can trigger a depression. A flexible scheme with plenty of options allows us, within limits, to match the light to our changing moods. Sometimes, lighting of a particular character makes it easier or more enjoyable to perform a specific activity. For example, while preparing a meal we need a high level of lighting (but not too harsh) that spurs us on to brisk efficiency. But while consuming the meal we may choose candle-flickering intimacy or chandeliered formality, and certainly we are unlikely to want the same bright lighting in which we did the cooking.

As a general rule, bright fluorescent tubes have a cool, efficient feel, conducive to work, while low-level tungsten lighting creates a relaxed, intimate atmosphere. We often use a shaded tungsten light to create a cosy

pool of light in a way that recreates the glow of a hearth. As a source of both light and heat, the hearth was for many centuries the focal point in the home. Perhaps because the emotional pull of the hearth is still strong, people often use lighting to emphasize a fireplace, or even to simulate one. In a room with subdued lighting, one or two tungsten table lamps may act as miniature hearths, drawing people toward them.

Also of interest is the way lighting can affect our appearance and behaviour. By carefully adjusting the lights to control the shadows and highlights cast on people's faces, we can encourage conviviality at parties. People can actually be made to look more attractive. However, if the lights glare into our eyes or throw deep shadows over our faces, the effect will be unsettling: everyone will be put on their guard and conversation may flag.

2

1

1 A traditional-style table lamp placed in a window acts as a potent symbol of welcome. The soft, mellow light on the drapes appeals to a deep-seated nostalgia.

2 A log fire serves as a focal point in a light and airy sitting room. By positioning lights around the fireplace, the owner has reinforced the sense of a hearth.

**3 A clinically functional
kitchen has its ambience of
hygienic efficiency underlined
by modern-style downlighters.
These provide an excellent
light to work by, as well as
creating attractive reflections
in the glossy white and satin-
steel surfaces.**

**4 A grand house in which
every window emits a warm
light has a reassuring, almost
joyous feel about it. Less
lavishly, you can create a
similar effect with a porch
light.**

When man first learned to control fire without getting his fingers burned, he hit upon what was to be the main source of artificial light throughout history. Even by the mid-20th century, more than half the world's population were still using flame as their principal light source in the home. Heat and light have always been closely linked: both are forms of electromagnetic radiation. However, heat has always been a problematic route to light from the point of view of cost and convenience.

The forms of combustion used to light interiors over a timespan of centuries have ranged from the most ancient flame torches to wax candles and tallow candles to the more sophisticated oil lamps and gas mantles that preceded the electric light bulb. None of these methods could truthfully be described as convenient or efficient, and all of them, in varying degrees, can be seen as luxuries when compared with the general availability of electric light today. From the Middle Ages to the 19th century, ordinary households used rushlights, while the wealthy illuminated their interiors with wax candles. It takes 120 candles to produce the light of a single 100-watt bulb, so we can easily imagine the heat given off in those days, and the vast byproduct of melted wax, when lighting a room to a reasonable level of brightness. The court of Louis XIV at the Palace of Versailles once consumed 25,000 precious candles in the course of an evening; his subjects, however, could rarely muster more than a handful in one year.

The 18th and 19th centuries were the period of real innovation in lighting, although no method completely replaced those that came before it. Oil lamps with reservoirs, reflectors and glass flues offered to the public for the first time a convenient source of reasonably intense light – and on a scale greatly increased by mass production. Two 19th-century inventions – the match (1827) and paraffin (1860) – further enlarged the possibilities.

Natural gas was first used as an illuminant by the ancient Egyptians, Persians and Chinese, but it was not until the 18th century that its use was developed in Europe. Gas mantles burned coal gas fuelled by piped supply systems. However, the systems were expensive to install, and were soon eclipsed by electric lighting when this became widely available at the end of the century.

The electric dawn

The first domestic electric lighting system employing filament bulbs was installed in 1880 by Lord Armstrong, the British armaments millionaire, in his fashionable new house at Cragside, Northumbria. However, the possibility of lighting by electricity had been known many years before.

It was the English chemist Humphry Davy who first generated electric light. As early as 1809, Davy had harnessed a battery of 2,000 cells to two carbon rods, producing a vivid arc-shaped

1

4

2

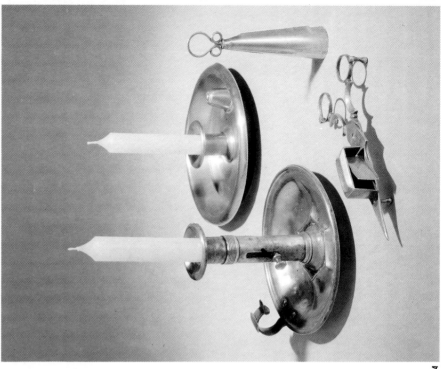

3

1 A floor-standing medieval-style metal candelabrum. The candles were held in place on spikes known as "prickets".

2 Whale-oil lamps of coloured pressed glass, made in New England in the mid-19th century.

3 An ornate gas fitting of 1851, styled to look like an exotic plant.

4 A group of 19th-century portable candlesticks with snuffers. The scissor-type snuffer contains a small box to hold charred pieces of wick.

"BRAY" INCANDESCENT GAS BURNERS & MANTLES

SAVE MY GAS BILLS

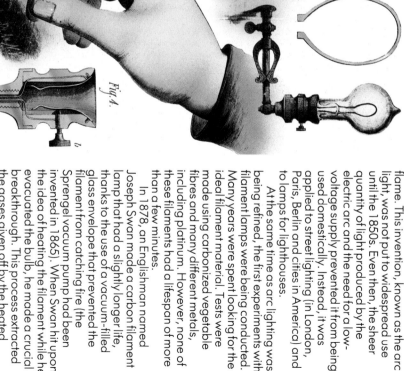

Fig.1. *Fig.2.* *Fig.3.* *Fig.4.*

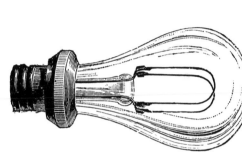

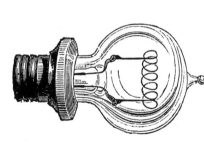

V. Rose

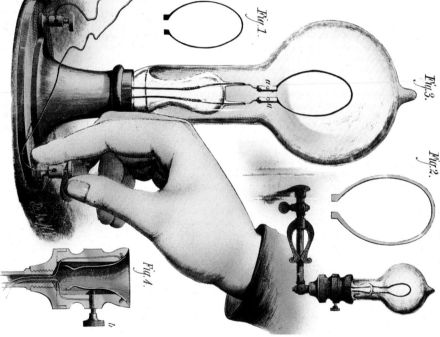

flame. This invention, known as the arc light, was not put to widespread use until the 1850s. Even then, the sheer quantity of light produced by the electric arc and the need for a low-voltage supply prevented it from being used domestically. Instead, it was applied to street lighting (in London, Paris, Berlin and cities in America) and to lamps for lighthouses.

At the same time as arc lighting was being refined, the first experiments with filament lamps were being conducted. Many years were spent looking for the ideal filament material. Tests were made using carbonized vegetable fibres and many different metals, including platinum. However, none of these filaments had a lifespan of more than a few minutes.

In 1878, an Englishman named Joseph Swan made a carbon filament lamp that had a slightly longer life, thanks to the use of a vacuum-filled glass envelope that prevented the filament from catching fire (the Sprengel vacuum pump had been invented in 1865). When Swan hit upon the idea of heating the filament while he evacuated the bulb, he made a crucial breakthrough. This process extracted the gases given off by the heated filament and prolonged lamp life. But it was the American scientist Thomas

5 A poster of about 1900. By this time, gas had been used for street lighting for almost a century, and had still not been superseded in the home.

6 Edison's carbon filament incandescent lamp heralded a lighting revolution. These diagrams, taken from an article in *Scientific American* in 1880, demonstrate the basic principles of the filament lamp.

7 After the launch of the carbon filament bulb, various refinements followed. Experimenters concentrated on ways of extending the life of the filament by looping and coiling it.

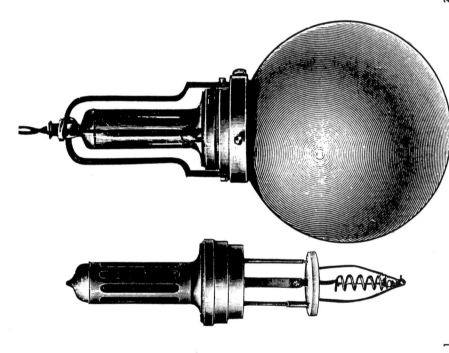

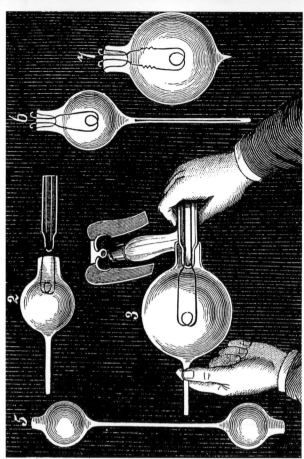

Alva Edison who, working independently along similar lines, produced the forerunner of the modern light bulb, at Menlo Park, New Jersey, in 1879. A resourceful experimenter, Edison had patented 157 inventions by this time. As reported by Edison, the first bulb "burnt like a star at night for 45 hours, and it went out with unexpected quickness".

Once the principle of the electric bulb was established, refinements soon followed. Two different methods of connecting light bulbs to the supply circuit were devised: the screw-in brass cap invented by Edison, and Swan's bayonet fitting, both of which are still in use today. The two inventors, who were both marketing their lamps in the UK by 1880, sensibly decided to go into partnership, forming the Edison and Swan United Lamp Company (later "Ediswan"). The first electricity supply network for household lighting — another Edison patent — was introduced in New York in 1882.

Experiments meanwhile attempted to make the filament bulb more efficient and more durable. Edison replaced his carbonized silk-thread filament with carbonized bamboo, while others experimented with different metals, such as osmium and tantalum. But the filament of the future was of the metal tungsten: although fragile, this proved the most efficient of all filament materials, and rapidly gained universal acceptance after its introduction in the United States in 1907. The first tungsten lamps made use of pressed tungsten, but in 1910 William Coolidge of Schenectady, New York, unveiled a process of producing drawn tungsten filaments, giving a greatly improved luminous efficacy.

To improve light output still more while using less power, Irving Langmuir, also at Schenectady, tried introducing inert gases into a bulb with a coiled filament. The gases had the effect of retarding the evaporation of the tungsten. At first nitrogen was used, and then varying mixtures of nitrogen and argon to create lamps of different wattages. A further advance came in 1913, when bulb life was extended dramatically by the use of a double-coiled filament. After that, no major

24

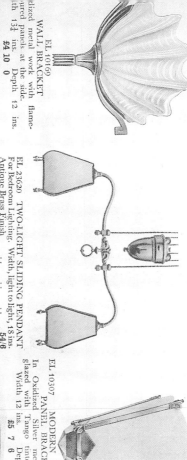

521

ELECTRICAL DEPARTMENT

Every Conceivable Electrical Lighting Fitting is Available at Harrods

EL 10169 WALL BRACKET with flame-oxidized metal work with the side. Coloured panels at the side. Depth 12 ins.
Length 13¼ ins. ... £4 10 0

EL 2951 BRASS FLEXIBLE READING LAMP
For Bedroom Lighting.
Can be focussed in any direction
Polished Brass Finished ... 17/6
Oxidized Copper Finish ... 21/-

EL 23620 TWO-LIGHT SLIDING PENDANT For Bedroom Lighting. Width, light to light, 18 ins.
Antique Brass Finish ... 54/6
Oxidized Silver ... 65/6
Silk Shades, extra ... Each 12/6

EL 10307 MODERN ONE-LIGHT PANEL BRACKET
In Oxidized Silver metalwork, and glazed with Tango tinted glassware. Width 12 ins. Depth 13 ins. ... £5 7 6

EL 10969 PENDANT
Four-light Rustless Iron Candle Pendant.
16th Century ... £10 18 6
Parchment Shades, extra. Each 12/6

EL 2122 CEILING LIGHT Orinula Finish Metalwork. Handsome Cut Glass Bowl. 9-in. diameter base ... £5 10 0

SHELL CRAFT

Made from the shell of the Tropical Oyster. Artistic and durable, easily cleaned and unaffected by heat or by water in washing.

No.	Size.	Natural Colour.
133	12½"×5½"	60/-
134	14½"×5½"	78/6
135	16"×6"	87/6
135A	19"×8"	102/6

SHELL.CRAFT

Bowls can be tinted any colour.

		Prices.
Size.	Plain	Tinted.
7 12½"×5½"	58/6	61/6
8 13½"×5½"	63/-	66/-
9 16"×6"	74/3	78/-
0 19"×8"	88/3	92/-

ALL PRICES ARE SUBJECT TO MARKET FLUCTUATIONS

Telephone SLOANE 1234 Telegrams 'EVERYTHING HARRODS LONDON'

HARRODS LTD LONDON S W 1

---

improvement was made in tungsten lighting until the introduction of tungsten-halogen lamps in 1964.

Discharge lighting

Meanwhile, there was a parallel line of research in the history of artificial lighting: the evolution of the electric discharge lamp. In 1850 a German scientist, Heinrich Geissler, demonstrated that an electric discharge through rarified gases could produce light. Discharge tubes of various colours were included in a display for Queen Victoria's Diamond Jubilee. Lights based on the discharge principle (known as "Moore tubes") were installed commercially for the first time in a store in Newark, New Jersey (1904). The tubes contained either nitrogen or carbon dioxide, depending on the colour of light required. However, they were never widely used, as they were difficult to install and maintain.

Peter Cooper-Hewitt's mercury-arc lamp (1901) was as much as twice or three times as efficient as the most advanced tungsten bulb; its first practical installation was in the composing room of the New York Evening Post. Within the same broad field of electric discharge lighting, another scientist of distinction was Georges Claude, whose discoveries were the bedrock of the neon sign industry. Sodium-vapour lights proved to have tremendous potential for outdoor lighting, but their characteristic yellow cast made them unsuitable for home, office or factory.

A wider range of applications was offered by the fluorescent tube, based on the phenomenon of fluorescence – the emission of light when phosphors are excited by ultraviolet radiation. The launch of fluorescent tubes in the American marketplace in 1938 was a milestone of lighting history, and they began to reach private homes in significant numbers from about 1942. After the Second World War a research effort was directed toward developing fluorescents of improved colour quality. Today, this remains one of the most active areas of lighting research along with the evolution of miniature types of fluorescent lamp.

1 The Nernst lamp was the first practical attempt to replace carbon by another incandescent substance (a mixture of oxides) in the filament of a light bulb. (The filament is shown here alongside a view of the whole lamp.) The inventor, a German scientist named H.W. Nernst, patented the device in 1901.

2 This poster of 1919 shows an Osram tungsten-filament bulb manufactured in the United States. The worker is sealing a glass socket and carbon filament into the outer envelope, or "flask", of an incandescent bulb.

3 An early illustration showing bulb manufacture in the United States. The worker is sealing a glass socket and carbon filament into the outer envelope, or "flask", of an incandescent bulb.

4 The same process in more detail. The central diagram (number 3) shows a glass stopper with a filament attached being fused together with a flask. Afterwards, the air would be drawn out through a long tube (6), and then the bulb would be sealed (7).

5 A page from the 1929 catalogue of Harrods department store in London. Most of the styles have become fashionable again. The shell-shaped desk lamp, for example, is available in a modern version, with a built-in dimmer, and the bowl-shaped pendants like those on the bottom row are sold today with mother-of-pearl shades.

Sources of Light

There is an expanding array of electric light sources on the market today, ranging from the familiar tungsten-filament bulb (shown opposite) to more advanced sources such as the new breed of miniature fluorescent lamps. The following section of the book profiles all the main types of bulb and tube available for home lighting, with helpful information on their efficiency, life expectancy, running costs, colour-rendering characteristics and practical applications.

There are various ways of modifying, to some extent, the characteristics of an artificial light source – for example, by careful choice of shade or fitting. However, this flexibility cannot absolve us of the need to select the appropriate type of light source at the outset. To make this choice, we need to juggle three more or less competing considerations. The order in which we tackle these factors will depend on our personal priorities, but certainly we should think about each of them before we make up our minds.

Cost may not seem like the greatest priority when the outlay required for buying and maintaining a lighting system is compared with the much greedier demands of other household electrical goods. For example, a one-kilowatt electric fire will use ten times

A representative selection of the wide variety of light sources available today:

1 The standard tungsten GLS bulb, in clear and pearl versions.

2 A tungsten candle bulb.

3 A golfball bulb, for decorative use.

4 Crown-silvered bulbs, used in combination with reflectors in specially designed fittings.

5 A Decor Round bulb, used principally for ornament.

6 Tungsten reflector lamps, for spotlighting.

7 A low-voltage tungsten-halogen reflector lamp for spotlighting.

8 A PAR 38 lamp, available in both spot and flood versions. This lamp is suitable for outdoor use.

9 A Philips SL miniature fluorescent lamp: one of a new breed of compact energy-saving lamps.

10 PL miniature fluorescents. Unlike the SL, these lamps need to be used with separate control gear.

11 Fluorescent tubes, available in two diameters: 26mm and 38mm.

as much power as a 100-watt tungsten light bulb. Nevertheless, the savings made possible by choosing energy-efficient light sources are by no means insignificant; and in any case, energy-saving is a global responsibility that everyone should share. For accurate budgeting, it is important to take a long-term view, balancing initial costs and running costs. A fluorescent will cost more to buy than a tungsten-filament bulb; but it will last much longer, use less electricity during the course of its life, and thus work out less expensive overall.

Another important factor to consider is the quality of light, in terms of both colour appearance and colour rendering. We have already noted how these aspects of a light source are related to its colour temperature (pages 12–13). Because they are lower on the colour temperature scale, tungsten bulbs are redder than fluorescents, in a way that we usually perceive as being homelier. However, it is also important to remember that considerable variations of lighting quality occur even within a single broad category of light source. Fluorescent tubes, although still regarded by many people as too cold-looking for the home, are now available in versions that more closely resemble tungsten lighting. Even tungsten bulbs vary widely in colour quality. Generally speaking, the hotter a tungsten bulb is able to run, the whiter and purer will be the light emitted. To achieve these higher temperatures, tungsten-halogen bulbs [used to give a powerful light more efficiently than tungsten-filament bulbs] often have a heat-resistant quartz envelope instead of the ordinary glass one.

Thirdly, the appearance or physical construction of the bulb can be a determining factor if we have already chosen a particular type of fitting. For example, tungsten-filament bulbs are sold in a compressed mushroom shape specially intended to be unobtrusive in shallow fittings. Or if the aim is to throw a narrow beam of light onto a particular object in a room, we would choose a reflector bulb in combination with a spotlight fitting. Or then again, we might require a low-wattage decorative bulb for the kind of installation in which the bulbs themselves are directly visible: such bulbs are made in a variety of more or less orthodox shapes, including imitation candle flames. Very occasionally, a specific decorative effect might call for a coloured light, in which case we would choose a bulb coated with pigment or, for more intense colour, one with a built-in colour reflector.

The tungsten bulb

For most households, the tungsten-filament bulb is still the mainstay of any lighting scheme. In essence, this lamp is still very much the one that Edison invented in 1879. His original carbon-coated thread has been replaced by a more reliable, longer-lasting coiled wire filament of the metal tungsten, and to the partial vacuum in the glass bulb a variety of inert gases have been added to improve performance. However, the basic principle remains the same. Electricity is passed through the filament, which consequently begins to heat up. When the temperature reaches 500°C (943°F), the filament begins to give off light as well as heat. The hotter the filament becomes, the more light is emitted, and the whiter the light appears. This effect occurs with all metals; however, tungsten is particularly suitable for lighting because of its high melting point. The gases inside the glass envelope of the bulb prevent the filament from oxidizing too quickly, and thus from wearing out. But the deterioration process cannot be halted altogether; it can only be slowed down. In time, as tungsten evaporates, the filament gets thinner and thinner and finally breaks.

Like all other types of bulb, tungsten bulbs are rated in watts – a measure of the electrical power consumed. The greater the power, the greater the light output – and the higher the running costs. The range of tungsten bulbs available rises from 15 watts to 1,000 watts, although for ordinary domestic use 200 watts is the upper limit.

Tungsten bulbs are inexpensive to buy and replace, but compared with fluorescent tubes they are costly to run on account of their inefficient performance: they produce fewer lumens per watt of electricity consumed. Most of the energy that a tungsten bulb uses is wasted in producing infrared radiation; only about six percent of the energy input goes into producing useful light. The average life of a conventional tungsten bulb is 1,000 hours. After that time the filament starts to fail. Using a bulb in a horizontal instead of a vertical position, or in an unventilated fitting, will shorten its life drastically. These days, manufacturers are able to make tungsten-filament bulbs that last longer than average; indeed, a Double Life version is available that will last at least 2,000 hours in normal use.

The earliest light bulbs were made of clear glass, but in time an alternative pearl finish was devised to provide a gentler source of light. The pearl effect is achieved by etching the inside surface of the glass. This is somewhat different from an opal finish – a white interior coating which obscures the filament and yields a more diffuse light source, with softer shadows. There is, of course, a price to pay for these refinements in terms of lighting

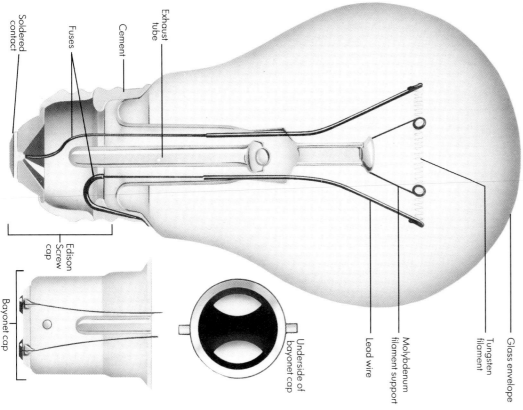

Tungsten GLS bulb

Exhaust tube

Cement

Fuses

Soldered contact

Edison Screw cap

Bayonet cap

Underside of bayonet cap

Lead wire

Molybdenum filament support

Tungsten filament

Glass envelope

efficiency. But today's opal bulbs are said to suffer a loss of no more than four percent of light output when compared with the clear-glass versions.

The tungsten-filament family

The earliest and most basic design of tungsten-filament bulb, and still the workhorse of most household lighting schemes, is termed the general lighting service (GLS) lamp. This is suitable for a vast range of fittings from ceiling pendants to desk and table lights.

However, for certain specific uses this is not necessarily the best type of light source. In theory, you could use an ordinary GLS bulb in a spotlight fitting, but this would produce an unfocussed source of light, radiating in all directions at random, in a way that would not make the most of the fitting. To give the kind of light that a true spotlight requires (an intense narrow beam for picking out a specific object or providing a strong accent of light and shade in a room), the ideal bulb is one with a built-in "silvered" reflector.

The simplest type of tungsten reflector is the crown-silvered (or bowl-silvered) reflector, which is characterized by its internally silvered front. The basic shape of this lamp may be the same as that of a standard tungsten bulb, or alternatively it may be spherical or lemon-shaped. Instead of scattering light all around, the front reflects light back into a curved reflective fitting with a parabola-shaped profile, which in turn throws a controlled beam back into the room. In fittings that leave the bulb clearly visible, the silvered crown adds a pleasing decorative touch.

A similar lighting effect is produced by the blown glass reflector lamp – a mushroom-shaped bulb whose interior surface is silvered all over except for the crown (thus reversing the principle and appearance of the crown-silvered reflector). The silvered part of the bulb reflects light through the crown a high-intensity beam.

In addition to this blown-glass range of lamps there is a pressed-glass range known as PAR (parabolic aluminized reflector) lamps. These robust, high-performance bulbs with a front of toughened, prismatic glass have double the life of other reflectors. Because they can withstand harsher treatment, they can be used outdoors without protection. They provide either a dispersed beam for floodlighting or a concentrated beam for spotlighting. A special "cool beam" version of the PAR spotlight, designed to remove 75 percent of radiant heat from the beam by means of a "dichroic" reflector, can be used only in fittings of suitable heat-resistant construction.

More recently, manufacturers have developed a category of spotlight bulbs which operate at low voltages; 12 volts is typical. These bulbs require a special fitting incorporating a transformer to adapt mains electricity. The reduced voltage allows the bulb to operate with a smaller filament, thus creating a more concentrated beam of light. Spotlights running on mains voltage are apt to leave unsightly scorch marks if they are too close to a wall or ceiling, but with low-voltage lamps this problem of scorching is alleviated.

For concealed lighting or picture lighting, or for use on mirrors or bedheads, tungsten strip lights combine the convenient linear shape of a fluorescent tube with simple installation. (See the lamp chart on page 185 for an indication of the wattages and lengths available.)

PAR 38 lamps are much more robust than ordinary reflector lamps, and have double the life. They may be either flood lamps or spot lamps. Some types are available with coloured pressed-glass covers for special effects.

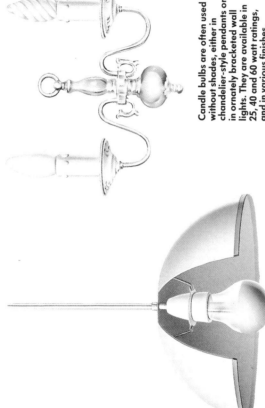

Candle bulbs are often used without shades, either in chandelier-style pendants or in ornately bracketed wall lights. They are available in 25, 40 and 60 watt ratings, and in various finishes, including amber and amber-tipped. This illustration shows both plain and twisted versions.

Tungsten reflector lamps, sometimes known as ISL (internally silvered) lamps, are still the mainstay of domestic spotlighting, despite growing competition from halogen lamps. Miniature 40-watt versions are available, with SES (small Edison screw) or SBC (small bayonet cap) attachments.

Crown-silvered bulbs offer an inexpensive way to achieve a narrow, sharply defined beam for effect lighting, provided that they are used with parabolic reflector fittings. In pendants such as this one (shown in a cutaway view) the bulb serves a decorative role and helps prevent glare by masking the filament.

BULBS IN SITU

These illustrations show four common tungsten-filament bulb types in appropriate fittings that made good use of the bulbs' special qualities.

Lamp type and beam width

Lamp type and beam width	Wattage	Spot dia. (for 1,000 lux)	Light 1m (lux)	Light 2m (lux)	Light 3m (lux)
Narrow beam (10°–25°)					
Crown-silvered (lemon-shaped) lamp in 90mm reflector, 16°	40W	0.5m spot dia.	3,000	750	330
Crown-silvered (GLS-shaped) lamp in 150mm reflector, 12°	60W	0.5m spot dia.	7,400	1,850	820
Crown-silvered (GLS-shaped) lamp in 190mm reflector, 12°	100W	0.7m spot dia. / 0.8m spot dia.	14,500	3,600	1,600
R25 spot, 22°	75W	0.5m spot dia.	1,350	330	150
R25 spot, 22°	100W	0.55m spot dia.	2,000	500	220
PAR 38 spot, 16°	100W	0.6m spot dia.	4,000	1,000	440
PAR 38 spot, 16°	150W	0.8m spot dia.	7,500	1,850	830
Medium beam (25°–40°)					
R16 Reflector, 30°	40W	0.4m spot dia.	425	105	45
R20 Reflector, 32°	60W	0.5m spot dia.	700	175	80
R30 Reflector, 35°	75W	0.55m spot dia.	700	175	80
R30 Reflector, 35°	100W	0.6m spot dia.	1,000	250	110
R40 Reflector, 35°	150W	0.9m spot dia.	2,000	500	220
PAR 38 Flood, 30°	100W	0.7m spot dia.	1,800	450	200
PAR 38 Flood, 30°	150W	0.9m spot dia.	3,100	775	345
Wide beam (over 40°)					
Ro80 Reflector, 70°	60W	0.7m spot dia.	276	70	30
Ro80 Reflector, 70°	75W	0.8m spot dia.	360	90	40
Ro80 Reflector, 70°	100W	1m spot dia.	350	135	60

Relative beam throw — and spot diameter for 1,000 lux (columns: 1m, 2m, 3m, 4m)

Approximate light levels — in centre of beam at specified distances (in lux) (columns: 1m, 2m, 3m)

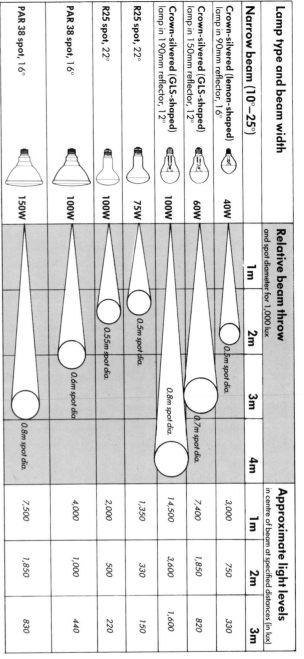

REFLECTOR LAMPS: TYPICAL BEAM CHARACTERISTICS

This chart shows beam throws and lighting strengths for a range of typical reflector lamps. For the purpose of describing the width of a beam, manufacturers measure the angle between the points in the beam at which the luminous intensity is half that of the beam's centre. To interpret the right-hand side of the chart, showing lighting strengths, bear in mind that normal lighting levels usually fall somewhere between 300 and 500 lux; for accent lighting, a level two or more times this value is required.

BEAM PROFILES

Many manufacturers publish beam profiles for every reflector lamp they produce. The example shown below (for a Thorn Decorspot 64) is typical. The vertical scale shows the distance from the light source, while the horizontal scale shows the beam diameter. The white profile is the angle at which the beam intensity is 50% of the illuminance of the beam's centre; this maximum is specified (in lux) for various distances in the central columns. The tinted profile is the angle at which the beam intensity is 10% of the maximum (usually regarded as the limit of useful spill light). Note that information is given for two different wattage ratings in this diagram.

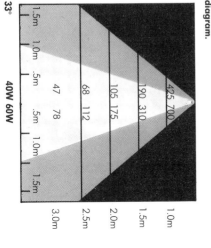

33°

Left scale: 1.5m 1.0m .5m .5m 1.0m 1.5m

425 700 / 190 310 / 105 175 / 68 112 / 47 78

Right scale: 1.0m 1.5m 2.0m 2.5m 3.0m

40W 60W

The tungsten-halogen bulb

With the growing interest in high-performance lighting in the home, tungsten-halogen bulbs (also known as quartz-halogen bulbs) are being increasingly deployed for domestic applications, although their original use was for floodlighting, shop displays and exhibitions.

The halogen bulb works on exactly the same principle as the ordinary domestic light bulb, despite its very different appearance. Contained inside a hard glass or quartz envelope is a tungsten wire filament which gives off light when heated electrically. However, the halogen gas introduced into the envelope results in a better performance. In a conventional tungsten bulb, vaporized tungsten particles gradually build up on the inside of the envelope, decreasing the filament size and blackening the bulb. Halogen lamps, however, have a special "regenerative cycle" that prevents this effect. Evaporated tungsten particles, instead of migrating to the envelope, combine with the halogen gas to form a compound. This compound redeposits the tungsten onto the filament, and in the process releases halogen to continue the cycle.

Although more expensive to buy and run than conventional lamps, halogen lamps last much longer – typically, between 2,000 and 4,000 hours. Their greater efficiency means that a much smaller bulb will provide the same amount of light as a GLS bulb of greater wattage. (A 500-watt halogen lamp is usually about the diameter of a pencil and about half as long.) Another advantage is the bulb's higher "maintained light output": at the end of their rated life, halogen sources emit as much as 94% of their original lumen output, compared with only 82% for other incandescent sources. The higher operating temperatures used in halogen lamps result in a whitish light, lacking the yellow tinge we normally associate with tungsten. As with all incandescent light bulbs, output can be reduced with a dimmer switch, which lowers the voltage. Dimming can prevent the regenerative cycle from functioning, making the lamp blacken in time just like a conventional bulb. However, running the lamp at full voltage for a few moments will start up the cycle again and clean the bulb surface.

Standard domestic light sockets are unsuitable for many halogen bulbs: instead you have to use special lampholders. Installation calls for a certain amount of care, as greasy fingermarks or scratches will cause some bulbs to fail prematurely. It is best to wear gloves when bulb-changing, except when the bulb has a special protective glass jacket. Fixtures must be specially designed to dissipate the high levels of heat given off, and must be carefully positioned away from vulnerable surfaces. Because the lamps are very bright, they must be carefully shielded from view.

Halogen bulbs take a number of distinctive forms. The standard tubular type has a glass or quartz tube with electrical contacts at either end, between which the tungsten filament is stretched. These lamps must usually be mounted horizontally, or the filament may fracture. Also now on the market are single-ended bulbs (rated at 75,100 and 150 watts) with conventional Edison screw or bayonet caps that obviate the need for special contacts.

Low-voltage miniaturized halogen

▶ **A low-voltage miniature halogen lamp of the kind often required by modern task lights with built-in transformers. This 12-volt, 50-watt version is the most common.**

All lamps on these two pages are shown at approximately 1⅕× actual size.

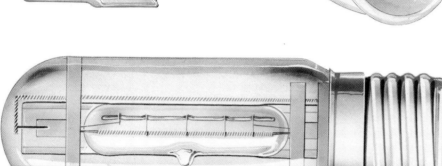

▲ **A single-ended tubular halogen lamp (standard voltage, 150 watts), manufactured by Thorn EMI. Essentially, this consists of a linear lamp inside an outer glass jacket. The ES cap obviates the need for a special double-contact lampholder.**

▲ **A low-voltage halogen dichroic reflector lamp. This particular example is rated at 12 volts, 75 watts and has a beam angle of 14°. The dichroic reflector reflects light forward but transmits heat backward, creating a "cool beam". The reflector also produces attractive sparkle. Dichroic lamps must be used in special heatproof fittings.**

TYPICAL BEAM PROFILES FOR TUNGSTEN-HALOGEN REFLECTOR LAMPS (with 56mm reflector)

Lamp type and beam width	Relative beam throw and spot diameter for 1,000 lux				Approx. light levels in centre of beam at set distances (lux)		
	1m	2m	3m	4m	1m	2m	3m
Pencil beam (less than 10°)							
6° 35 watts (6 volts)				0.3m spot dia.	17,000	4,250	1,890
Narrow beam (10°–25°)							
14° 35 watts (6 volts)			0.5m spot dia.		4,000	1,000	445

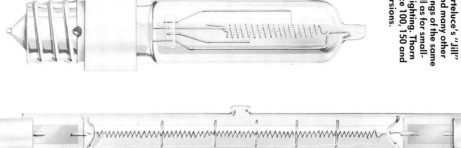

A mains voltage linear halogen lamp. This 300-watt lamp would be suitable for use in the Arteluce's "Jill" uplighter and many other modern fittings of the same type, as well as for small-scale floodlighting. Thorn also produce 100, 150 and 200 watt versions.

▶ A standard-voltage single-ended tubular halogen lamp. This type is available in 50, 100, 150 and 250 watt ratings. It is suitable for many desk lights and uplighters.

lamps, designed for use in special fittings equipped with a transformer, are becoming increasingly popular. One type from Thorn EMI takes the form of a truncated sealed-glass tube, about one inch long, with a two-pin cap at one end. The bulb was originally developed for highly specialized use in microfilm readers, but is now finding its way into imaginative new lighting for the home. Its sealed construction makes it easier to handle than the mains-voltage halogen bulb, and you can use it in any operating position. Also available are low-voltage halogen reflector lamps suitable for spotlighting and floodlighting.

An important innovation in halogen technology is the Philips Light Point – a 6-volt halogen lamp with an integral transformer, built-in reflector, protective glass front, and an Edison screw cap compatible with conventional spotlight fittings

Applications

The small size of tungsten-halogen bulbs in relation to their output has made it possible today to create easily portable indirect lighting systems in the home. A single 250-watt tungsten-halogen tube is powerful enough to provide indirect background lighting in a room of average proportions, provided that walls and ceilings are white or pale-coloured. Their modest dimensions make these tubes easy to incorporate in elegant uplighters for indirect lighting; such fittings are now being produced in large numbers, especially by the Italian manufacturers. Wall-mounted lights are also among the applications. For all these kinds of background lighting, it is important to keep the intense halogen light source out of direct sight, or it would cause severe dazzle. To avoid this pitfall, considerable ingenuity is being invested in fittings provided with glass or perforated metal diffusers or with reflecting surfaces which bounce the light into the room. Tungsten-halogen bulbs are also widely used for outdoor floodlighting.

Low-voltage halogen bulbs have special uses of their own. For example, they are small enough to fit into desk

lights, for delivering a concentrated beam onto a work surface. Unlike GLS lamps or fluorescents, they can be focussed into a narrow beam, which also makes them suitable for spotlighting. They give excellent sparkle on glassware and other reflective objects.

The fluorescent tube

Fluorescent lights, commercially available since the end of World War Two, provide such an efficient way to convert electricity into light that they have become the almost universal method of lighting shops and offices. However, beyond the bathroom, kitchen and garage, they have still not made a major impression in the home.

In an energy-conscious era, the fact that a fluorescent tube uses up to five times less electricity than a tungsten bulb to provide the same amount of light would strike one as a compelling attraction. Fluorescent tubes also radiate less heat and have a longer life. However, these arguments have proved unable to outweigh certain prejudices against using fluorescents in domestic settings. The quality of light produced is seen as harsh and unappealing; the strongly linear nature of the lamps makes them seem too obtrusive for living areas; and they require special fittings that are not normally found in the home. But in fact, the poor image of the fluorescent is not entirely deserved. For example, the flickering effect that people often complain about is the result of poor maintenance. The tubes do not give up the ghost suddenly, in the manner of tungsten bulbs, but instead deteriorate very slowly, sometimes beginning to flicker after their rated life has expired.

Basic principles

Unlike a tungsten-filament bulb, a fluorescent does not work on the principle of heating a wire. It produces light not by incandescence but by electric discharge. Each end of the glass tube contains a tungsten-wire electrode, connected to a two-pin cap. Inside the tube are minute droplets of mercury together with vapours of an inert gas (argon, an argon-neon mixture, or more recently krypton).

INSIDE A FLUORESCENT TUBE

The diagram below shows the basic construction of a fluorescent tube.

The lower illustration diagrams the basic principle by which fluorescent tubes operate. An electric arc discharge struck between the two electrodes vaporizes droplets of mercury in the tube. The electrons in the arc bombard the vaporized mercury, causing an emission of UV radiation. When the UV rays contact the phosphor coating, they are converted to light.

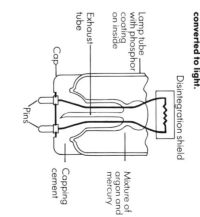

Visible light
UV
Electrons
Electrode
Vaporized mercury

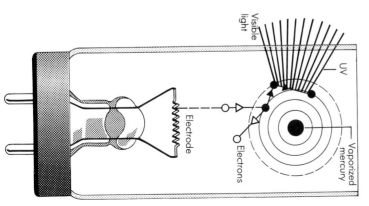

Lamp tube with phosphor coating on inside
Exhaust tube
Cap
Pins
Disintegration shield
Mixture of argon and mercury
Capping cement

Passing a high-voltage current across the electrodes causes them to emit electrons, ionizing (that is, imparting an electric charge to) the gases and creating a flow of current (an arc). The heat of the arc vaporizes the mercury, which takes over the arc and emits ultraviolet radiation. Invisible UV rays bombard a phosphor coating on the inside of the tube, which glows brightly and evenly.

Impurities mixed with the fluorescent coating determine the colour appearance and colour-rendering properties of a tube. Until recently good colour rendering could only be achieved by sacrificing luminous efficacy – the number of lumens emitted per watt of electricity consumed. However, new technology based on triphosphor chemistry has made available high-efficacy lamps that also show good colour rendering. These are more expensive than conventional fluorescents, because they depend on rare-earth phosphors, but they are more economical to run as fewer lamps are needed to produce the same lighting level.

Control gear

All fluorescents need to be operated with special control gear, which may be housed within the fitting, or, if required, at some distance from it. It is essential to make sure that a lamp and its control gear are compatible with each other: a mismatch could cause a variety of problems, including reduced lamp life, noisy operation, overheating of the control gear components or wiring, or unstable colour qualities.

An essential component of the control gear is the ballast (or choke) – a coil of wire which provides an initial surge of electricity to start the tube and controls the current once the arc has struck. In "switch-start" lamps the ballast is accompanied by a glow-switch starter, which generally consists of two bimetallic strip electrodes enclosed in a glass bulb containing an inert gas. When the lamp is switched on, the full mains voltage is developed across these electrodes causing a discharge to take place between them. The discharge warms the bimetallic strips, which bend toward each other and make contact. This allows current to flow through the lamp's electrodes, heating them so that they become enveloped in clouds of electrons. It is this that causes the characteristic white glow at each end of the tube. Meanwhile, the starter switch cools down and springs apart. Because there is a choke in series with the lamp, the breaking of the inductive circuit causes a voltage surge across the lamp electrodes and the main arc strikes. If the lamp fails to start, the discharge is established again in the starter and the cycle repeated. It is this process of repeated attempts by the glow-switch starter that causes the blinking of a switch-start circuit with a lamp that has failed. Once the lamp has started, the ballast serves to regulate the current, preventing the electrodes from burning out prematurely. Provided that the starter is replaced periodically, this kind of circuit is efficient and reliable. It is suitable for both krypton-filled and argon-filled lamps.

Some modern fluorescent tubes have no starter but instead use a quick-start transformer or similar device, which allows the lamp to reach full output instantaneously, without the two- or three-second delay of a switch-start tube. A drawback of quick-start tubes is their slightly greater consumption of power: a small current from the ballast continues to heat the electrodes for as long as the lamp is left on. However, offsetting this factor are the rapid start and a slightly higher light output than is possible with a switch-start circuit. Electrodes suffer some erosion every time the tube is switched on, reducing the life of the lamp.

Electronic start circuits are essentially switch-start circuits in which the starter is replaced by a solid-state component that has no moving parts and lasts as long as the fitting. They therefore combine the advantage of switch-start (lower power) and quick-start (maintenance-free) circuits, without the limitations of either.

Fluorescent tubes are available in lengths between 600mm (2 feet/18 watts) and 2,400mm (8 feet/100 watts). Until recently the standard diameter was 38mm (1½ inches). However, there is now also a family of 26mm krypton-tubes which are more energy-saving. These tubes are restricted to switch-start or approved electronic start circuits.

Circular fluorescent tubes (40 watts) are used mostly in decorative ceiling fittings.

Applications

Fluorescent light is diffuse: it cannot be focussed in the way that tungsten and tungsten–halogen light can. Moreover, fluorescent light cannot easily be dimmed. These factors influence the way that fluorescents are used in the home. In general, the main function is that of providing a high overall level of light, which on its own will create a flat, shadowless effect. An attractive and stimulating fluorescent-based scheme would need supplementary point sources of light to add interest to the background lighting. Unless the tube is concealed, a diffuser is normally necessary, or the light emitted will be too bright.

In recent years, increasing attention has been given to the design and detailing of fluorescent fittings, which are now available in more attractive shapes and a wider palette of colours than in the past. In parallel with this trend, there have been recent signs of an awakening interest in fluorescent lighting in the home – for example, in the form of rise-and-fall lights over dining tables.

Miniature fluorescents

The most rapid technological advances in lighting in recent years have been in the development of new, miniaturized fluorescent lamps, combining the convenience of tungsten-filament bulbs with the low running costs of fluorescent tubes. Although special fittings are available, some types can also be plugged into an ordinary screw or bayonet tungsten-bulb fitting via an adaptor. The control gear that all fluorescents require may be housed in the fitting or the adaptor. However, there is also a category of miniature fluorescents (notably the Philips SL lamp) which house the control gear within the lamp itself; these can directly replace a GLS bulb, without any adaptor or circuit modification, in existing lampholders. All miniature fluorescents are low-wattage, ranging from 7 to 28 watts. A 25-watt rating produces at least as much light as a 100-watt GLS bulb.

An optional accessory for the Thorn 2D is an integral plug and control gear which fits a conventional socket outlet, allowing remote siting of the control away from the lamp and fitting.

The savings to be made with miniature fluorescents are considerable. The SL, for example, uses one quarter the electricity of a GLS bulb and lasts five times longer. The economic factor makes these lamps popular for commercial and institutional applications. However, the major manufacturers hope that the unique formula of compact size, low cost and ease of installation will at last overcome the prejudice against fluorescent lights for the home.

The colour quality of miniature fluorescents is similar to that of ordinary bulbs, thanks to the latest developments in phosphor powder

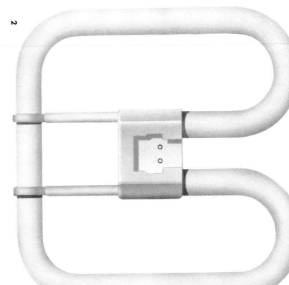

The illustrations on these pages show some of the principal kinds of miniature fluorescent lamp available today.

1 The Toshiba Neoball. An 18-watt globe-shaped fluorescent with a life of 6,000 hours. The control gear is integral, and the lamp comes with either a bayonet cap or Edison screw fitting. The polycarbonate bowl is available in opal or clear.

2 The Thorn 2-D. Available in 16 or 28 watt ratings. The lamp is suitable for some wall and ceiling fittings and for specially designed task lights. A special adaptor allows it to be plugged into a ordinary BC lampholder.

3 The Philips SL, designed to replace an ordinary tungsten bulb in a wide range of fittings. The outer envelope, which may have either an opal or prismatic finish, conceals a folded miniature tube. The base contains the control gear. A similar lamp from Wotan is the Compacta.

4 The Wotan Circolux. Available in 12, 18, 24 and 25 watt ratings and with either a BC or ES fitting.

5 The Philips PL. Made in four ratings: 5, 7, 9 and 11 watts. The average life expectancy is 5,000 hours. The starter is integral, but the lamp must be used with a separate ballast. A similar double-limb lamp is the Wotan Dulux.

Other lamp types

Many important new lamp types have evolved in the past few decades in response to the demand for energy-saving lighting for commercial uses and for public spaces. Most of these are high-intensity discharge (or HID) lamps. It is likely that some of these new technologies will eventually spread into the home. Already, many home owners are using these kinds of lamp for floodlighting gardens.

Among the most important subdivisions of the HID category are high-pressure sodium (SON) lamps and mercury halide lamps. SON lamps differ from the low-pressure sodium lights used for streetlighting in having reduced efficacy, but with a tremendous gain in colour rendering. Like SON lamps, metal halide lamps were introduced in the early 1960s. Since then they have been rapidly developed, as they offer a light source that is three times more efficient than a tungsten-halogen lamp but with excellent colour qualities. Efficacy decreases with wattage, which has restricted the applications of metal halide lamps for interior use. However, it seems that low-wattage versions will soon become available.

Blended lamps are discharge lamps that require no control gear. A mercury discharge arc tube and an incandescent filament operate in the same bulb. The filament controls the arc tube and at the same time contributes its own light. The combination of fluorescent, mercury and incandescent radiation creates a diffused white light with good colour qualities. The long life, luminous efficacy and balanced spectral distribution of blended lamps makes them suitable for promoting plant growth indoors.

Neon lamps can be used decoratively in the home. Pure neon gas produces a warm, red-orange glow but additives can be used to produce other colours. Neon is also used in flickering candle-effect bulbs.

chemistry. Because they give a diffuse, all-round light, these lamps cannot be used for spotlighting, but are well-suited for most general lighting purposes.

The Hardware

In the last ten years or so, the design of light fittings has entered an exciting new phase, characterized by innovation and elegance. This section of the book attempts to capture something of the creative upsurge.

The section begins with a survey of the basic principles involved in the design of light fittings, followed by individual chapters on the main types – downlighters, spotlights, pendants and so on. For each category, advice is given on choosing and using the fittings, with photographs showing classic designs as well as fittings used *in situ* in successful room schemes. This general introduction to each fitting type is accompanied by a visual index illustrating some of the most attractive designs from the major manufacturers. (In the captions to the visual index pages, designers are named in brackets where appropriate.)

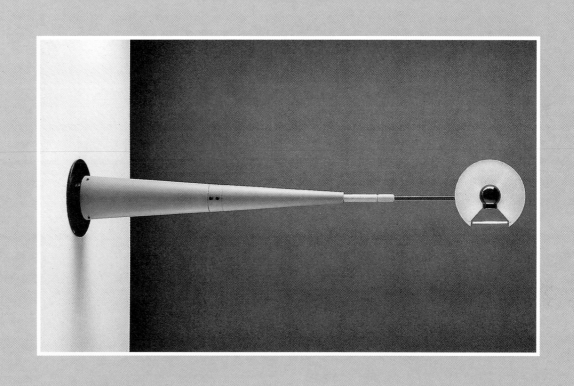

N o lamp is sufficient to light a room by itself. At the very least, a lamp needs some means of connection to an electricity supply and a device to protect it from damage and hold it in place. A light fitting (technically termed a "luminaire") fulfils these basic requirements, and performs the additional function of directing and controlling the light flow. Indeed, the fitting plays as important a role in shaping the character of the overall lighting in a room as does the light source itself.

Fundamentals

Many people think only in terms of aesthetic appeal when choosing a light fitting. However, also important are factors such as: ease of installation, ease of maintenance, durability, portability, adjustability and economy.

The first requirement of a light fitting is that it should be of sound and intelligent construction. The standards to which a fitting is designed and manufactured are as much responsible for the safety of the fitting as is the electrical circuit that supplies the power. Just one faulty component can sometimes have very serious consequences.

Compatibility is another key factor. You should always take care to select a fitting that is matched to the proposed light source, in two different ways: the lamps should suit the fitting from a safety point of view, and should also make the most of the fitting's characteristics. For example, choosing a PAR "cool beam" lamp for a conventional spotlight fitting without special heat-resistant qualities would incur a risk of overheating; while using a standard bulb in a spotlight designed for a silvered reflector lamp would wastefully dissipate some of the light output within the fitting. Fitting manufacturers always specify the range of suitable lamps, and also indicate the maximum wattage. Exceeding this wattage limit can lead to overheating inside the fitting or in one of the electrical connections, and scorching of the shade. For economic as well as safety reasons, good fittings are designed not to get too hot. Most

lamps are designed to operate at optimum temperatures, and their life can be shortened if the temperature builds up beyond a certain point. Fluorescent tubes are particularly sensitive in this respect, and need ventilation.

To choose the right fitting for a lighting scheme, you need to be able to visualize the lighting effect you seek. The appearance and the cost of the fitting will obviously play a part in your final choice. But before you look at these factors, you should work out exactly what you want the fittings to do and how this intended function relates to the tasks performed by other lights within your room scheme. In order to carry out this evaluation successfully, it is important to understand how various

kinds of fitting can control and modify the light source for which they are intended.

How fittings control light

Some light fittings – for example, those in which a bare, decorative bulb gives an all-round illumination – exert only a minimal effect on the distribution of light. Other fittings, however, are finely tuned pieces of engineering that offer a precise and predictable influence over the lighting they emit into the room. Certain desk lights, spotlights and ceiling-mounted downlighters are among the fittings that fall into this latter category.

Fittings can determine the distribution of light by employing the principles of reflection, diffusion or

refraction. The shape of the fitting, and the materials of which it is constructed, also have a crucial effect.

Some lamps (for example, blown-glass reflector lamps) have their own built-in reflectors to narrow, spread or redirect the beam, but very often this reflective function is performed instead (or in addition) by the fitting. A shiny surface behind the light source bounces a beam of light forward into the room. This surface is generally metallic (for example, highly polished, anodized aluminium) but in theory could also be of some other reflective material, such as chromium. "Dimpled" reflectors bounce off light less efficiently, but with the advantage that they reduce glare when the beam falls on a shiny object, such as a glass

HOW SHADES DISTRIBUTE LIGHT
To obtain a broader spread of downward light you can either lower the bulb within the shade (a) or choose a shade with a wider bottom opening (c, d and e). Note that the shape of the shade does not affect the beam angle.

Diagram f shows the three different types of light produced by a fitting with an open, translucent shade: direct, diffused and indirect.

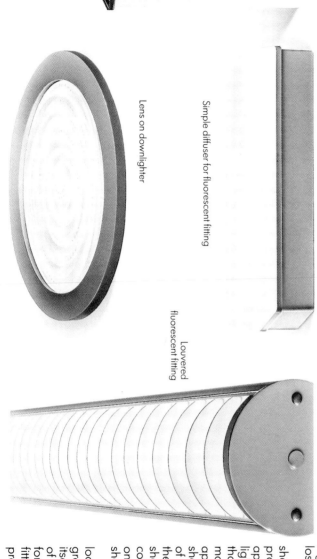

Baffle on downlighter

Lens on downlighter

Simple diffuser for fluorescent fitting

Louvered fluorescent fitting

cover over a painting. The shape of the reflector is no less important than its material. Reflectors with a parabolic profile focus the light and train it into a parallel beam instead of radiating it out in all directions, as would happen with a hemispherical reflector. Some fittings can be equipped with detachable reflectors that clip inside when a standard bulb is being used instead of a silvered reflector lamp. In some fittings, the reflector is tinted gold to bestow a warmer hue to the lighting.

Diffusers offer the simplest method of regulating a light source. They take the form of translucent covers, commonly made of opal glass, etched glass or plastic, whose intention is to conceal the exact source of the light (thus avoiding glare) and to put out a uniform brightness over the whole of the diffusing surface. This effect, however, only occurs if the lamp is placed sufficiently far from the diffuser. Diffusers enlarge the apparent size of the light source, and emit a general, undirected light, creating a relatively shadowless interior.

Among the light fittings that exploit the principle of refraction are those that make use of lenses to spread and soften the beam or deflect it in a chosen direction — for example, certain kinds of downlighter. Combined with reflectors, lenses also have a somewhat specialized use in high-performance "framing projectors"; in these fittings, which are intended to throw a precisely defined beam, the lamp and reflector can be adjusted closer to or farther away from the lens to broaden or narrow the beam angle. Refraction is also the scientific basis of diffusing covers that are moulded into a pattern of tiny plastic prisms; these both reflect and refract light to achieve an even level of brightness. A more traditional use of prisms is in the classic crystal chandelier, where they create an attractive sparkle.

Baffles, louvers and shades

In addition to reflectors, diffusers and lenses, the armoury of light-manipulating devices used in fittings also embraces baffles, louvers and shades. The term "baffles" is generally used to describe the grooved indentations found on the inner surfaces of many cylindrically shaped fittings, mainly spots and downlighters. The grooves are finished in matt black and have the effect of reducing apparent brightness when you look into the fitting from an angle that enables you to see its inner surface. They also minimize the unwanted spill-over of light, beyond the narrowly defined edges of a particular beam profile.

Louvers take the form of a series of blades, usually of opaque or translucent plastic or metal. The blades minimize glare by preventing a direct view through the opening of the fitting to the light source. The precise arrangement of louvers varies according to the fitting's shape. For example, louvers for fluorescent tubes are usually set at right angles to the lamp axis, whereas louvers in drum-shaped downlighters form a series of concentric blades.

Despite the increasing sophistication of designs, the most common method of modifying artificial light in the home is still the shade, which may be either integral to the fitting (as in a spotlight) or sold separately (as with traditional table lights). People commonly discriminate between shades mainly in terms of colour and decorative appearance. However, it is the functional characteristics of shades — the material, the method of construction and the size — that have the greatest influence on how a room looks at night.

The crucial thing, of course, is whether the material is opaque or translucent. Opaque shades confine the light emitted in one or two directions, depending on the disposition of openings. Usually, there are apertures at the top and bottom. It is the size of the openings, not the general profile of the shade, that determines the spread of light emitted. The uppermost aperture throws light up onto the ceiling, which directs it back into the room as "indirect" lighting. The lowermost opening casts light downward onto the floor as "direct" light (although some of it may be bounced as indirect light off the floor covering).

Indirect lighting is the less efficient (which is not to say the less desirable) of these methods by which shades put out light. It relies on a high level of ceiling reflectance (see page 15). Direct lighting from a shade, although more efficient, may distribute the light too narrowly, and require supplementary light sources — especially if the shade bounces little or no light off the ceiling.

Bear in mind that light output is affected by the nature of the shade's internal surfaces: unless these are of high reflectance, the proportion of light lost within the fitting will be high.

Translucent shades, like opaque shades, have a directional function, provided that they have at least one aperture. However, any directional light is supplemented by a soft light that diffuses through the shade's material. A shade of wide radius will appear less bright than a narrower shade of identical shape, on account of the greater distance from the bulb to the inner surface. The fabric of the shade can give an unpredictable colour effect when the lamp is switched on, so if possible you should view a shade in action before purchasing it.

The higher or lower a shade is located in relation to eye level, the greater the risk of glare, as the lamp itself will be visible from a wider range of positions within the room. Shades for ceiling-hung pendants are often fitted with one of the various glare-preventing devices described above.

Choosing a fitting

Light fittings can be categorized in five distinct groups, according to the proportion of upward light they emit. The illustrations on this page show one representative design of fitting for each group. (All fittings are in the current Tronconi range.)

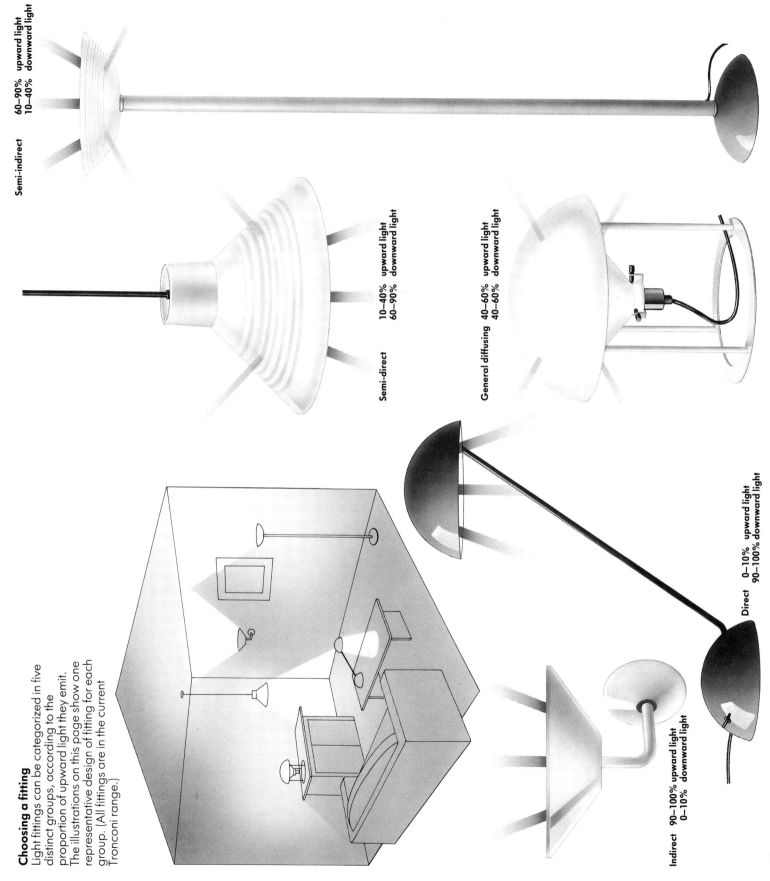

Semi-indirect   60–90% upward light
                 10–40% downward light

Semi-direct   10–40% upward light
                 60–90% downward light

General diffusing 40–60% upward light
                   40–60% downward light

Direct   0–10%   upward light
         90–100% downward light

Indirect 90–100% upward light
          0–10%   downward light

Design features

In the design of contemporary light fittings, certain basic shapes and construction principles occur again and again, together making up what might be termed a basic vocabulary of fitting design. A selection of these recurrent motifs is shown below and on the following pages.

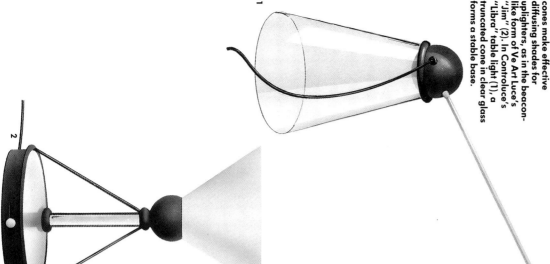

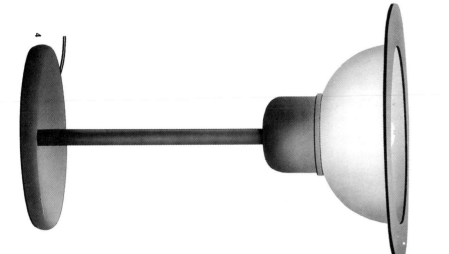

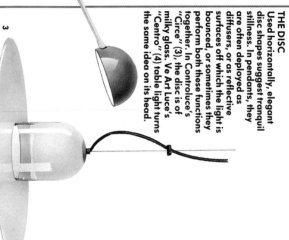

THE CONE

Cone shapes are commonly used for shades: their geometry suggests a beam of light spreading out from its apex, the bulb. Inverted cones make effective diffusing shades for uplighters, as in the beacon-like form of Ve Art Luce's "Jim" (2). In Controluce's "Libra" table light (1), a truncated cone in clear glass forms a stable base.

THE DISC

Used horizontally, elegant disc shapes suggest tranquil stillness. In pendants, they are often deployed as diffusers, or as reflective surfaces off which the light is bounced, or sometimes they perform both these functions together. In Controluce's "Circe" (3), the disc is of milky glass. Ve Art Luce's "Centro" (4) table light turns the same idea on its head.

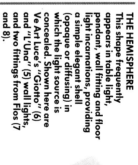

THE HEMISPHERE

This shape frequently appears in table light, pendant, wall fitting and floor light incarnations, providing a simple elegant shell (opaque or diffusing) in which the light source is concealed. Shown here are Ve Art Luce's "Giotto" (5) and "L'Una" (6) wall lights, and two fittings from Flos (7 and 8).

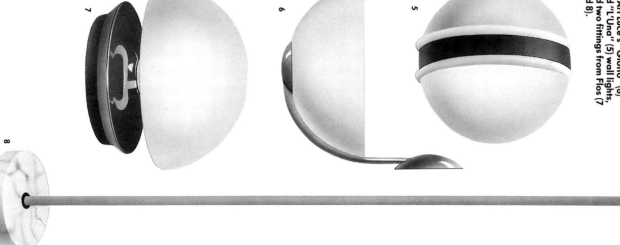

41

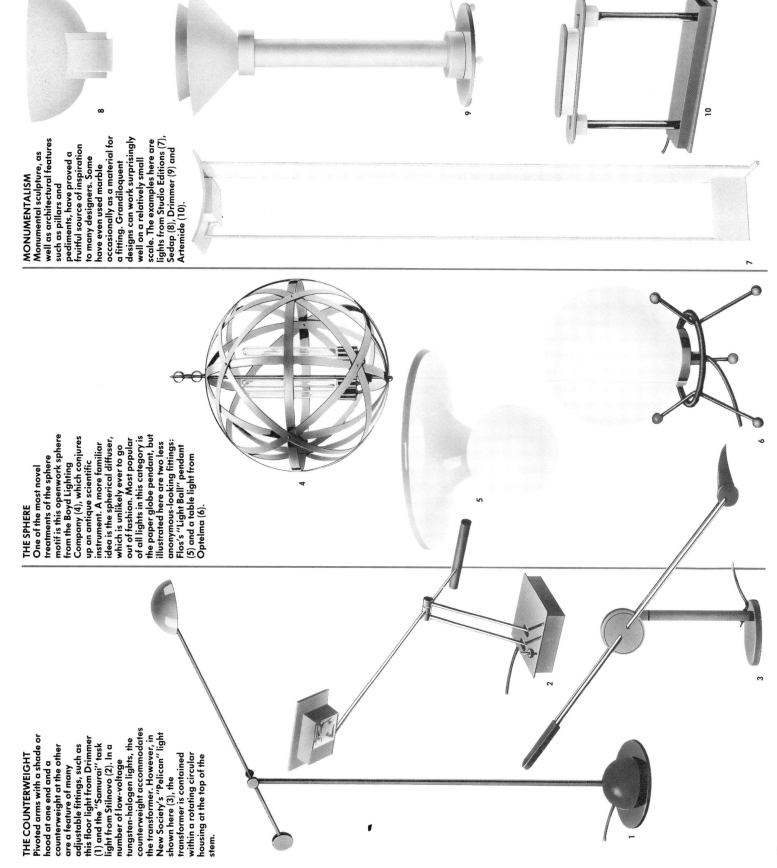

THE COUNTERWEIGHT

Pivoted arms with a shade or hood at one end and a counterweight at the other are a feature of many adjustable fittings, such as this floor light from Drimmer (1) and the "Samurai" task light from Stilnovo (2). In a number of low-voltage tungsten-halogen lights, the counterweight accommodates the transformer. However, in New Society's "Pelican" light shown here (3), the transformer is contained within a rotating circular housing at the top of the stem.

THE SPHERE

One of the most novel treatments of the sphere motif is this openwork sphere from the Boyd Lighting Company (4), which conjures up an antique scientific instrument. A more familiar idea is the spherical diffuser, which is unlikely ever to go out of fashion. Most popular of all lights in this category is the paper globe pendant, but illustrated here are two less anonymous-looking fittings: Flos's "Light Ball" pendant (5) and a table light from Optelma (6).

MONUMENTALISM

Monumental sculpture, as well as architectural features such as pillars and pediments, have proved a fruitful source of inspiration to many designers. Some have even used marble occasionally as a material for a fitting. Grandiloquent designs can work surprisingly well on a relatively small scale. The examples here are lights from Studio Editions (7), Sedap (8), Drimmer (9) and Artemide (10).

42

THE RIGHT-ANGLE
Right-angle designs are often favoured for uplighters, wall lights and table lights. Usually, the angles are softened by a touch of roundness, as in Bilumen's "Composto" pendant (11) and "Curve" table light (12). Luci's "Veronica" (13) is a half-way stage toward the more rigid angularity of PRC's halogen table light (14).

12

13

11

14

15

16

17

18

THE CURVE
Arcing curves are the backbone of some of the most elegant modern fittings. A unique variant is Studio Editions' "Omega" table light (15). Ci's "Arcobalena" floor light (16), designed by Marco Zotta, won a treasured place in the Design Collection of New York's Museum of Modern Art. Also much imitated is Flos's "Arco" (18), a creation of Achille Castiglioni. Stilnovo's "Elle" (17) arcs more modestly.

43

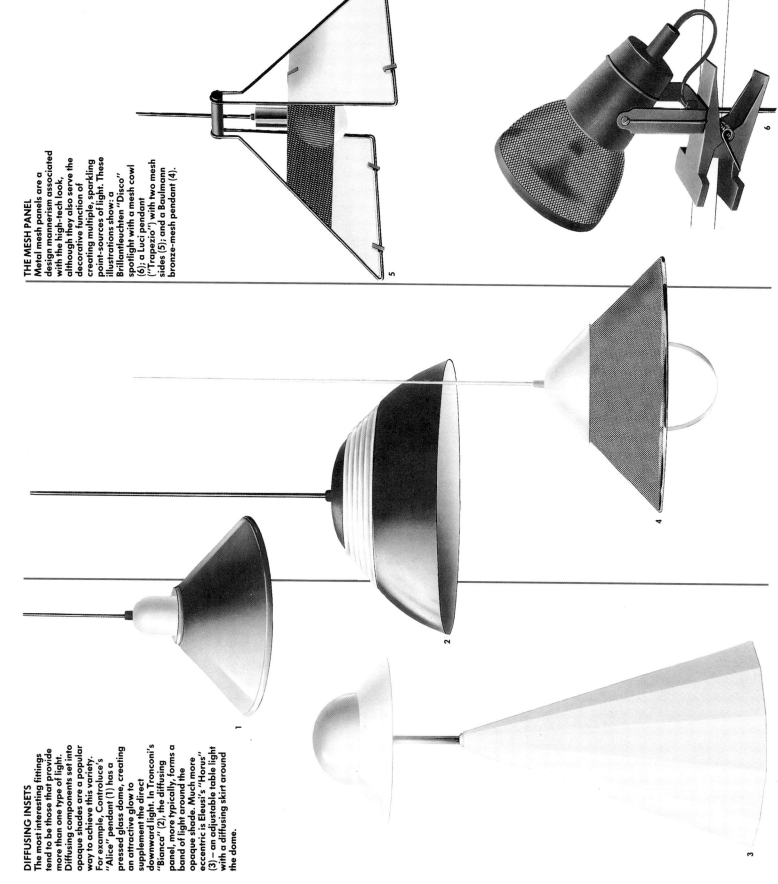

DIFFUSING INSETS

The most interesting fittings tend to be those that provide more than one type of light. Diffusing components set into opaque shades are a popular way to achieve this variety. For example, Controluce's "Alice" pendant (1) has a pressed glass dome, creating an attractive glow to supplement the direct downward light. In Tronconi's "Bianca" (2), the diffusing panel, more typically, forms a band of light around the opaque shade. Much more eccentric is Eleusi's "Horus" (3) – an adjustable table light with a diffusing skirt around the dome.

THE MESH PANEL

Metal mesh panels are a design mannerism associated with the high-tech look, although they also serve the decorative function of creating multiple, sparkling point-sources of light. These illustrations show: a Brillantleuchten "Disco" spotlight with a mesh cowl (6); a Luci pendant ("Trapezio") with two mesh sides (5); and a Baulmann bronze-mesh pendant (4).

44

THE STEPPED SHADE

Stepped shades make an emphatic design statement. The material may be metal as in Cil's "Bizzy" (7); however, moulded glass is more common, as in Stilnovo's "Ziggurat" (8) and "Sofio" (9).

THE BARE BULB

Fittings which show off the bulb instead of disguising it were especially popular in the 1960s, along with harsh, glittery lighting and brash primary colours. To avoid glare with these fittings, bulbs must be low-voltage or crown-silvered. Optelma's tin-can fitting (10) and Stilnovo's "Fante" pendant (10) take an opal spherical bulb. Also from Stilnovo are the "Disco" pendant (11), which makes use of a crown-silvered reflector lamp, and the "Pharo" spotlight, which unashamedly shows off a blown-glass reflector (13).

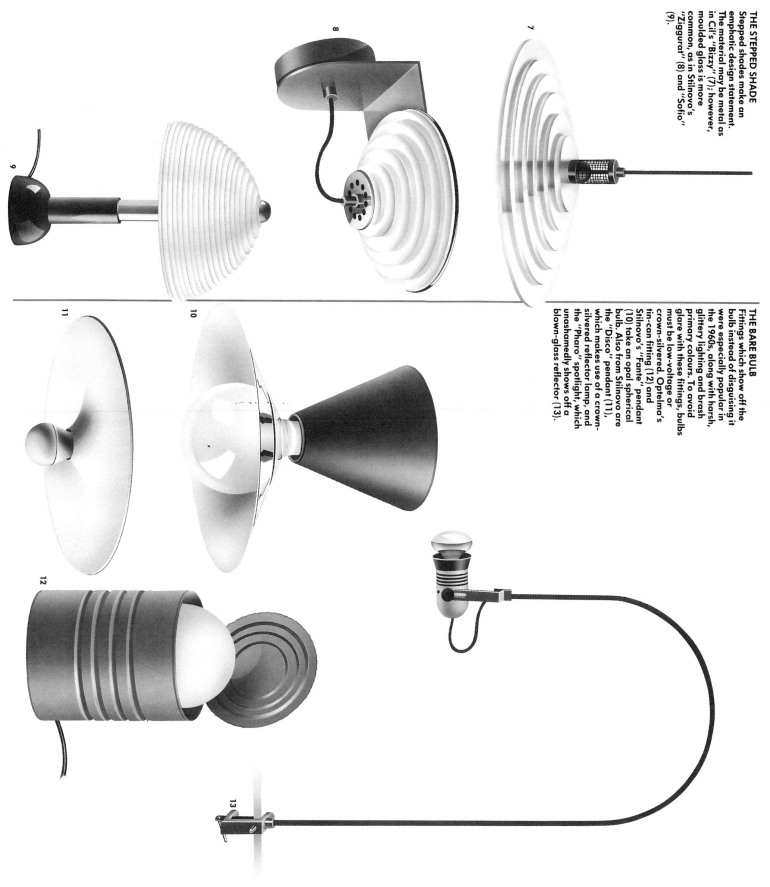

45

FABRIC

The reaction against hard-edged, machine-made forms is most clearly expressed in the use of fabrics in many modern fittings. The organic formlessness of Stilnovo's "Torre" table light (3) – a fabric flounce on a cylindrical glass base – looks less aggressive than rigid geometry. Stretched fabric is commonly used in fittings based on kite and umbrella motifs; the examples here are from Optelma (2) and Shiu Kay Kan (1).

ADJUSTABILITY

Desk lights (typified by the Anglepoise range) are not the only kind of adjustable fitting, as these illustrations show. Adjustable table lights, wall lights and floor lights offer a useful number of alternative lighting options, but also often have a play value: quite simply, they are fun to use. Hinges and springs can play an important decorative role. Cil's "Le Bagnanti" (6) is one of the more complex types: the shade and diffusing/reflecting screen are individually adjustable. A more conventional range of options is offered by Stilnovo's "Alfiere" table light (4) and "67533" table light (5), both with swivelling shades.

Manufacturers

Many of the world's most important manufacturers of light fittings are small-scale companies run virtually on the scale of cottage industries. Output is often fairly restricted. Some of the designers working within this sector produce innovative, experimental fittings which in some cases come close to being works of art.

There are also large-scale manufacturers, whose output may consist of either high-volume utilitarian products – or sometimes a mixture of both. Many of the most adventurous companies are linked with furniture manufacturers, and most are Italian: it is no accident that Italian names recur constantly throughout this book. For such firms, the design and presentation of new fittings is carried on very much in the manner of the fashion industry. That is to say, new designs are created each season, and prototypes are prepared to show at trade fairs. Those that elicit a favourable response go ahead to full production.

This is a highly competitive field in which a small number of élite firms set the pace, while more cynically minded companies produce cheaper copies of the same designs – or at least, turn out products inspired by the pace-setters. The true innovators depend on skilled craftsmen who can assemble metal or glass components to a high degree of finish. Cheaper versions, while they may have a similar shape or form, will rarely match the quality of the originals.

Major firms who may be counted among the market leaders include: Flos, Arteluce, (Flos's sister company), Artemide, Tronconi, i Guzzini and Stilnovo, all in Italy; Concord in Britain; Brillantleuchten and Ingo Maurer in West Germany. These companies tend to share the services of a group of leading independent designers – for example, Achille Castiglioni, Perry King, Santiago Miranda, Ettore Sottsass and Vico Magistretti. The levels of both technological and artistic innovation are high. New-technology light sources are increasingly put to work in imaginative ways.

Most manufacturers will produce a basic design for a range of specific fitting types. For example, a floor-standing uplighter may spin off a lookalike wall light, and perhaps a ceiling pendant too. This makes it possible to light a whole interior using fittings that have a strong family identity.

Most of these leading manufacturers initially catered only for specialist interior designers. However, now that domestic lighting is becoming more adventurous, their products are becoming much more widely available in retail lighting outlets. In a somewhat watered-down form, comparable designs are also to be found in mass-market department stores, which are filling a useful role in offering quality lighting at a reasonable cost.

Control hardware

To give you maximum control over your lighting arrangements, in theory each fitting must be separately switched. However, in practice, groups of fittings that work collectively (for example, a cluster of downlighters) are often run off one circuit.

Wall switches vary more widely in style than is commonly believed. In addition to the ubiquitous white or ivory-coloured plastic rocker switch (which may be single or multiple), there are various other finishes, such as aluminium, brass, copper or coloured plastic. Ornate mock-antique switches are best avoided, even in the most traditional-style interiors, as they tend to look much too ostentatious.

The introduction of the dimmer switch was a major landmark in domestic lighting. The "old-style" resistance dimmers wasted power at low levels and tended to hum noisily, but today's solid-state versions are a great improvement. Not only do they allow you to reduce lighting levels to suit different moods, but they are also energy-saving.

One of the most popular types of wall dimmer has a rotary action to select any brightness level from very dim to full, and an independent push-pull action to switch the light on and off. This means that you do not have to reset a particular brightness level every time you switch on, as you do with some units. Touch-sensitive wall dimmers are also now available. Dimming fluorescent lights is not really practicable: you have to use special equipment, which is more expensive than the benefits would justify. Whatever dimmer you use, take care not to exceed the maximum wattage prescribed for it.

A recent development in control hardware is a handheld infrared unit (with appropriate receivers) that allows you to switch or dim lights in a room from some distance away; the principle is the same as that used for remote-control TV channel changing devices.

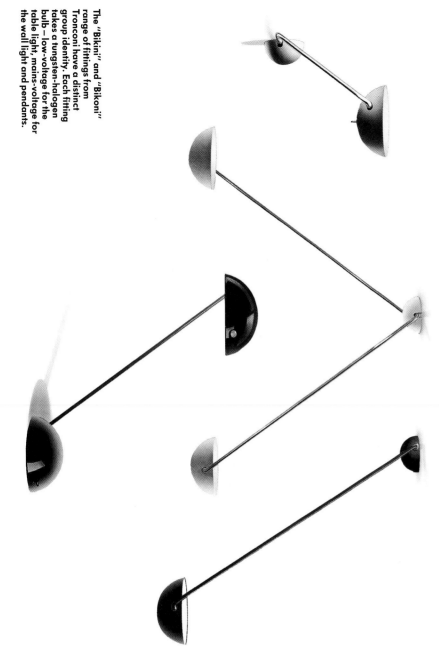

The "Bikini" and "Bikoni" range of fittings from Tronconi have a distinct group identity. Each fitting takes a tungsten-halogen bulb – low-voltage for the table light, mains-voltage for the wall light and pendants.

Downlighters can be broadly categorized under two headings: those that are wholly or partially recessed into the ceiling, leaving the source of light all but invisible; and those that are mounted on the surface of a ceiling. Both types, as their generic name suggests, are essentially fittings that concentrate all the light output downward into a room. The light takes the shape of a precisely controlled beam, whose profile is determined by the size and shape of the fitting, the bulb type and the disposition and character of the reflectors. Each fitting is specified for use with a particular bulb, which may be a GLS, reflector spot, PAR spot or flood, or miniature fluorescent.

There are also some types that take low-voltage halogen lamps, which reduce the size of the fitting and minimize over-heating problems; these units require a separate, remote transformer.

Black multigroove baffles fitted to some downlighters greatly reduce the brightness apparent within the aperture. Other models have a mirror black reflector which presents the appearance of a black hole when lit. Silver- and gold-finish reflectors are also commonly available, providing a soft glow of brightness around each aperture. Additionally, there are downlighters with louvers, diffusers and fresnel lenses for a fairly broad, soft-edged light. In none of these examples is the lamp itself directly visible from normal viewing angles. Some fittings allow precise fine-tuning of beam direction, either by internal adjustments or by swivelling an "eyeball". Directional control is useful not only for spotlighting collectibles or architectural features but also to provide a vertical beam from within a sloping or vaulted ceiling. A few directional downlighters both recessed and surface-mounted are specifically intended for washing a wall with light. Some special fittings come with masking devices that can produce a precise rectangle of light of a given size on a vertical surface: the usual way to exploit this facility would be to pick out a wall-hung painting, framing it against relatively dark surroundings.

Choosing and installing downlighters

You cannot tell just by looking at a downlighter exactly what its capabilities are. Before buying, you should therefore ask for technical information from the retailer or manufacturer. All manufacturers publish "performance cones", which illustrate the beam profile for a specified lamp and provide a basis for working out the optimum spacing. This, of course, will depend on ceiling height.

The recessed variety of downlighter looks singularly unimpressive in a shop. These are simple, functional items of equipment without decorative

frills – although some exceptional types make a modest concession to ornament, for example in the form of brass rims. Do not be put off by the utilitarian austerity of these fittings; they are specially designed to be unobtrusive in a room, taking up no space at all.

It is important to check that your ceiling is deep enough for a recessed downlighter. Some fittings are suitable only for non-domestic uses, with ceilings much deeper than those in the average home. In some cases, you can solve the problem by choosing a fitting that is only partially recessed. Variable recess units may be installed

with any projection from zero up to about 6 inches (15 cm).

Installing recessed fittings requires considerable effort or expense. Rewiring will be necessary, as well as a good deal of building and decorating work to pierce the holes and make good any damage afterwards. Once installed, recessed lights cannot be tidily removed. These factors make them a much more likely proposition for an owner than a renter.

Surface-mounted downlighters take the form of a metal cylinder or square "can" with a white, bronze or silvered finish. They are available in a narrower range of types than the recessed type.

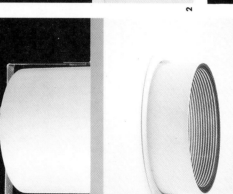

7

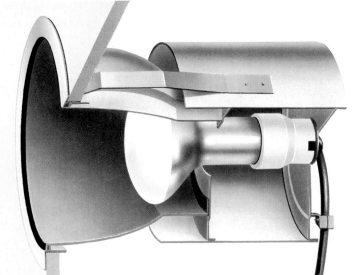

The views above and on the opposite page illustrate the basic construction of some of the principal types of downlighter, shown *in situ* in a ceiling installation. All the fittings (except 7) are from Concord, but designs show little variation from one manufacturer to another.

1 A variable-depth downlighter with a sharply grooved baffle to reduce aperture brightness. This fitting takes a 40- or 100-watt reflector lamp.

2 A pinhole downlighter for general lighting. Light from a 100-watt pearl bulb is concentrated through a very small aperture to produce a wide-angle beam with minimum visible source.

3 A directional downlighter, which gives a narrow, high-intensity beam with a soft edge. The adjustable parabolic reflector takes a low-voltage halogen lamp. (The separate transformer is not shown.)

4 A cone downlighter, which offers soft-edged, wide distribution of light from a 100-watt pearl bulb. Available with a black aperture or a gold or silver reflector.

5 The "Darklighter", a directional light for emphasizing a picture, sculpture or other feature, using a concealed low-brightness source. The angle of the fitting can be adjusted through 30°, with 358° of horizontal rotation.

6 A low-energy downlighter, for use with a 9-watt compact fluorescent.

7 A cutaway view of the Marlin "Dark Cone" downlighter. The fixing arms spring open to hold the downlighter in place after it has been inserted in the ceiling hole from below.

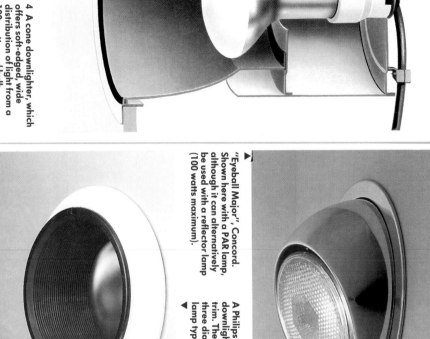

"Eyeball Major", Concord. Shown here with a PAR lamp, although it can alternatively be used with a reflector lamp (100 watts maximum).

A Philips recessed downlighter with a flanged trim. The fitting comes with three diameters for different lamp types.

A variable-depth recessed fitting from Marlin, shown in two of its positions. The fitting has a black milligroove baffle and an attractive gold-finish trim.

A surface-mounted "Mini-Multigroove" fitting (Concord). The finish may be brushed aluminium (as here) or satin white.

An all-purpose Philips downlighter ("W4001") that adjusts to accommodate a variety of light sources, including a PAR "cool beam" lamp and a special mercury-blended reflector lamp for plant lighting.

A surface-mounted cylindrical downlighter from Philips, with a distinctive ventilation grille.

A semi-recessed light in the Philips range, available with an optional clip-on wall-washing attachment.

Applications

When used in a co-ordinated system instead of singly, downlighters can provide overall lighting in a room in a way that accentuates horizontal surfaces, and to a lesser extent the walls. Emphasis is thrown away from the ceiling, which appears relatively dark, onto the room's contents — furniture, flowers, pictures and so on. Whereas indirect light sources, such as uplighters, rely on a pale-coloured, highly reflective ceiling, downlighters are the type of fitting to use if you prefer a darker ceiling tone.

Recessed downlighters are often positioned in a grid pattern, in a single row, either along a hallway or close to a wall, or in groups over surfaces that need to be given their own intense light, such as table tops. When placing lights over tables, choose a fitting that will not cause glare by reflecting the light source in a varnished or otherwise glossy surface.

To use multiple downlighters to maximum effect, arrange them in groups on different electrical circuits. This makes the scheme more versatile. For example, you can use one switch to turn on a row of wall-washing lights, another for a separately wired group concentrated over a table. That way, the latter do not have to be on every time you want the wall-washers on, and vice versa.

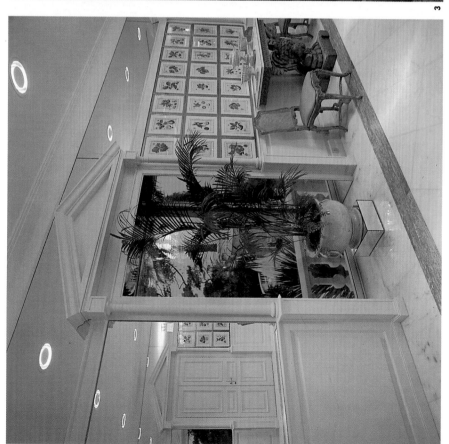

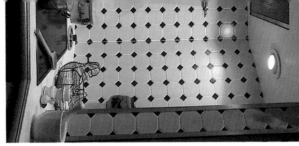

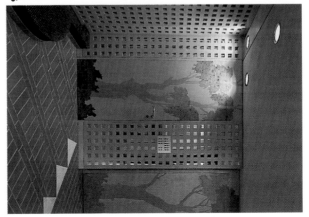

1 Recessed downlighters positioned well away from the wall provide background lighting in this corridor lined with botanical illustrations. Each light has a spill ring to combat glare and prevent the shiny floor from picking up reflections of the bulbs.

2 A bathroom lit entirely by downlighters. The two eyeball fittings close to the wall are spaced to give a double arch effect, while a third fitting dispels gloom from the entrance.

3 Adjustable downlighters are ideal for displaying a collection that is regularly rearranged. These are low-voltage halogen fittings.

4 A pair of eyeball fittings shed useful light over a kitchen range, as well as creating sparkling reflections in a well-polished *batterie de cuisine*.

5 A series of box-shaped downlighters, elaborately built to spread diffused light over a dining table, offers an interesting variation on the downlighter theme.

6 In this unusual entrance hall, recessed downlighters used as wall-washers contribute to the atmosphere and strike a note of welcome.

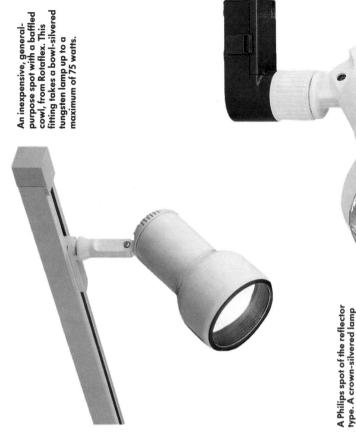

An inexpensive, general-purpose spot with a baffled cowl, from Rotaflex. This fitting takes a bowl-silvered tungsten lamp up to a maximum of 75 watts.

A Philips spot of the reflector type. A crown-silvered lamp (100 or 60 watts) reflects light back into the highly polished integral reflector, which in turn throws a high-intensity beam into the room. The knuckle joint adjusts over a wide range – 350° on the horizontal plane, 180° on the vertical.

A display spotlight from Philips, designed for use with any reflector lamp but shown here with a PAR lamp. The mount adjusts through 260° horizontally and 85° vertically. A black cowl is available as an optional extra.

The central purpose of a spotlight is to provide a concentrated light over a limited area to highlight a particular object or surface. One of the key features of the fitting is the flexibility with which it can be adjusted, thanks to a multidirectional joint; this typically allows up to 360° of horizontal rotation and 90° of vertical swivel. Usually, there is a safety stop, which prevents the lamp from pointing toward the mounting surface, with consequent risk of overheating.

At its simplest, a spotlight can consist of an internally silvered lamp with a socket. But to improve efficiency and increase beam concentration, the fitting also normally contains a built-in reflector. This opens up the possibility of creating decorative effects; spotlights are very often used as much for the sparkle that shines off their reflectors as for the characteristics of the light that they emit.

Various kinds of cowls and reflectors are available, sometimes as interchangeable options. As with downlighters, a baffled reflector is common. The finish for the cowl may be metallized, or stove-enamelled in black, white, red or brown. But with some fittings the cowl is replaced by a sleeve, which leaves the whole head of the lamp visible. The most common lamp type used with spots is the reflector, although many fittings can also be used with a conventional bulb or PAR lamp (spot or flood). Some types take crown-silvered bulbs. A recent development is the low-voltage tungsten-halogen spot, which is designed for use with a halogen reflector lamp.

Spotlights are sold as single, double or triple fittings with a mount that can be attached to a ceiling or wall. With double or triple spots, the mount sometimes takes the form of a bar, although a circular mount (similar to a ceiling "rose" for a pendant) is perhaps more familiar. You can also buy spots with a clamp for attachment to a shelf or pole. However, the most fashionable approach these days is to mount spotlights on tracks which are fixed flush to a wall or ceiling (or sometimes suspended at some distance below the ceiling).

Track-mounted spots

Track-mounted spotlighting originated as a technique for shops and exhibitions, providing an easily adjustable, easily installed lighting system for picking out items on display that might regularly have to be rearranged. From there, the idea spread to enjoy an enormous vogue in domestic interiors. Tracks can also be used for pendant lights, but it is with spotlighting that they are most commonly associated.

The track is a strip, usually ceiling-mounted, at which a light fitting can be positioned at any point, via an adaptor, and locked into place by pushing a lever or tightening a screw. The track also carries the power; it can take as many lights as you need, up to the maximum wattage imposed by the electrical circuit. You can easily check that you have not exceeded this safety limit by applying a mathematical formula: watts = volts × amps. For example, a circuit rated at 5 amps and running at the standard 240 volts for the UK gives you a total wattage of 5 × 240 = 1,200 – enough to run 12 100-watt bulbs or 20 60-watt bulbs safely.

Generally, lighting track is made up of lengths of aluminium with a U-shaped profile. These are screwed to the wall or ceiling, attached via metal brackets, or sometimes recessed. Housed in an insulated channel within the track is a set of electrical contact strips, set well back out of reach of straying fingers for safety. A live-feed end unit connects with the main circuit wiring, while the opposite end terminates in a "dead-end" stop.

The track is sold in standard lengths which may be clipped together to make longer runs. Normally, you can cut a standard length shorter without special tools. Corner junctions, T junctions and flexible, concertina-like connectors allow more elaborate layouts, including grid patterns.

Although some track/spotlight adaptors have individual switches, these would obviously be out of reach in a ceiling-mounted system, so wall-switches are normally preferred. Special multi-tracks take three or four separately switched circuits, although

Methods of mounting spotlights

Circular mount

Track

Pole

Wall bar

Clamp

Stem types

Knuckle

Multi-directional bracket

Cross-section of track (single circuit)

Earth

N terminal

L terminal

Cutaway view of a Marlin spotlight, showing the lampholder.

Cutaway view of a Concord "Targa" low-voltage spot with framing projector attachment.

Lens

Levers to control the beam shape

A Marlin floodlight for interior use. The linear tungsten-halogen lamp is protected by a toughened glass visor.

Cowl types

1 Mini-bullet 2 Bullet (or acorn). 3 Drum. 4 Reflector (for use with crown-silvered bulb). 5 Ventilated (shown with dichroic reflector lamp). 6 Eyeball. 7 Sleeve. 8 Cone.

1 Drum spotlights on a ceiling track illuminate a dining table and a checkerboard wall hanging. Had the ceiling been any lower, these bulky lights would have tended to look obtrusive.

2 A suspended metal grid provides a housing for ceiling-level clip-on spots. The effect is certainly glittering; many people, however, might find the light sources too bright for comfort.

3 Wall-mounted spotlights with broad reflectors and crown-silvered bulbs are angled upward to supply indirect kitchen lighting. An unusual way to combat glare from spotlights and banish distracting shadows from work surfaces.

4 The "Parentesi" light (Flos, designed by Achille Castiglioni) puts a 150-watt reflector lamp to work in a unique way. You can slide the light source up or down a flexible steel wire to provide versatile task lighting.

single circuits are still more usual for domestic applications. Tube-shaped tracks, finished in polished silver-anodized aluminium, offer a novel alternative to the more conventional square-section track. Some track-mounted lights can be operated from a skirting-board socket outlet via a length of flex and a plug.

There are two special pitfalls that you should bear in mind when planning track-mounted spotlighting. One is that track-spot systems are not generally interchangeable from one manufacturer to another: you cannot rely on being able to use one firm's track with another firm's light. The second danger is a matter of aesthetics. Long lengths of track can become an unsightly intrusion, unless handled with tact and care. Tracks look best when they echo the geometry of the room; they should be parallel to the walls to create a minimum of visual disruption.

You should never use track in a bathroom, or in other humid environments where the electrics may come into contact with water.

Changing fashions

During the 1960s and 70s there was a general mania for spotlights, which had a lot to do with the appeal of glistening metal and the quest for low-budget modernity. This vogue resulted in spots being used in many quite unsuitable positions: their directional flexibility was insufficiently exploited, and their looks often clashed with the style of the surroundings. Today, spotlights can appear very dated. But it would be a pity if changing fashions were to kill them off altogether. Provided that they are sensitively deployed, spots are an important tool in the art of lighting an interior. For example, they can play a major role in providing strong contrasts of light and shade that will bring a flat

lighting scheme to life, and they are invaluable for display lighting (see pages 112–115).

If you feel uncomfortable about the somewhat obtrusive, high-tech appearance of spotlights, you could always conceal them behind a pelmet at cornice level or in an alcove, or even behind a houseplant or other suitable object. The current generation of minispots are in any case fairly discreet in appearance.

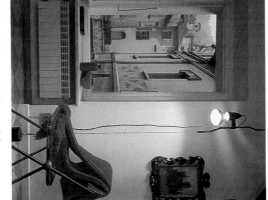

4

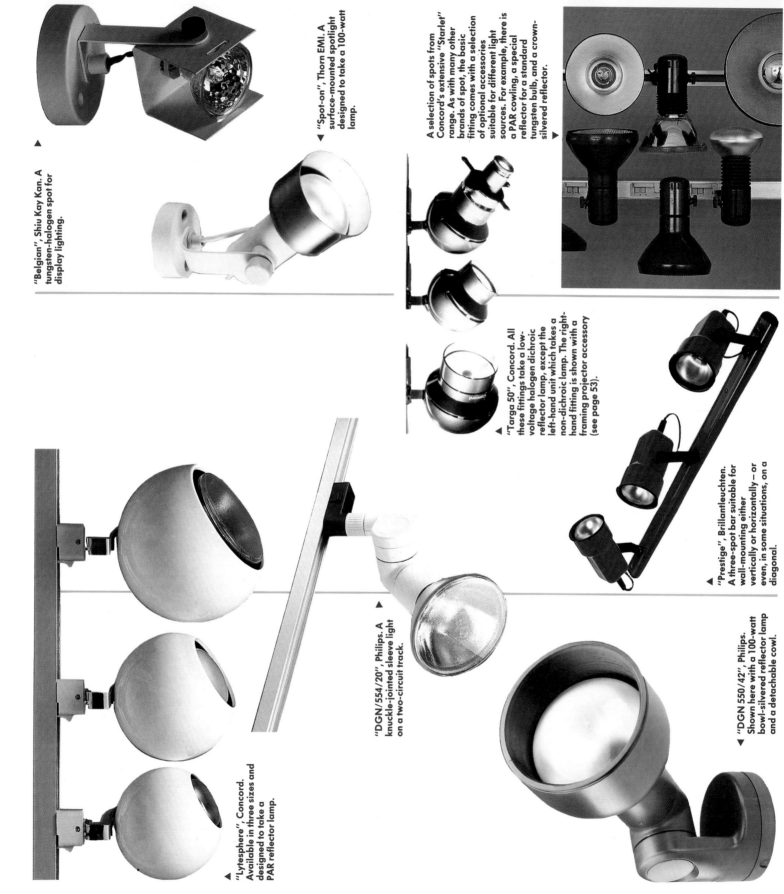

Spotlights

"Belgian", Shiu Kay Kan. A tungsten-halogen spot for display lighting.

▼ "Spot-on", Thorn EMI. A surface-mounted spotlight designed to take a 100-watt lamp.

A selection of spots from Concord's extensive "Starler" range. As with many other brands of spot, the basic fitting comes with a selection of optional accessories suitable for different light sources. For example, there is a PAR cowling, a special reflector for a standard tungsten bulb, and a crown-silvered reflector. ▼

▲ "Targa 50", Concord. All these fittings take a low-voltage halogen dichroic reflector lamp, except the left-hand unit which takes a non-dichroic lamp. The right-hand fitting is shown with a framing projector accessory (see page 53).

▲ "Prestige", Brillantleuchten. A three-spot bar suitable for wall-mounting either vertically or horizontally – or even, in some situations, on a diagonal.

▲ "Lytesphere", Concord. Available in three sizes and designed to take a PAR reflector lamp.

▲ "DGN/554/20", Philips. A knuckle-jointed sleeve light on a two-circuit track.

▼ "DGN 550/42", Philips. Shown here with a 100-watt bowl-silvered reflector lamp and a detachable cowl.

56

"Click", Brillantleuchten. Adjustable spots intended for wall-mounting. The white interior surface of the cowl reflects light from a 40-watt standard bulb (clear or pearl).

"Lytesphere", Concord. The "Mini" spot in this range is shown here with a silvered reflector bowl, designed to take a 40-watt crown-silvered bulb.

▶ "Bullet Major", Concord. The highly polished aluminium cowl houses a 150-watt PAR lamp. The light is shown here on tubular track.

"Dardo", Luci (Toshyuki Kita). A low-voltage halogen spot, with integral transformer. The baffle is an optional extra. ▶

▼ "Monkey", Arteluce. A track-mounted fitting with a glass reflector which also acts as a partial diffuser.

"Powerwasher", Concord. A track-mounted floodlight designed for wall-washing. This fitting, which uses a 300-watt halogen lamp, is suitable only for large rooms.

Another "Prestige" fitting from Brillantleuchten: a wall-mounted spot with its own push-button switch. ▼

▶ "Quartet Major", Concord. For high-intensity accent or display lighting with a 300-watt PAR spot or flood lamp. The louver attachment prevents side glare.

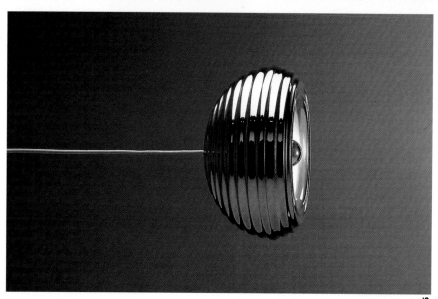

Pendants are still the most common type of light fitting found in the home. Baldly defined, a pendant is a fitting that relies on an electrical flex falling directly from a ceiling attachment to provide the power. At the lower end of the cable is a holder for the light source, which is shielded from view by a shade of some kind. The heavier types of shade may require a special means of support; it is unwise to place too much loading on the flex itself, or it may come loose from its fixings.

This broad description of a pendant embraces a wide spectrum of lights, all the way from costly crystal chandeliers to low-budget paper globes. The chandelier is the ancestor of all other pendants, and was used in pre-electric days to carry groups of candles. Many pendant fittings made today try to recapture this flavour of the past, by imitation of historic styles. Because pendants are conspicuous objects within a room, it is important to give some careful thought to this stylistic aspect. The question of whether a pseudo-antique look is desirable, and if so how far it is permissible to follow this path, is likely to be contentious. Not everyone could live with light sockets designed to look like candles, with flame-shaped bulbs.

To determine the quality of light from a pendant, there are many crucial considerations, quite apart from the

1 Achille Castiglioni's
influential "Frisbi", designed
for Flos, not only diffuses and
reflects but also sends down
a narrow shaft of direct light.

2 Note the simplicity of the
rise-and-fall mechanism on
Stilnovo's "Multiplica" fitting.

3 Pendants lend themselves
easily to ornamental
treatment. These fittings are
redolent of the 1920s.

4 The faithful paper globe –
inexpensive and easy to pack
– is often used for its
dominating shape.

5 A polished aluminium
shade, jokingly named
"Splügen Bräu after a brand
of beer: Castiglioni, its
designer, thought it looked
like a bottle top.

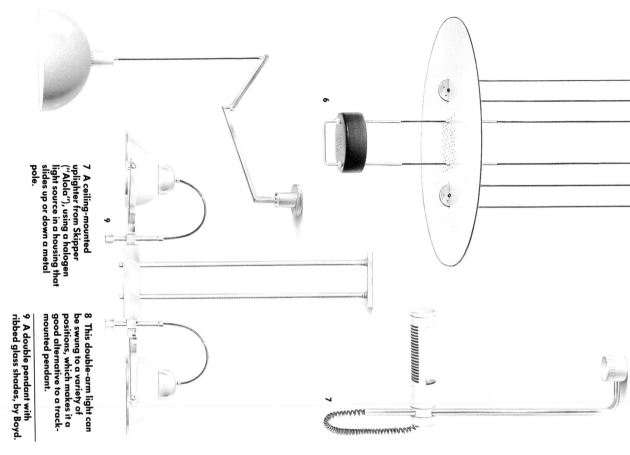

6 Controluce's "Ippogrifo": an ingenious rise-and-fall halogen fitting. The support wires pass over four wheels and then through a reflector disc that directs light back into the room.

7 A ceiling-mounted uplighter ("Alola"), using a halogen light source that slides up or down a metal pole.

8 This double-arm light can be swung to a variety of positions, which makes it a good alternative to a track-mounted pendant.

9 A double pendant with ribbed glass shades, by Boyd.

choice of bulb. For example, key factors are the height of the light source above the floor, the disposition of openings (if any) in the shade, the size of the openings, the material the shade is made of, and the proportions of the room. How this last factor comes into play may not at first be obvious, but can be illustrated clearly enough by an example.

Take a shade made of an opaque material, with an opening only at its lower end. This will produce a light only in a downward direction, in the profile of a cone. In a low-slung position, such a pendant will create an intense, localized pool of light immediately beneath it. This is true regardless of the size of the room. However, when the same pendant is used on a short drop much nearer the ceiling, room size becomes a significant factor. In a small room, some of the light will be reflected off the walls (assuming that they are pale-coloured) back into the room to create a high overall level of illumination. But in a larger room, the light from the pendant will fall off before it reaches the walls, leaving patches of gloom around the edges of the light cone.

Rise-and-fall fittings have been developed that allow pendants to be converted to either of these extremes – low-slung or high-slung – as required. These types are most often used over dining tables. At mealtimes they are used in the lowered position for intimate mood lighting, while at other times during the evening they are raised for more general illumination. Rise-and-fall pendants have advantages for the aged or infirm, who might find it difficult to change a bulb in a fixed, high-level fitting.

Just as some pendants produce only a downward light, there are other types that throw indirect light up toward the ceiling and walls by bouncing all the light output off a silvered bowl or disc fitting. Between these two categories are general diffusers (for example, the paper globe), which distribute light evenly in all directions, and fittings that send some light up as well as down.

Arguably, the most successful pendant lights are those that manage to give off light in more than one way.

For example, Achille Castiglioni's modern "Frisbi" light combines a downlighter with a white plastic diffusing disc that hangs just below the metallic shade, so that the total light emission is made up of both direct and indirect light. In a rather different way, the traditional chandelier has a double function: the overall light that a chandelier supplies is supplemented by decorative light sparklingly refracted through cut glass.

The standard light source for a pendant is a tungsten-filament bulb, and because pendants are often the principal light source in a room, the bulb will be of relatively high wattage – say up to 100 watts. However, if the light is at eye level, a lower wattage is preferable – 15 watts if the bulb is visible, up to 40 watts if it is obscured. Other light sources are also possible. Miniature fluorescent lights can be put to work in pendant fittings, and so can miniature low-voltage halogen bulbs, although these will give light primarily for accent lighting.

Applications

Because pendants are such a familiar kind of light source, it is all too easy to view pendant lighting uncritically, without thinking how current stereotypes can be varied. For example, we tend to assume that a single pendant should be placed in the centre of a living room or bedroom, as a general light source. However, there are various drawbacks to this approach. A central pendant, unaccompanied by other lighting, provides little flexibility for matching light to mood (even with a dimmer), and casts radial shadows beneath and behind furniture. It may also cause glare problems for anyone in the centre of the room.

To some extent these difficulties can be overcome by using supplementary lighting, in addition to the central pendant. A more creative approach, however, is to consider less orthodox applications – for example, using pendants in off-centre positions to complement the architecture or furnishings of a room, or mark off areas of space. In seating areas where glare is a potential danger, you can often solve the problem by choosing a fitting with louvers that cut off the view of the bulb. We have already referred to the practice of putting pendants over dining tables, but you could equally well adopt this strategy with a coffee table.

When thinking about positional possibilities, bear in mind that pendants can serve to emphasize the loftiness of tall rooms and spaces. For example, you may be able to use one effectively in a stairwell or other double-height space. In these circumstances, the flex itself becomes a design element in the room, and to turn it into more of a positive feature you could try using coloured flex and a coloured ceiling rose matched to the shade.

Of course, shades too are a major decorative element in their own right, and it is important to consider their effect when the light is off, as well as when it is switched on. A white paper globe lampshade obviously makes a strong impact on the look of a room; but less obvious is the way that you can use the shade for bouncing light from a spot, as well as for providing diffused illumination. Purely as furnishings, pendants often look best when used in multiples. A single pendant of distinctive design or colour may look simply lost, or jarringly isolated. But add one or more identical fittings, and the result is a recurring motif that may tie different parts of an interior together. Consider, for example, the effectiveness of putting pendants with matching shades over a kitchen work surface. With some pendants, instead of adding extra fittings you can create the same kind of visual echo by choosing matching wall lights made by the same manufacturer.

In circulation areas, the lowest part of a pendant should be at least 78 inches (198cm) above the floor. On the other hand, if the bulb is fairly close to the ceiling, you may notice a build-up of dirt, lifted onto the ceiling surface by air currents caused by convected heat from the bulb; this is a minor problem, as the dirt can easily be wiped off.

1 This aluminium mesh shade over a table grouping is relatively complex. The tungsten bulb is concealed by an upturned metal bowl, which reflects light upward into the shade. The mesh allows some of the light to percolate through, while the rest is bounced downward onto the table.

2 A low-slung pendant used in the classic way to emphasize an eating area. Observe how the spiralling flex adds a decorative flourish: with a taut, straight flex the effect would be very different.

3 An inverted oriental umbrella, made of paper and bamboo, makes an ingenious pendant, which goes well with the wickerwork chairs.

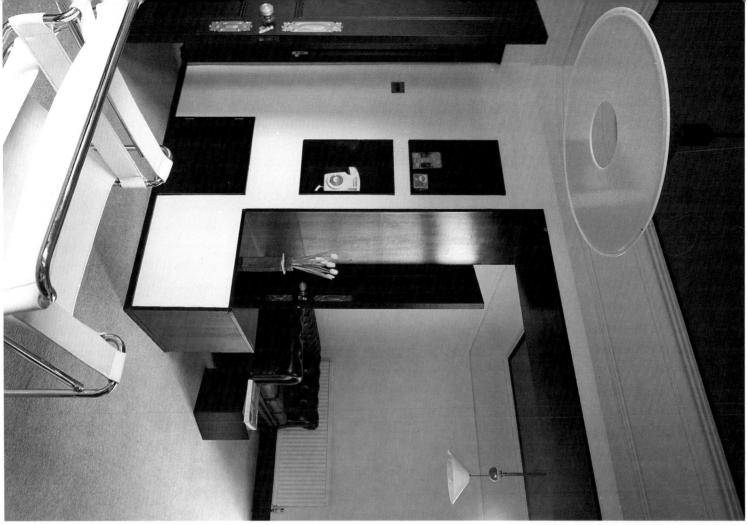

4 Pendants in different parts of a room do not have to match, provided that they have a stylistic affinity. Here, the "Frisbi" light in the foreground is a perfect companion to the rise-and-fall fitting with conical shade.

5 A pendant with concentric diffusing rings provides a soft source of light that can be brought down low over a table without causing glare problems.

6 Light from a spun aluminium pendant creates an enclosed, intimate atmosphere at twilight. A delicate counterweight system means that the fitting can be raised or lowered at the touch of a finger.

Pendants

▲ ▲

"Maria Theresa", Chelsom, above. A traditional glass-and-brass chandelier designed for use with candle-shaped tungsten bulbs.

"SP/13–14–15", Arteluce (Gino Sarfatti), above left. Colourful ceiling or wall fittings available in a variety of sizes. The recommended light source is a 40-watt spherical pearl bulb.

▲ One of a range of pendants by Brillantleuchten. The metal shade has a handle to facilitate rise-and-fall adjustments.

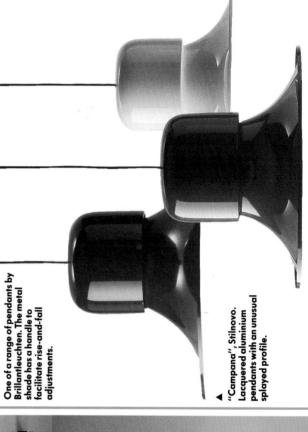

◀ "Campana", Stilnovo. Lacquered aluminium pendants with an unusual splayed profile.

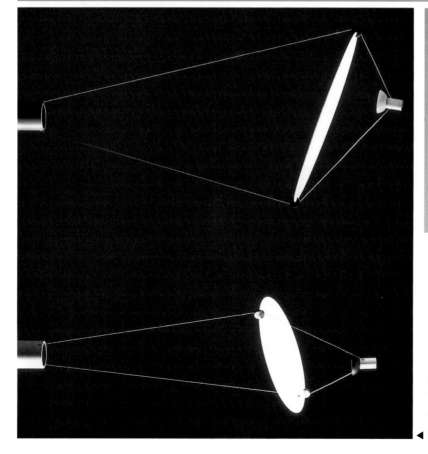

▲ "Aquilone", Eleusi (Georges Seris). A low-wattage halogen pendant with an upward-facing lampholder at the bottom which bounces light off and through the translucent shade.

"Kandido", Luci (F. A. Porsche). Adjustable, telescopic chromium arms support a low-voltage halogen bulb.

"Moni", Flos (Castiglioni). A close-mounted halogen fitting. The perforated metal support casts attractive spoke-like shadows. ▶

62

"Germana", Luci (Gianfranco Frattini). A functional-looking pendant with a glass diffuser. Grey or black rubber baffles prevent glare.

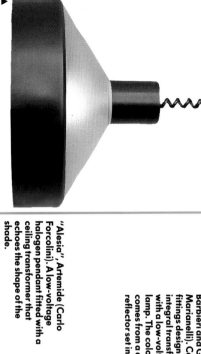

"Solitaire", Tronconi (Paul Barbieri and Giorgio Marianelli). Cast metal fittings designed with an integral transformer for use with a low-voltage halogen lamp. The colourful sparkle comes from a dichroic reflector set in the rosette.

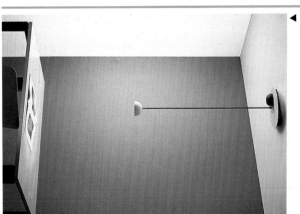

"Alesia", Artemide (Carlo Forcolini). A low-voltage halogen pendant fitted with a ceiling transformer that echoes the shape of the shade.

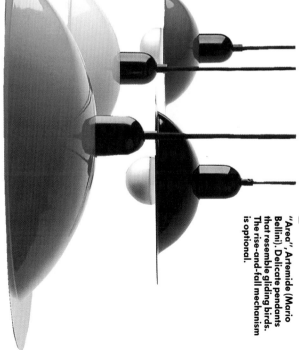

"Piatto", Stilnovo (De Pas, D'Urbino and Lomazzi). Lacquered aluminium pendants in a flying-saucer shape.

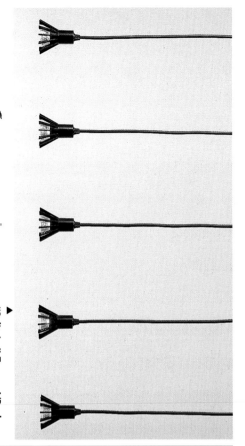

"Area", Artemide (Mario Bellini). Delicate pendants that resemble gliding birds. The rise-and-fall mechanism is optional.

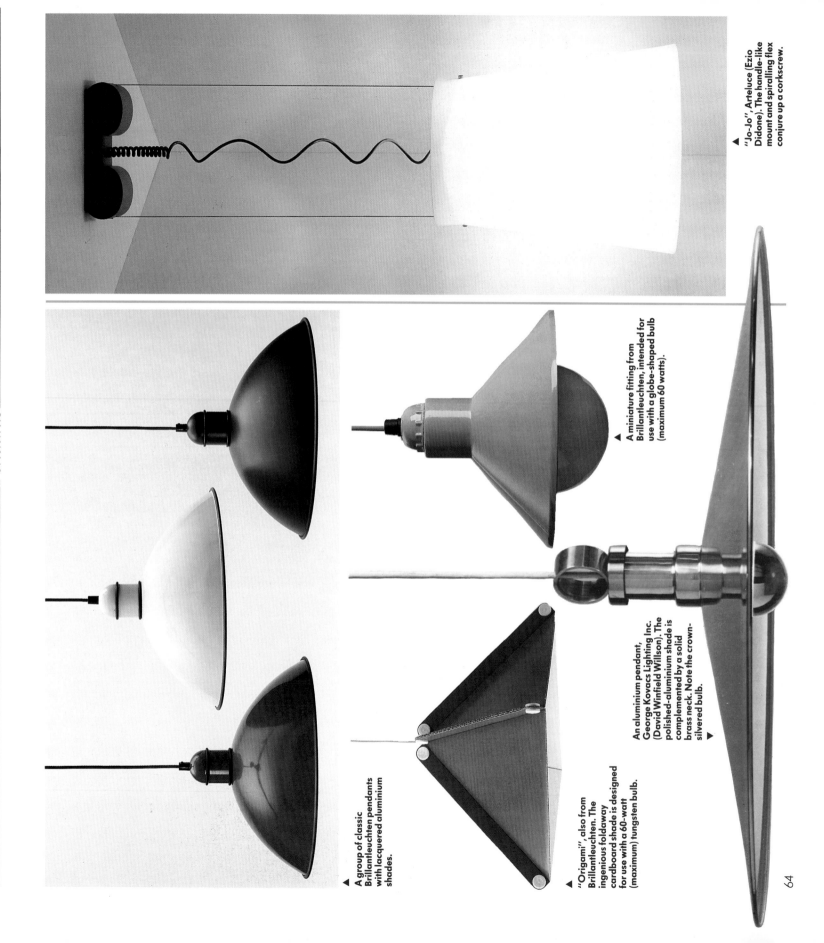

▲ "Jo-Jo", Arteluce (Ezio Didone). The handle-like mount and spiralling flex conjure up a corkscrew.

▲ A group of classic Brillantleuchten pendants with lacquered aluminium shades.

▲ A miniature fitting from Brillantleuchten, intended for use with a globe-shaped bulb (maximum 60 watts).

▲ "Origami", also from Brillantleuchten. The ingenious foldaway cardboard shade is designed for use with a 60-watt (maximum) tungsten bulb.

▲ An aluminium pendant, George Kovacs Lighting Inc. (David Winfield Willson). The polished-aluminium shade is complemented by a solid brass neck. Note the crown-silvered bulb.

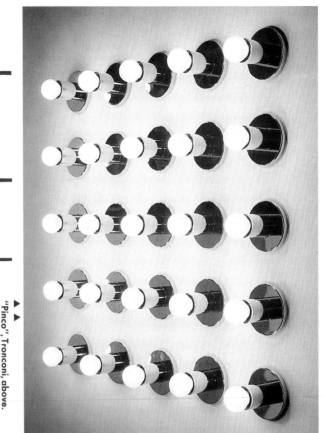

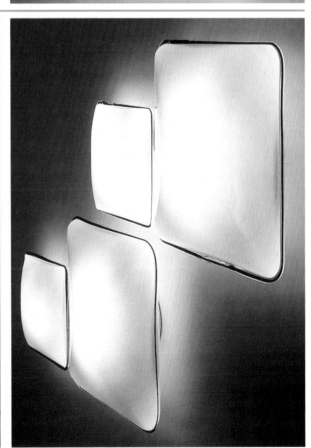

▶ ▶ **"Pinco"**, Tronconi, above.
These small-scale brass
fittings look good in a group.

"Kea", Leucos (Studio
Tecnico), above right. Black
trim is available as an
alternative to red.

▲ A range of chrome-finished
pendants by Stilnovo (Gae
Aulenti and Livio Castiglioni).
The inner surfaces are white,
silver and matt-black baffled.

"Crisol", Arteluce (King, ▶
Miranda and Arnaldi). A low-
voltage halogen pendant with
a diffuser of pressed, etched
glass.

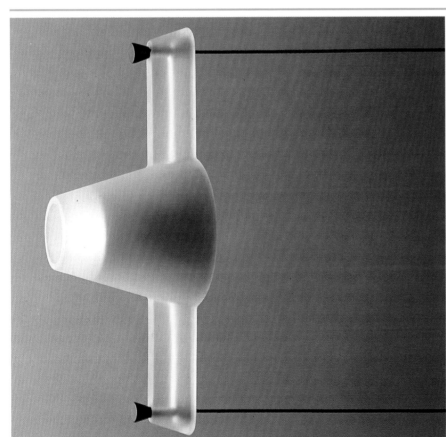

It is not merely the colour characteristics of fluorescent tubes that have kept them, undeservedly, out of most rooms in the house. Also to blame is the scarcity of attractive fittings. Too many of the fittings available look blandly utilitarian, like pieces of office equipment. This is not surprising: the market, after all, is geared to large commercial and institutional installations, and a major aim is to design fittings that can be mass-produced at low cost. Consequently a premium is placed on clean, simple lines, which streamlines the production process. A product that looked overpowering or fussy when used in large numbers would in any case be out of place on purely visual grounds. So, for the most part, fluorescent fittings take the form of simple boxes, screened by diffusers or louvers.

The first fluorescent fittings designed to make a dash in interiors have been less than inspiring in looks – in most settings, a decorative glass cover is not enough to prevent a fitting from looking dull and cheap. However, in recent years there have been attempts to make fittings with more flair, especially ones designed for the new generation of miniature fluorescents. One of the most unusual, originally designed for the office or the studio though with great potential in the home, is a rise-and-fall pendant fitting with a brightly coloured, perforated metal shade; in its low-slung position, this can serve as a task light. Another cause for optimism is the fairly recent appearance on the market of suspended track systems that incorporate fluorescent fittings – for example, Thorn's "Pipeline" and Luci's "Rio" systems. Circular fluorescents have inspired a few close-mounted ceiling fittings that are worthy of attention.

Fittings for fluorescents have a number of important tasks to perform if they are to function properly. As explained earlier (see page 34), a starter mechanism is required to start the electric discharge and a ballast to control the consumption of electricity. This "control gear", which is relatively bulky, is normally accommodated

within the fitting. For example, in most tubular fittings it is housed in a long, thin metal box above the tube, whereas in table lights that take miniature fluorescents it is usually concealed within the base.

Another important factor is the visual role of the fitting. In most domestic installations, bare fluorescent tubes are used, but this does little to help the fluorescent's tainted popular image. Like most other light sources, fluorescents tend to look easier on the eye when used with some kind of screening or shielding device. For example, one or more tubes (they are often mounted in pairs) might be entirely enclosed inside a diffusing material, such as translucent plastic. Alternatively, they might be partially screened by plastic or metal louvers. Fittings are available for fluorescent bathroom lights, sometimes with integral shaving points.

Fluorescents are often used as a source of indirect light, hidden by purpose-built screens that blend with the architectural style of a room. For example, in bedrooms, living rooms and kitchens, the tubes are very often to be found concealed behind timber fascias, or housed in cornice-level coving units. Curtain pelmets are another favoured location. Luminous ceiling kits are also now available, consisting of a set of diffusing panels which you hang below one or two fluorescent tubes. Tubes housed in an open-topped diffusing canopy suspended in pendant fashion will cast diffused light downward while bouncing supplementary indirect light off the ceiling. Because of their linear nature, fluorescent tubes also fit neatly into display cabinets for concealed lighting of collectibles.

1 Circular fluorescent tubes
are here used as novel
decorative elements in a
hallway. The flex oscillates
eyecatchingly over support
wires.

2 A fluorescent tube fitting
sits neatly inside the channel
of a ceiling-supporting
girder. Additional fluorescent
light in this room comes from
fittings hidden inside the
platform where the urn
stands.

3 A streamlined fluorescent
system from Arteluce is put to
effective use in this bathroom,
although it was designed
chiefly with an office
environment in mind.

"90PL", Anglepoise. This
desk light takes an 11-watt PL
fluorescent. The head is matt-
black plastic with a white-
painted interior. ▶

"FWN 30S", Philips. A wall
fitting for a PL miniature
fluorescent. ▶

"Flu", Luci (Gianfranco
Frattini). A wall- or ceiling-
mounted double fitting with
arms that can be turned
through 180° and
directionally adjustable
reflectors. ▶

"Main Street Due", Eleusi
(Sergio Asti). A highly
decorative wall fitting. ▶

"Dinos", Megalit (Nemo). A
miniature-fluorescent desk
light with the control gear in
the base. ▶

"Rio", Luci (Rudolfo Bonetto).
A halogen uplighter with a
fluorescent tube along the
side. There is a separate
switch for each light source. ▶

"Aster", Luci (Gianfranco
Frattini). Slimline fittings with
rotatable reflectors for direct
or indirect lighting. ▶

Luci's "Carrera" wall light, with a pressed glass cover, is derived from the classic utilitarian bulkhead style fitting. It is suitable for interior or exterior use.

A historical-style bracket light manufactured by Chelsom. The etched glass shade recalls turn-of-the-century gas fittings.

Wall lights may be either fixed or plug-in. This plug-in kite-shaped diffusing light from Brillantleuchten proudly displays its curling, bright yellow flex.

Quarter-spherical bowl-shaped wall lights often create a subdued halo effect. These examples in the i Guzzini range are made of translucent acrylic and take a 100-watt bulb.

Early wall lights took the form of simple bracket fittings, which provided an early alternative to the tyranny of the central ceiling pendant. Like pendants, they derived from a light source that predated electricity. This probably accounts for the archaic shapes in which wall lights are still often to be found. The folk memory of burning torches stuck in wall holders, or of wall-mounted candleholders, seems to have been too much for some designers of light fittings. Many of them still delight in turning out primitive-looking fittings that recreate in plastic and bakelite the shapes of huge, dripping wax candles intended for flame-shaped bulbs. Some even go as far as real brass candleholders and rough-hewn timber supports. Actually, the wall light's true ancestor, if we need to look for one, is the gas fitting. Indeed, many 19th-century gas fittings were converted to electricity as the new power source became more widely available.

Many wall light designs are simply adaptations of other types of fitting. For example, most wall-mounted uplighters derive from floor-standing uplighters. Like their more portable cousins, they tend to use tungsten-halogen light sources, and have shades in metal or thick glass; the glass ones diffuse some light as well as

bouncing light off the ceiling. Similarly, you can buy wall-mounted downlighters of a simple box or drum construction that closely echo the appearance of non-recessed ceiling downlighters. These are particularly useful for bedside lighting. Some drum types have an open top, casting a beam upward onto the wall to form a reverse image of the curving beam shape below the fitting.

Many people use spotlights in wall positions, usually to fill a purely decorative role. However, there are limitations to this practice: unless the

which it is made, this fitting can be given exactly the same decorative finish as the wall around it, and thus blend into virtually any room scheme. Another interesting wall fitting has been designed in the form of a metal framework that fits into a corner, with a diffusing screen to hide the bulb.

Globe lights, based on turn-of-the-century café fittings, are perennially popular, and come with a range of plain or flamboyant brackets. Fittings with a highly reflective finish, such as polished plated brass, often pick up intriguing reflections of the room's finishes and furnishings; this effect can be tiresome, however, unless the polished surface has a distinctive shape that distorts the reflections beyond recognition. Directional wall lights include those with a pivot that allow you to angle them in any direction along the wall plane – for example, Flos's "Bollo".

ceiling is very low, a ceiling-mounted position would normally be a better bet for a spotlight, as it offers greater directional freedom. Some wall spots project into the room on long limbs, which can either be fixed or on an adjustable elbow joint.

In addition, there are fittings that have been specially tailored as wall lights, instead of being derived from other species. One particularly useful variety is in the form of a moulded plasterwork bowl, shaped to provide uplighting from a low-voltage halogen bulb; because of the material from

When you choose a wall light, it is worth considering the type of beam pattern that will form on the wall. The examples on this page show some of the possible effects.

A chrome hemispherical fitting from Boyd with an acrylic inset that refracts some of the light downward, creating decorative sparkle.

This novel wheel light ("Giovi" from Flos) has a ring of plastic slats which are hidden from view by the circular back plate. The slats fracture the light decoratively into spokes of light and shadow.

A Franklite double wall light in polished brass with etched glass shades.

The shade on this Baulmann wall light is actually only a half-shade: light escapes through the gap between the shade and the wall to yield a subtle halo effect.

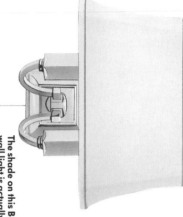

"Caltha": an adjustable, wall-mounted halogen uplighter from Luci. The 300-watt linear halogen lamp casts a clearly defined wedge-shaped beam.

A Goccia bulkhead light used in a vertical position instead of the more conventional horizontal position.

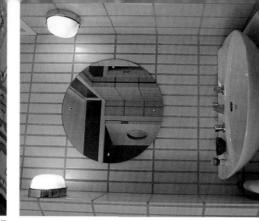

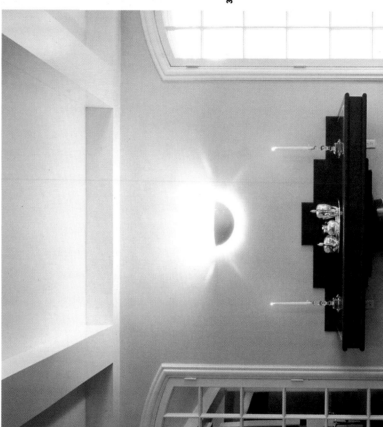

1 A pair of "Gomito" lights, made by Stilnovo, is ideal for bringing out the form of an old brick vault in a converted cellar. Each fitting contains a 300-watt halogen bulb.

2 A "Quarto" wall fitting from the Flos range creates a dramatic burst of light over a side-table display. The twin candles reinforce the symmetry of the overall arrangement.

3 Fan-shaped lights draw the eye to a doorway and from there to the dining area beyond. They make attractive decorative elements in a room that is otherwise fairly austere.

4 Bulkhead fittings either side of a bathroom mirror provide even, shadowless lighting suitable for shaving.

Applications

Stylistic considerations apart, the wall light has its own special kinds of contribution to make to a lighting scheme. Fittings with a shade placed close to a wall can mix direct, indirect and diffused light. The direct light (mainly downward) washes the wall and horizontal surfaces below the fitting, while the wall area behind the fitting and the ceiling above reflect light back into the room. At the same time, the shade, if it is translucent, acts as a diffuser. Unless you choose wall lights entirely for decorative purposes, it makes sense to opt for fittings that make the most of these possibilities.

Wall lights offer a neat, unobtrusive way of supplying light. They do not take up precious floor space or shelf space, neither do they encroach upon headroom. However, installation can present problems to those who, for

whatever reasons, are anxious not to penetrate wall surfaces. Wiring circuits for lighting are not usually found in walls, and you will have to chase in special drops to provide the power. Although you could use cables rising visibly from skirting board outlets, these inevitably look unsightly. Switches or dimmers may be positioned either at the fitting itself, or remote from it.

To position a wall light successfully, you need to analyse its intended function. For example, if you want to use wall fittings for general lighting you should place them high enough up the walls to be able to bounce light off the ceiling. However, in other roles (for example, bulkhead lights in bathrooms or reading lights in bedrooms), you should place the lights at a suitable distance from the task they are intended to facilitate.

5 These finely balanced wall-mounted task lights are used partly for their sculptural contribution to the interior design. Unlike most other wall lights, they take up a lot of room space, but the sacrifice in this case is well worthwhile.

6 An industrial-style gooseneck fitting, originally intended for use at a work bench, has been recycled as an improvised wall light angled to bounce indirect light off the ceiling.

"By the sea", Koch and Lowy. ▲
A diffusing wall light in opal glass, available in both permanent and "pin-up" (flex and plug) versions.

Picture lights in three different finishes, Studio Editions. Each fitting takes a 300-watt halogen bulb and has a built-in dimmer.

"Lichtballon", ▲
Brillantleuchten. Intended for use above a wall socket. Each balloon takes a 60-watt bulb (maximum).

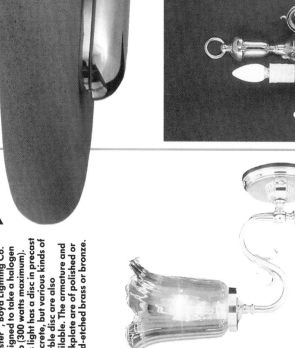

"Pfister", Boyd Lighting Co. ▲
Designed to take a halogen bulb (300 watts maximum). This light has a disc in precast concrete, but various kinds of marble disc are also available. The armature and backplate are of polished or sand-etched brass or bronze.

A bracket light in the style of ▲
a 19th-century gas fitting. The upturned frilled glass shade is an authentic period touch.

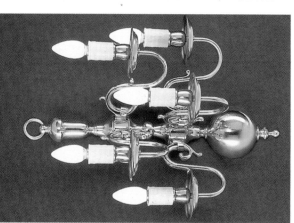

"Flemish-style" wall fitting, ▲
Chelsom. A faithful reproduction of a 17th-century fitting, in solid brass.

A wall-mounted version of Areluce's famous "Jill" floor light (King, Miranda and Arnaldi). The fitting is used with a 500-watt halogen bulb.
▼

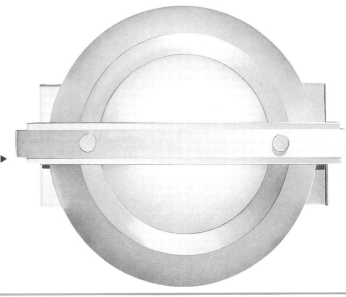

"Deco Disc", Boyd Lighting Co. A glass diffuser light with a strong geometrical design.

▲

"Glass form I", Boyd Lighting Co. The light from a 100-watt bulb is diffused through the rippled glass lozenge.

▲

"Drachen" (Kies), Brillantleuchten. These brightly coloured fittings can be used singly, or neatly interlocked to create a pattern.

▲

"Bollo", Flos (Tobia Scarpa). A halogen fitting which can be rotated to alter the lighting direction. The light is diffused through a prismatic glass cover.

▶

A Koch and Lowy cone light with a smoked-glass diffuser.

▶

"Flopi", Luci (Salvati and Tresoldi). A classically simple fitting for wall or ceiling use.

▲

A mirror light unit from Brillantleuchten. Three-bulb fittings are also available. Finishes vary ranging from brass and chrome to brown, red, beige and white.

▶

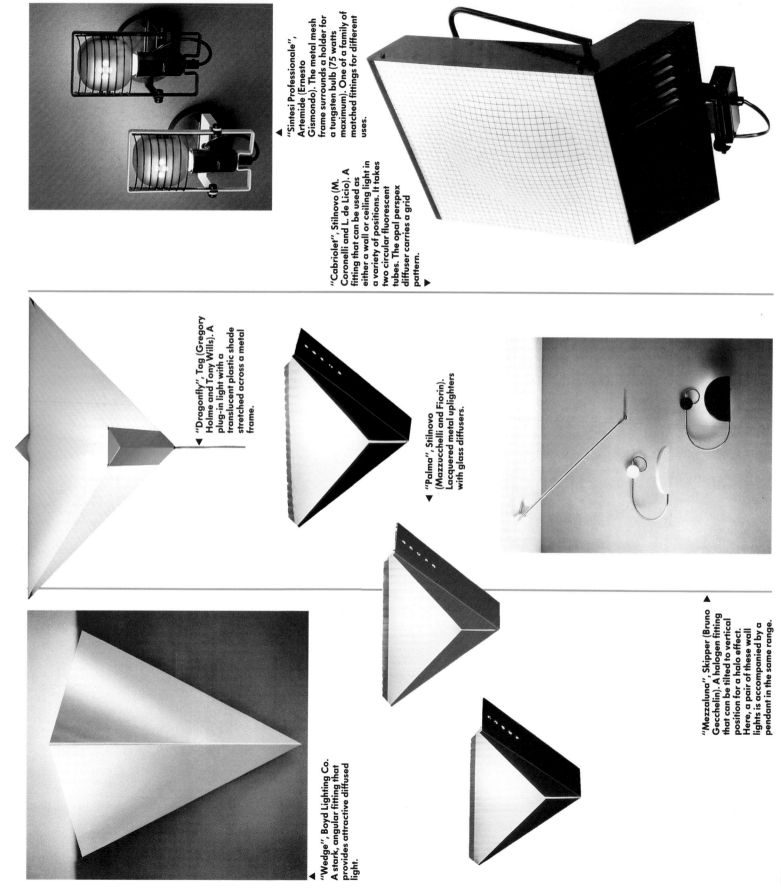

Wall Lights

"Sintesi Professionale", Artemide (Ernesto Gismondi). The metal mesh frame surrounds a holder for a tungsten bulb (75 watts maximum). One of a family of matched fittings for different uses. ▲

"Cabriolet", Stilnovo (M. Coronelli and L. de Licio). A fitting that can be used as either a wall or ceiling light in a variety of positions. It takes two circular fluorescent tubes. The opal perspex diffuser carries a grid pattern. ▼

"Dragonfly", Tag (Gregory Holme and Tony Wills). A plug-in light with a translucent plastic shade stretched across a metal frame. ▼

"Palma", Stilnovo (Mazzucchelli and Fiorin). Lacquered metal uplighters with glass diffusers. ▼

"Wedge", Boyd Lighting Co. A stark, angular fitting that provides attractive diffused light. ▲

"Mezzaluna", Skipper (Bruno Gecchelin). A halogen fitting that can be tilted to vertical position for a halo effect. Here, a pair of these wall lights is accompanied by a pendant in the same range. ▲

▶ **"265"**, Arteluce (Paolo Rizatto). A large-scale, wall-mounted version of a conventional desk light, with a pierced hood.

▶ **"Minibox"**, Stilnovo (Gae Aulenti and Piero Castiglioni). The reflectors, which are attached by a magnet, take low-voltage halogen bulbs.

◀ **"Elle"**, Stilnovo (R. Beretta and A. Macchi Cassia). A swivelling fitting with a crown-silvered bulb.

▶ **"Techlinea"**, Boyd Lighting Co. An adjustable standard-voltage halogen wall-bracket, for wall washing.

◀ **"Ala"**, Luci (Gianfranco Frattini). A directional wall-mounted uplighter with an extruded aluminium body. Takes a 300-watt linear halogen lamp.

▶ **"Lotus"**, Boyd Lighting Co. A wall fitting that provides both direct and diffused light from either two 60-watt tungsten bulbs or a miniature fluorescent.

▶ **"Conus"**, Orit Militscher. An unusual plug-in fitting with a colourful coiled flex.

Table lights fall naturally into two distinct groups. First, there are task lights (also known as desk lights), whose purpose is to deliver enough light to a given surface or area to enable the user to carry out a visually demanding task. And secondly, there are table lights proper. While these also may have a specific functional role (for example, providing light for armchair reading), their primary purpose is to provide low-level decorative or background light. Usually, the fitting itself is a conspicuous ornamental object which makes a positive contribution to the overall look of an interior even when switched off.

Task lights

Task lights are often complicated pieces of engineering, contrived to combine maximum adjustability with fingertip control. Together, these characteristics allow you to make small alterations to the lighting direction as you work, without interrupting your concentration. You should be able to lift one hand to make an adjustment very quickly, almost instinctively. And the light should be jointed in such a way that an infinite range of settings is possible.

The original "Anglepoise" light, designed by George Carwardine in 1933, achieved this degree of flexibility with a design solution whose elegance has never been beaten. Taking as his model the jointing of the human arm, Carwardine used a combination of pivots and springs, the latter performing a role parallel to that of the arm's muscles. The lighting angle could be fine-tuned with the gentlest of touches – a great improvement upon other hinged task lights of the time, which needed the use of both hands, and considerable force, to make an adjustment. Stability in the "Anglepoise" was ensured by a heavily weighted base.

The Anglepoise Company still produces a task light that differs little from their original, revolutionary design. In every sense, the light is a classic. As this word implies, it retains features that could now be regarded as old-fashioned: it operates only with a conventional tungsten bulb, and the wattage has to be kept low to avoid overheating. However, the enduring popularity of this fitting is a sure index of quality. Even against new designs based on new lighting technologies, the historic "Anglepoise" holds its own.

By contrast, modern types of task lights are increasingly using tungsten-halogen light sources (and are often fitted with an integral dimmer). The classic fitting in this field is Artemide's "Tizio", which Richard Sapper designed at the start of the 1970s as a desk light with maximum stability yet minimum intrusion upon usable desk space. It was the first low-voltage halogen fitting that became widely available for the home. The requisite transformer is sited in the base, adding to stability, which benefits from the lightweight bulb. Available in black or white versions, with the plastic hinges picked out in red, the "Tizio" demonstrates the dangers of making too rigid a distinction between decorative and functional lights. Its gawky elegance has made it something of a cult-object among the design-conscious, and earned it a well-deserved place in the living room.

Some manufacturers, including Anglepoise, now make task lights that take a concealed fluorescent tube or miniature fluorescent. One example is the "Anglepoise 433T", which is designed for use with a 2D lamp and comes with a range of optional accessories, including louvers, a prismatic diffuser or a clamp-on magnifier.

Clamp-on task lights have the merit of taking up very little desk space, but they can only be used in a limited number of positions throughout the home; for example, you would be unable to stand one on a coffee table or sideboard. If you need to have the base well away from your working area, a better choice might be a

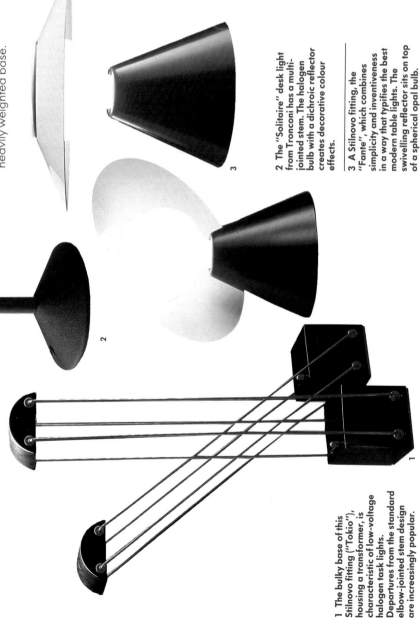

1 The bulky base of this Stilnovo fitting ("Tokio"), housing a transformer, is characteristic of low-voltage halogen task lights. Departures from the standard elbow-jointed stem design are increasingly popular.

2 The "Solitaire" desk light from Troncini has a multi-jointed stem. The halogen bulb with a dichroic reflector creates decorative colour effects.

3 A Stilnovo fitting, the "Fante", which combines simplicity and inventiveness in a way that typifies the best modern table lights. The swivelling reflector sits on top of a spherical opal bulb.

heavy-based double-arm halogen light.

Table lights

The popular image of the table light is of a decorative base, a lampholder and a detachable shade, usually sold separately from the fitting. The flex is threaded through a hole in the base and from there, invisibly, to the lampholder.

This, mercifully, is only a part of the picture. Today, table lights are available in an extraordinary variety of shapes and sizes, often exploiting the principles of diffusion and reflection in complicated ways. Some, like task lights, are adjustable; for example, one model has a pivoted shade that you can adjust to vary the amount of direct light put out. Others are solid pieces of sculpture in expensive materials such as marble, or extrovert fabrications in coloured metals. There are even some table lights in which the flex, far from being concealed, adds to the visual impact by wriggling up inside a see-through base or on the outside of the fitting.

Because table lights lend themselves to a highly personal design approach, there are inevitably some designers who have not been able to resist the whimsical. Animals, cars, aeroplanes and top hats are among the countless manifestations. These fittings may appeal to some tastes, but their charms seldom last as long as the objects themselves.

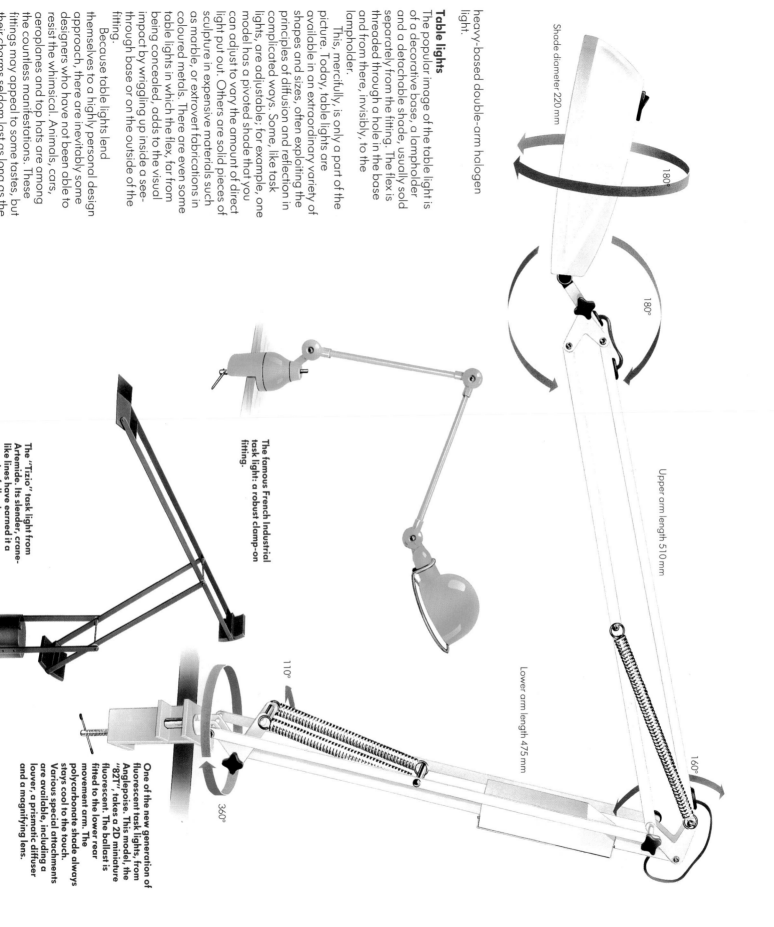

Shade diameter 220 mm

180°

180°

Upper arm length 510 mm

Lower arm length 475 mm

110°

160°

360°

The famous French Industrial task light: a robust clamp-on fitting.

The "Tizio" task light from Artemide. Its slender, crane-like lines have earned it a massive following.

One of the new generation of fluorescent task lights, from Anglepoise. This model, the "82T", takes a 2D miniature fluorescent. The ballast is fitted to the lower rear movement arm. The polycarbonate shade always stays cool to the touch. Various special attachments are available, including a louver, a prismatic diffuser and a magnifying lens.

1

2

1 A pair of "Tizio" lights makes an effective frame for a double bed. Built-in dimmers allow the lighting to be subdued enough for casual bedtime reading or bright enough to provide indirect, off-the-wall illumination throughout the room.

2 This table light was chosen for its simple geometrical lines to provide a neat contrast with an antique mirror. At a pinch, it can also be used as a makeup light.

3 and 4 Two variations on the theme of twinned table lights positioned in a way that concentrates our attention on cherished objects. Conical shades cut down the amount of upward light: too much would spoil the effect. With this kind of arrangement, the bulbs should not exceed 60 watts.

5 On such a high table, this shaded light is perfectly suitable for armchair reading. It also provides diffuse background lighting.

Applications

The visual appeal of many modern task lights is indebted to the interplay of slender stems and bulkier bases and hoods, and to a sense of precarious balance: some models seem positively to defy gravity. These elements, together with the marked angularity of many task lights, makes them work very well as table sculptures when set off against a blank wall. Used in this way, adjustability has aesthetic as well as practical advantages, enabling you to change the shape of a fitting whenever it begins to look too familiar. Pairing task lights that are identically matched but adjusted to different positions can look particularly effective.

Some guidelines on using task lights for specific activities are given on pages

102–103. In living rooms, dining rooms or bedrooms, they are excellent sources of indirect lighting when used to bounce light off a white or pale-coloured wall or, for a greater spread of illumination, off the junction between wall and ceiling. Even types that take conventional tungsten bulbs can produce a surprising breadth and level of background lighting by this method. Fluorescent task lights can be deployed in the same way, but with some loss of atmosphere.

The traditional function of a non-task table light is to create a sense of intimacy around a seating area. To avoid glare, you should pay attention not only to the height of the lamp but also to the choice of shade. Usually, a fairly deep shade is needed to eliminate

glare from both standing and sitting positions.

The downward beam cast by a shaded table light makes an excellent showcase for a collection of objects – or perhaps just one treasured item, such as a framed family photograph. A glass or polished-wood table top may catch a distracting reflection of the light source, in which case it may be preferable to cover it with an attractive piece of fabric.

Placed next to a wall, shaded table lights are useful for picture lighting. Or against a bare wall, they will cast an intriguing shadow pattern: a dark band where light dimly penetrates through the shade, paler cusps of shadow above and below (where some light is reflected off the shade's inner surface)

and U-shaped areas of brightness where direct light hits the wall. You can vary the geometry of the effect by placing a light in a corner, to create double instead of single shadow cusps.

Materials for shades should be chosen to blend in with the furnishings. If you want a direct match, you can have shades made professionally, or alternatively you could try making your own using white cardboard for the inner surface.

Many of the diffusing table lights now being produced by the most imaginative manufacturers have an extraordinary luminous beauty when switched on. These are ideal fittings to bring an alcove or shelving unit to life. They can also serve a more practical purpose as TV lights.

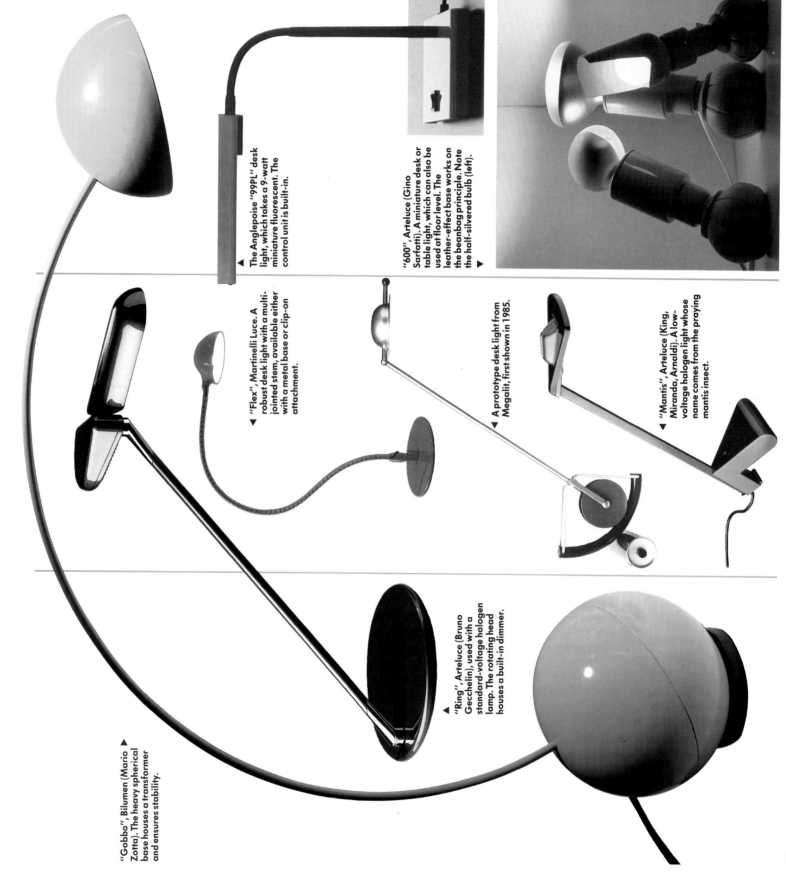

The Anglepoise "99PL" desk light, which takes a 9-watt miniature fluorescent. The control unit is built-in. ◄

"600", Arteluce (Gino Sarfatti). A miniature desk or table light, which can also be used at floor level. The leather-effect base works on the beanbag principle. Note the half-silvered bulb (left). ▶

"Flex", Martinelli Luce. A robust desk light with a multi-jointed stem, available either with a metal base or clip-on attachment. ◄

A prototype desk light from Megalit, first shown in 1985. ◄

"Mantis", Arteluce (King, Miranda, Arnaldi). A low-voltage halogen light whose name comes from the praying mantis insect. ◄

"Ring", Arteluce (Bruno Gecchelin), used with a standard-voltage halogen lamp. The rotating head houses a built-in dimmer. ◄

"Gobbo", Bilumen (Mario Zotta). The heavy spherical base houses a transformer and ensures stability. ▲

"Swan Line", ▼
Brillantleuchten, another
low-voltage halogen lamp
with the transformer in the
base.

▼ "Dogale", Oluce (Bruno
Gecchelin). A desk light
intended for use with a 12-volt
halogen bulb. The shade also
comes in white.

"Periscopio", Stilnovo (D. and
C. Aroldi). The stiffened nylon
joint with rubber covering
both tilts and rotates. Used
with a 60-watt pearl or half-
silvered bulb.

▶ A low-voltage halogen fitting
from Martinelli Luce.

▶ "Donald", Arteluce (King,
Miranda, Arnaldi), so-called
because the beak-like visor
suggests the cartoon figure
Donald Duck. Available with
a clamp or heavy base.

▶ A task light from Sirrah (Gino
Sarfatti), with a touch of gun-
metal austerity. Unusually for
such a modern-looking light,
the switch is in the traditional
style.

▶ "Bestlite", Best and Lloyd,
designed in 1930 and still in
production.

"The Calder", Boyd Lighting Co. (Enrique Franch). A low-voltage halogen desk light with integral dimmer.

A low-voltage task light from Megalit (B. Brousse). The head is adjusted by an ingenious sliding mechanism, and may be reversed for uplighting.

"Alistro Morsetto", Artemide (Ernesto Gismondi). An 11-watt miniature fluorescent creates shadowless lighting.

An Anglepoise task light ("433T") which accommodates a 16-watt 2D miniature fluorescent. The robust polycarbonate shade stays cool to the touch. Various special accessories are available, including a prismatic diffuser, clip-on magnifier, and low-brightness louver.

"Tomos", Sirrah. Its perspex diffusing head is a distinctive feature. There is a choice of a heavy base or a clamp attachment.

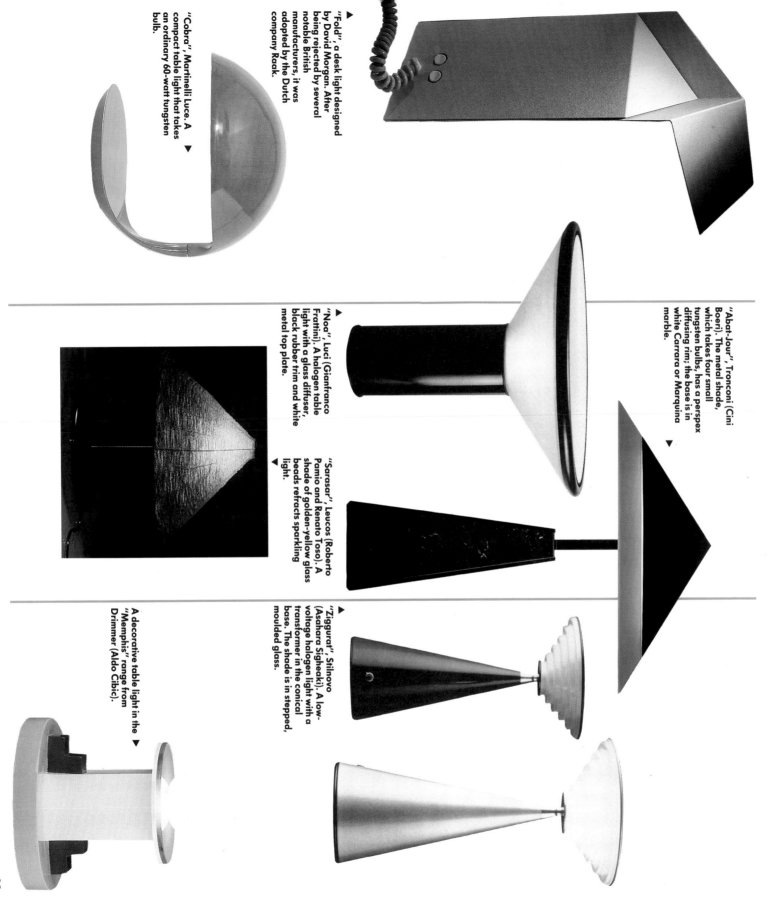

"Fold", a desk light designed by David Morgan. After being rejected by several notable British manufacturers, it was adopted by the Dutch company Raak.

"Cobra", Martinelli Luce. A compact table light that takes an ordinary 60-watt tungsten bulb.

"Abat-Jour", Tronconi (Cini Boeri). The metal shade, which takes four small tungsten bulbs, has a perspex diffusing rim; the base is in white Carrara or Marquina marble.

"Noa", Luci (Gianfranco Frattini). A halogen table light with a glass diffuser, black rubber trim and white metal top plate.

"Sarasar", Leucos (Roberto Pamio and Renato Toso). A shade of golden-yellow glass beads refracts sparkling light.

"Ziggurat", Stilnovo (Asahara Sigheaki). A low-voltage halogen light with a transformer in the conical base. The shade is in stepped, moulded glass.

A decorative table light in the "Memphis" range from Drimmer (Aldo Cibic).

▲ "Gibigiana", Flos (Achille Castiglioni). A 12-volt halogen bulb is housed in the base of the stem, its light directed upward onto a small adjustable mirror. The head includes a built-in dimmer.

"Minibasket", Eleusi (Davide Mercatali and Paolo Pedrizze). A low-voltage halogen fitting with integral dimmer. The bulb in the base reflects light off the stepped glass cone. ▲

A brass table light ("4740") from George Kovacs Lighting Inc. The polished brass stand is fitted with a tan-coloured pleated linen shade and equipped to take three tungsten bulbs.

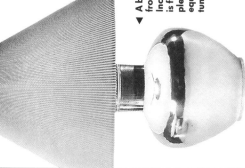

"Bugis", ¡ Guzzini. A table light designed for bedside use. The metal housing can be tilted to shade the pearl bulb.

"Pall", Tronconi (Raul Barbieri and Giorgio Marianelli). A miniature fluorescent fitting with a perspex diffuser ring. ▶

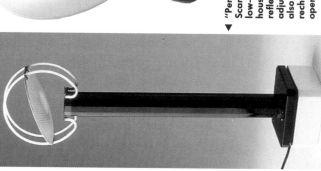

"Perpetua", Flos (Tobia Scarpa). A table light with a low-voltage halogen bulb housed in its base. Light is reflected into the room off the adjustable disc. This fitting is also available in a rechargeable battery-operated version. ▶

▲ "Halo Beam", Brillantleuchten. A low-voltage halogen table spot with an adjustable head.

"Tobia", Tronconi (Gabriella Montaguti). A decorative diffusing light, whose opal glass shade is supported by a simple metal stand available in white, black, red or yellow. ▶

"Alfiere", Stilnovo (De Pas, D'Urbino, Lomazzi). A glass diffusing table light with a swivelling reflector of lacquered metal.

"Tender", Tronconi (Romolo Lanciani). A satin-finish opal-glass diffusing light, with a coloured metal handle. The height of the fitting is only 11 inches (28 cm), although there is a larger version available, known as the "Tenderone", (16 inches, 41 cm).

"Taccia", Flos (Achille and Pier Giacomo Castiglioni). The column-like base is surmounted by a clear-glass diffuser, which houses an enamelled metal reflector.

"Totem", Lampes Drimmer (Albert Lehé). A mushroom-like table light with ceramic base and shade.

"Suitcase", Shiu Kay Kan. A low-wattage pearl tungsten bulb provides diffused light through a moulded plastic shade.

"Lampiata", Stilnovo (De Pas, D'Urbino, Lomazzi). These lights have a separate shade that can be slotted into any one of a series of grooves at the top of the enamelled aluminium base.

"Petite Fleur", Brillantleuchten. A bunch of thirty tulips, each containing a miniature tungsten bulb, provides a novel table arrangement.

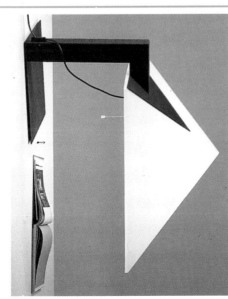

"Pitagora", Martinelli Luce. The design owes much to the stark contrast of black and white.

Even though they lack the directional versatility of spotlights or task lights, floor lights offer a surprising range of lighting options. They can provide at least as much general light as a pendant, yet because they are plug-in fittings they are easily portable. This makes them an ideal choice for tenants, or for anyone who is reluctant to carry out rewiring or to make a commitment to a less flexible lighting scheme using fixed fittings.

Until tungsten-halogen light sources became generally available for home use, floor lights mostly took the form of the conventional standard lamp. This resembles an elongated table light, with a sturdy base and a wooden stem four to five feet (1.2–1.5 metres) high supporting a lampholder and fabric shade. The fitting is designed to supply three different kinds of illumination: light diffused laterally through the shade fabric, direct light in a downward direction, and indirect light from an upward beam reflected off the ceiling.

One early exotic variation, which has recently undergone something of a revival, was a studio light created by the fashion designer Mario Fortuny. This fitting used a tripod to carry an umbrella-like reflector. A bright tungsten light source bounced light off the umbrella and back into the room.

A third type of design is the floor-standing spotlight unit, which consists of a freestanding vertical pole on which a number of spotlights are clamped. You can add or subtract lights at will, and adjust the lighting direction by giving the spots a firm twist.

Another popular category is the growing range of flexible or jointed tungsten floor lights, which are a spin-off from task lights. Notable examples are Stilnovo's "Periscopio" and Artemide's "Aggregato Terra".

Uplighters

Today the standard lamp is rapidly losing ground to the halogen uplighter, which reflects all or most of its light output off the ceiling, with little or no direct or diffused light. The intensity of a 300- or 500-watt tungsten-halogen light source means that background lighting for a whole room can be provided by a single fitting.

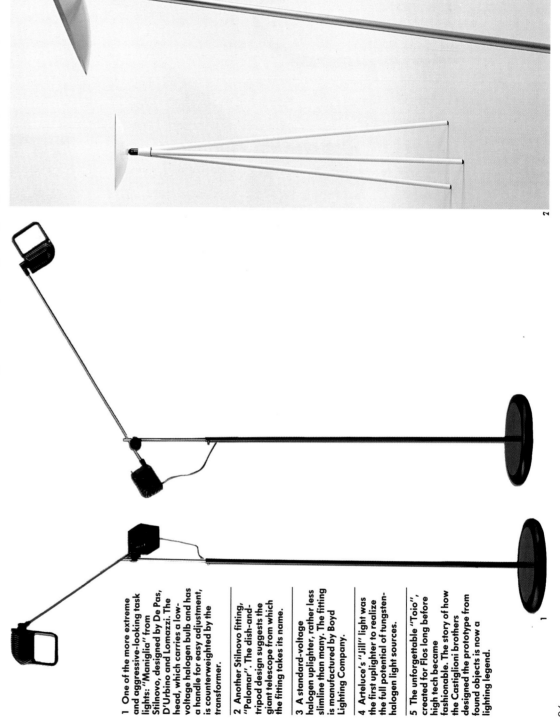

1 One of the more extreme and aggressive-looking task lights: "Maniglia" from Stilnovo, designed by De Pas, D'Urbino and Lomazzi. The head, which carries a low-voltage halogen bulb and has a handle for easy adjustment, is counterweighted by the transformer.

2 Another Stilnovo fitting, "Palomar". The dish-and-tripod design suggests the giant telescope from which the fitting takes its name.

3 A standard-voltage halogen uplighter, rather less slimline than many. The fitting is manufactured by Boyd Lighting Company.

4 Arteluce's "Jill" light was the first uplighter to realize the full potential of tungsten-halogen light sources.

5 The unforgettable "Toio", created for Flos long before high tech became fashionable. The story of how the Castiglioni brothers designed the prototype from found objects is now a lighting legend.

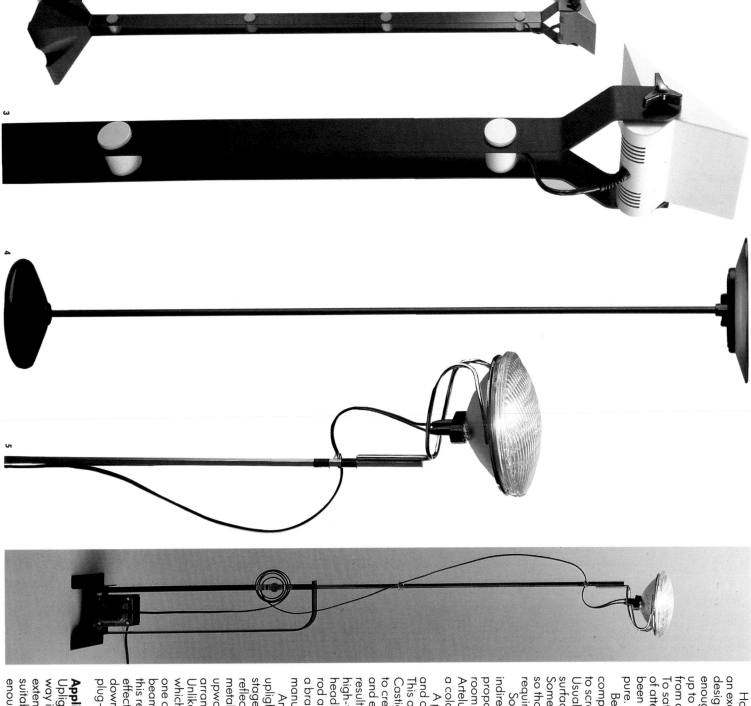

Halogen uplighters have created an exciting new aesthetic for lighting designers. The fittings need to be tall enough to send most of the light output up to the ceiling and to shield the bulb from our eyes in order to avoid glare. To satisfy these requirements, a range of attenuated sculptural shapes has been developed – tall, elegant and pure.

Because halogen bulbs are comparatively small, the shades used to screen them can be very compact. Usually they have a reflective inner surface that helps to direct the light. Sometimes they sit on a pivot or hinge so that the beam can be angled as required.

Some uplighters supplement the indirect light output by allowing a small proportion of the light to filter into the room through a diffuser. For example, Arteluce's "Jill" does this by means of a coloured glass scoop.

A particularly ingenious uplighter, and one of the earliest, is the "Toio". This originated in 1965 when the Castiglioni brothers were challenged to create a light fitting from some odds and ends piled up in a garage. The result was an extraordinary exercise in high-tech design, with a halogen car headlamp as the light source, a fishing rod as the support and a band saw as a brace. Today, this light is manufactured by Flos.

Another, very different type of uplighter, based on the principle of stage footlights, consists of a silvered reflector lamp housed inside a small metal drum or box. The light is directed upward and to one side by an arrangement of mirrors and baffles. Unlike the more usual kind of uplighter, which produces soft, indirect light, this one creates a dramatic sharp-edged beam, suitable for display purposes. In this respect, it is comparable in its effect to a ceiling-mounted downlighter, but with the advantage of plug-in wiring.

Applications
Uplighters are increasingly finding their way into living rooms – and to a lesser extent into bedrooms. They are suitable for halls only if there is space enough to keep both the flex and the

fitting well away from circulation routes, to avoid the risk of a mishap.

As with all indirect-light fittings, uplighters work most efficiently in alliance with high-reflectance surfaces. Because these lights are generally given a peripheral position, some of the light emitted will bounce twice before angling down usefully into the room – once off the ceiling, then off the nearby wall. Therefore, to maximize the light output, both the ceiling and upper part of the appropriate wall should be white or pale-coloured. The lower part of the wall can be much darker, if you wish, without any serious diminution of overall brightness; but, of course, to make visual sense of a sharp colour contrast part-way up a wall you really need a picture rail or some kind of decorative frieze as a boundary.

Uplighters fitted with a powerful halogen bulb give a light that is bright

enough for reading. They are especially useful at the bedside, as the switch is within easy reach at floor level. However, many people prefer to read in a direct pool of light, and for armchair reading incline toward the standard lamp, which balances the direct beam with a certain proportion of diffused and indirect light, thereby reducing contrast.

The contribution made by uplighters on a purely visual level should not be overlooked. They make an emphatic design statement, especially when used in pairs. Twinned fittings may overwhelm some rooms, but the technique can be very effective if handled with a blend of confidence and sensitivity.

1

2

1 **The three-legged Fortuny light can never be inconspicuous. Here, its eyecatching circular shape is offset against the triangles of the adjacent painting.**

2 **The "Jill" light adds a touch of restrained colour to this predominantly white room scheme, and casts its characteristic straight-bottomed beam onto the wall behind it.**

3 In this room, the uplighter blends in relatively unobtrusively, forming a reticent design element. By bouncing light off the ceiling, it draws attention to the interior's lofty proportions.

4 A polished-steel uplighter used to underscore the Art Deco mood of a decorative arrangement. The fitting is being used as a geometrical shape in a kind of giant still life.

5 A custom-made halogen uplighter for a special installation. The fitting has overtones of neo-classical dignity.

6 These stark modern uplighters by no means detract from the historic architecture. As this picture shows, a visible plug and flex do not necessarily strike a false note, provided that you do not make a half-hearted attempt at concealment.

"Stelo", Tronconi (Raul Barbieri and Giorgio Marianelli). A halogen light, with a stem available in brass or various colours. The shade is in moulded neutral-coloured glass. ▼

"Zagar", Stilnovo (D.S. Carpani). A swivel-top light that takes a 300- or 500-watt halogen tube. The dimmer control matches the handle for adjusting the beam direction. ▼

▲ A low-voltage halogen light, designed by Ronald Sportes for the Elysée Palace, Paris. There are two separate light sources – one in the base (reflected off the lower bowl) and one in the upper bowl.

"Delta", Koch and Lowy (Piotr Sierakowski). A 500-watt halogen uplighter with an unusual forked stem. ▲

"Shell" floor light, Boyd Lighting Co. The alternative finishes available are antiqued brass, polished brass and chrome.

▼ A floor-standing task light designed by Ronald Sportes for the Elysée Palace, Paris.

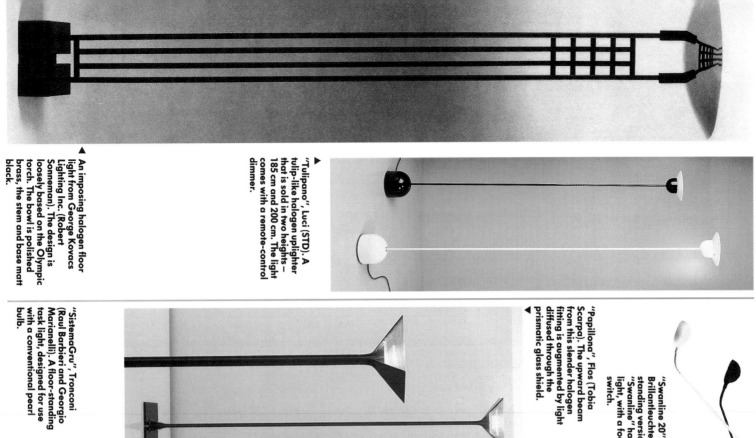

▲ An imposing halogen floor light from George Kovacs Lighting Inc. (Robert Sonneman). The design is loosely based on the Olympic torch. The bowl is polished brass, the stem and base matt black.

▲ "Tulipano", Luci (STD). A tulip-like halogen uplighter that is sold in two heights – 185 cm and 200 cm. The light comes with a remote-control dimmer.

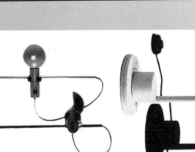

▲ "Papillona", Flos (Tobia Scarpa). The upward beam from this slender halogen fitting is augmented by light diffused through the prismatic glass shield.

"SistemaGru", Tronconi (Raul Barbieri and Georgio Marianelli). A floor-standing task light, designed for use with a conventional pearl bulb.

"Swanline 20", Brillantleuchten. A floor-standing version of the "Swanline" halogen desk light, with a foot-operated switch.

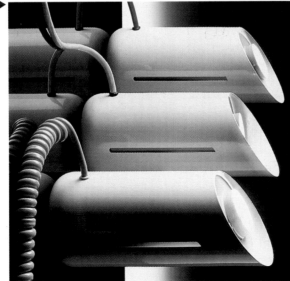

▲ A trio of portable uplighters from John Cullen Lighting Design Ltd.

▲ "Toltec", Concord. A new uplighter designed to take a metal-halide light source. Metal-halide lamps are likely to be used increasingly in the home.

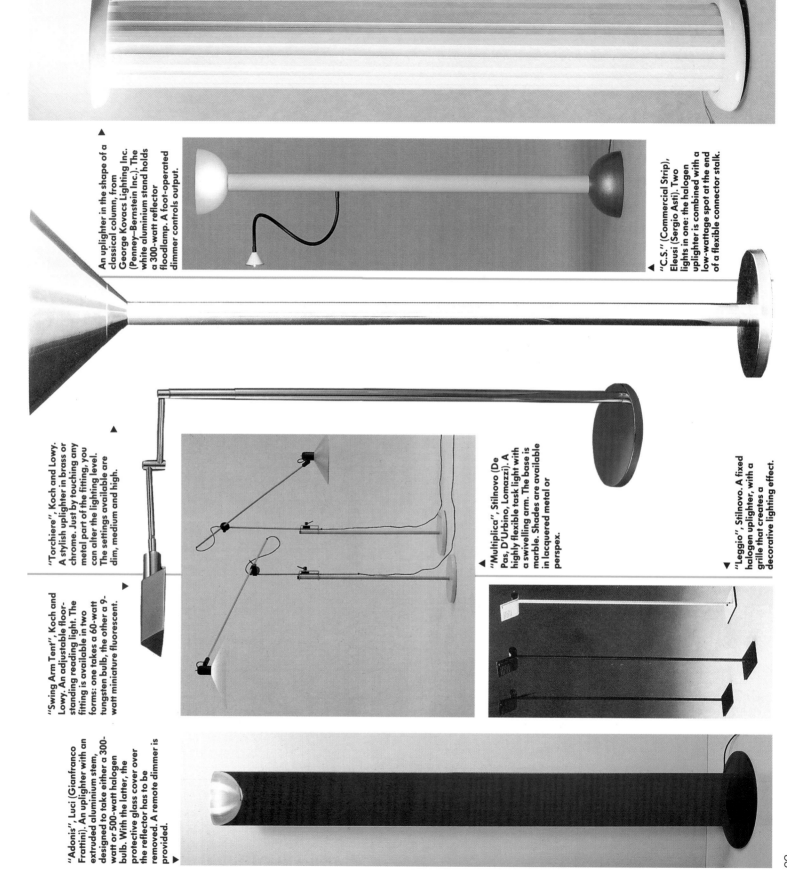

An uplighter in the shape of a classical column, from George Kovacs Lighting Inc. (Penney–Bernstein Inc.). The white aluminium stand holds a 300-watt reflector floodlamp. A foot-operated dimmer controls output.

"C.S." (Commercial Strip), Eleusi (Sergio Asti). Two lights in one: the halogen uplighter is combined with a low-wattage spot at the end of a flexible connector stalk.

"Torchiere", Koch and Lowy. A stylish uplighter in brass or chrome. Just by touching any metal part of the fitting, you can alter the lighting level. The settings available are dim, medium and high.

"Swing Arm Tent", Koch and Lowy. An adjustable floor-standing reading light. The fitting is available in two forms: one takes a 60-watt tungsten bulb, the other a 9-watt miniature fluorescent.

"Multiplica", Stilnovo (De Pas, D'Urbino, Lomazzi). A highly flexible task light with a swivelling arm. The base is marble. Shades are available in lacquered metal or perspex.

"Leggio", Stilnovo. A fixed halogen uplighter, with a grille that creates a decorative lighting effect.

"Adonis", Luci (Gianfranco Frattini). An uplighter with an extruded aluminium stem, designed to take either a 300-watt or 500-watt halogen bulb. With the latter, the protective glass cover over the reflector has to be removed. A remote dimmer is provided.

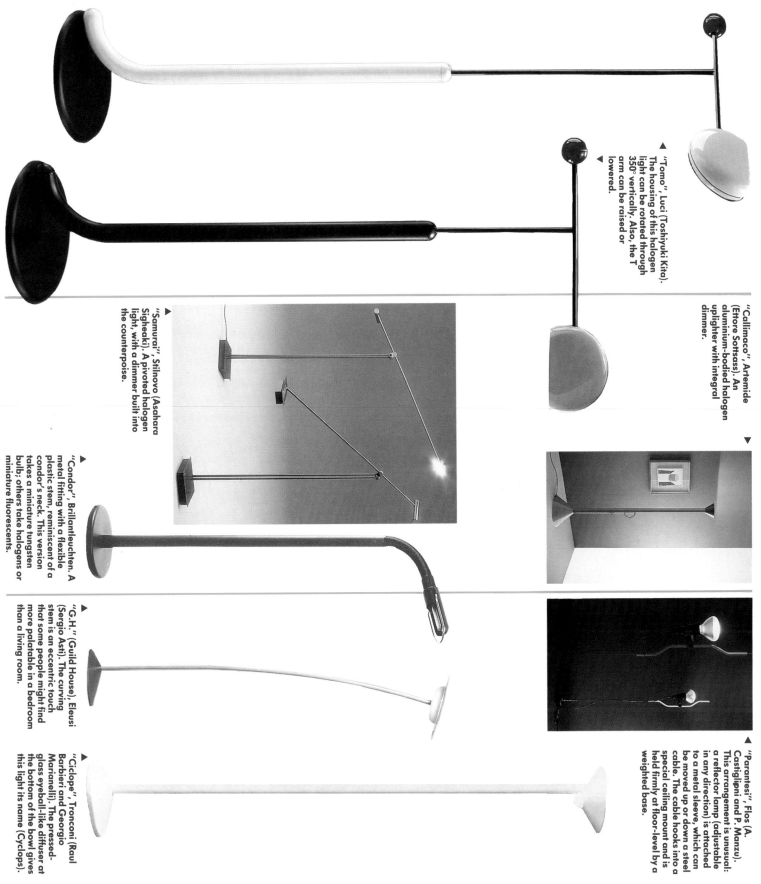

▲ "Tomo", Luci (Toshiyuki Kita). The housing of this halogen light can be rotated through 350° vertically. Also, the T arm can be raised or lowered.

► "Callimaco", Artemide (Ettore Sottsass). An aluminium-bodied halogen uplighter with integral dimmer.

► "Samurai", Stilnovo (Asahara Sigheaki). A pivoted halogen light, with a dimmer built into the counterpoise.

► "Condor", Brillantleuchten. A metal fitting with a flexible plastic stem, reminiscent of a condor's neck. This version takes a miniature tungsten bulb; others take halogens or miniature fluorescents.

► "G.H." (Guild House), Eleusi (Sergio Asti). The curving stem is an eccentric touch that some people might find more palatable in a bedroom than a living room.

▲ "Parantesi", Flos (A. Castiglioni and P. Manzu). This arrangement is unusual: a reflector lamp (adjustable in any direction) is attached to a metal sleeve, which can be moved up or down a steel cable. The cable hooks into a special ceiling mount and is held firmly at floor-level by a weighted base.

► "Ciclope", Tronconi (Raul Barbieri and Georgio Marianelli). The pressed-glass eyeball-like diffuser at the bottom of the bowl gives this light its name (Cyclops).

93

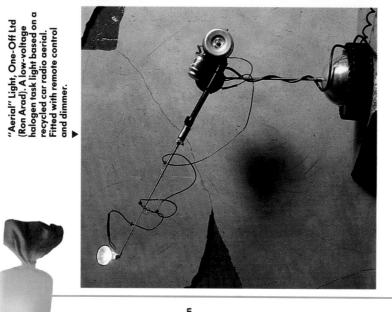

"Aerial" Light, One-Off Ltd (Ron Arad). A low-voltage halogen task light based on a recycled car radio aerial. Fitted with remote control and dimmer. ▶

"Nastro", Stilnovo (Albert Fraser). An extraordinary low-voltage halogen desk light with a multi-coloured plastic arm. ▶

Plastics can be moulded into any shape to form a suitable diffuser for a tungsten light bulb. These "Bonbon" plug-in lights are manufactured by Brillantleuchten. ▶

D esigners of light fittings are often encouraged to give free reign to their imagination, subordinating function to ornament, or to ingenuity for its own sake. This miscellaneous selection ranges from visual jokes to highly elaborate fittings that function almost as adult playthings.

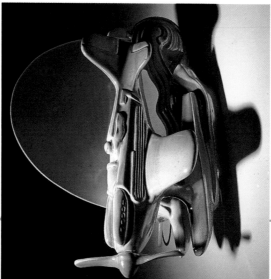

A ceramic "Aeroplane" table light from Sunset Ceramics, designed with a shelf or mantelpiece in mind. The bulb is screened by a disc-shaped diffuser. ▲

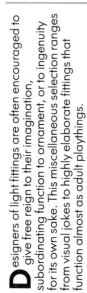

▼ A fashion mannequin, ironically sanctified with a halo of neon. This concoction exemplifies the startling effects that can be achieved by improvisation.

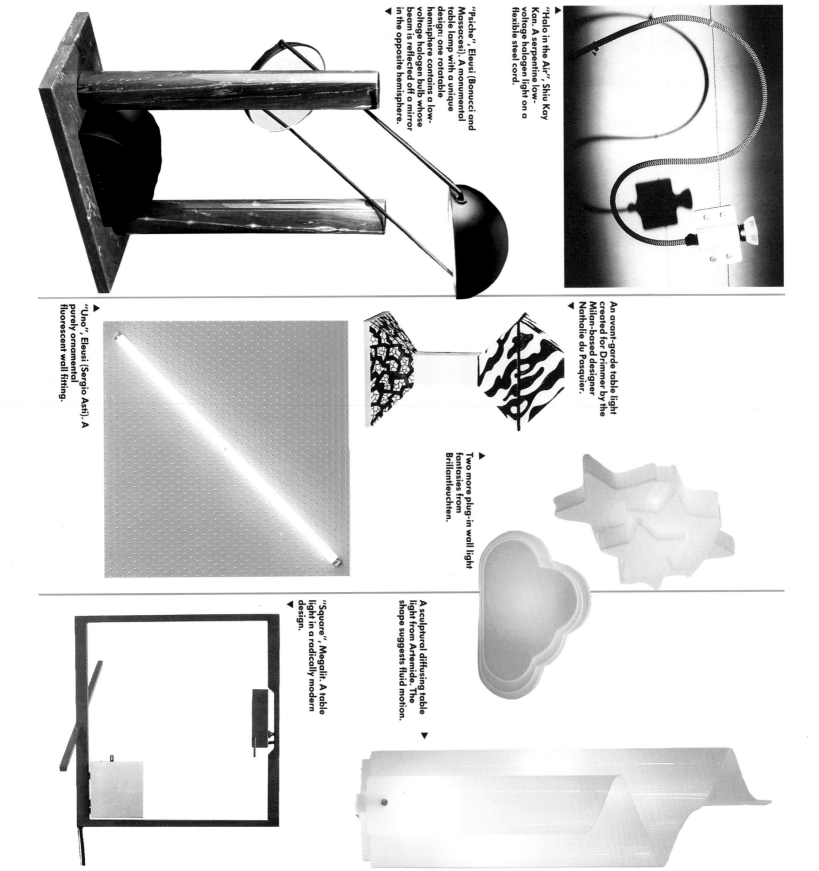

"Halo in the Air", Shiu Kay Kan. A serpentine low-voltage halogen light on a flexible steel cord. ▶

"Psiche", Eleusi (Bonucci and Massacesi). A monumental table lamp with a unique design: one rotatable hemisphere contains a low-voltage halogen bulb whose beam is reflected off a mirror in the opposite hemisphere. ◀

An avant-garde table light created for Drimmer by the Milan-based designer Nathalie du Pasquier. ◀

"Uno", Eleusi (Sergio Asti). A purely ornamental fluorescent wall fitting. ▶

Two more plug-in wall light fantasies from Brillantleuchten. ▶

A sculptural diffusing table light from Artemide. The shape suggests fluid motion.

"Square", Megalit. A table light in a radically modern design. ◀

▼

Oddities

Light fittings for outdoor use are designed for a wide variety of roles – from illuminated house-number plates or address signs to powerful floodlights for displaying garden features or exterior walls. But despite this variety, all exterior lights have certain features in common: they must be weatherproof, durable, easy to maintain and economic to run. Weatherproof, of course, means corrosion-resistant as well as watertight. Commonly used materials that meet this demand are cast aluminium or stainless steel. Shatterproof glass or plastic diffusers protect against stone-throwing vandals. As an additional safety measure, many lights are also tamper-

proof, in that they can only be dismantled with special tools: this is a useful deterrent against children playing unsupervised in the garden who might try to take a fitting apart.

Another important factor is that outdoor lights must be as glare-free as possible. At night, when our eyes have adapted themselves to dim light, any artificial lights will seem all the brighter by contrast with their surroundings, and may dazzle. To overcome this potential difficulty, most exterior fittings are designed for use with low-wattage lamps or alternatively with special shades or anti-glare attachments – such as baffles, louvers or barndoors.

The principal categories of outdoor lighting are wall lights, floodlights, path

lights, accent lights and special fittings for pools and fountains. Wall lights have the major advantage that the wiring and switching can be kept indoors, with power coming from conventional domestic circuits. All other kinds of exterior lighting require special installation, preferably by a qualified and registered electrical contractor who is conversant with the strict safety regulations. You should never attempt this type of work yourself unless you know exactly what you are doing. Sockets for portable lights must be totally weatherproof. Underground cables must be buried at least a specified distance below the ground to avoid the possibility of being damaged by garden tools.

Wall lights

One of the most common varieties of exterior wall light is the bulkhead fitting – a classically simple type with a glass or plastic diffuser, sometimes protected by steel or aluminium bars. The glass-covered types tend to age better, and have greater light transmission.

Many wall lights have a decidedly municipal look, while others are questionably historical in style. You should be prepared for a determined search if you require a stylish-looking fitting that falls between these two extremes.

Illuminated house numbers often have the numeral clearly defined in black over a glass or plastic diffuser; a

1 A post-mounted double downlighter can be used to cast ample light over garden pathways. There are many variations on this principle. This fitting, 30 inches (76cm) high, is from Brillamleuchten (as are the lights in pictures 2, 4, and 5).

2 As well as being useful for path lighting, downlighters offer an effective way to show off foliage or flower beds. The dome of this fitting has a white reflective inner surface to maximize light output.

3 Globe-shaped wall lights are available in clear or opal versions. This one from Marlin has a vandal-proof polycarbonate diffuser, and takes either an ordinary tungsten bulb or an SL miniature fluorescent. It is also sold in pole-mounted and plinth-mounted versions.

4 A clamp-on exterior spotlight attached to a tree should be adjusted carefully so as not to damage the branch. You will need to loosen the clamp at intervals to allow for the tree's growth.

5 A tough, weatherproof bulkhead light with a prismatic glass cover.

low-wattage lamp ensures that the contrast between the figures and the light source is not too great. Some fittings in this category are specially designed to accommodate an energy-saving miniature fluorescent. An integral bell push is also a popular feature. As an alternative to buying a special fitting, you can either paint the house number onto a bulkhead diffuser, or use a mini spotlight to illuminate a name or number board.

Some wall-mounted fluorescent fittings are sold specifically as security lights, to deter intruders and reassure nightowls returning home. If you wish, you can install photocell units, which switch lamps on and off automatically as daylight fades and returns.

Floodlights and spotlights

If your home and garden are of a scale and a style that warrant extensive floodlighting most nights of the year, it is sensible to consider low-energy light sources, such as mercury fluorescents or high-pressure sodium lights. But for more modest applications, the long-term savings in running costs would not accrue soon enough to offset the initial expense of this kind of lighting. Tungsten or tungsten-halogen floodlighting is a better bet.

Broad-beam wallwasher-type halogen fittings with a scooped reflector are a standard option that is modestly priced. However, if they are to be angled upward – for example, to light the front of a house – they must be equipped with special heat-resistant glass shields or they will gather rainwater.

Parabolic reflector (PAR 38) lamps are very useful in the garden for accent lighting. Their sealed construction means that they can be used without protection, provided that they are fitted in rainproof lampholders with appropriate electrical connections. They can be clamped to trees or other suitable supports, or alternatively can be embedded into the ground on long spikes. Sealed-beam PAR 56 lamps yield a stronger light than PAR 38 lamps, but are not designed to resist temperature extremes: they must therefore be fitted with a toughened glass cover.

For illuminating greenery, flowers or paths, pole-mounted downlighter fittings offer a convenient light source. The mushroom style of fitting, with a domed cover (white inside) protecting two tungsten bulbs, is also deservedly popular. Some single-bulb mushroom lights are directionally adjustable. Various kinds of slimline bollard fitting, usually standing 3 feet (1 m) high, are also available.

For paths, the most discreet type of lighting comes from a recessed fitting let into the path's surface, so that its toughened glass top lies flush with paving stones.

Submersible lights

Beautiful effects can be created with illuminated fountains or waterfalls, or even simple pool lighting. A number of low-voltage submersible fittings are made by specialist manufacturers. Some types are designed either to float or to be tethered below the surface of a pool. Fountain lights are available which channel the water directly up through the centre of the fitting, so that the whole of the jet traps light.

7

6 The white walls of this small patio play an important role in reflecting light from an exterior spotlight positioned high on the side of the house.

7 Spike spots are the most convenient of garden lights, as they can easily be moved around to highlight different flowers as the seasons progress.

"Lotto", Luci (STD). This waterproof fitting can be used with a 100-watt tungsten bulb or an 80-watt mercury-vapour lamp. Two heights are available: 155cm (61 inches) and 87cm (34 inches). ▲

"Giardino", Goccia. A robust ▲ light with a body of zinc-plated steel. All lamps in the Goccia range are available with sockets for tungsten bulbs, high-pressure mercury or sodium vapour lamps, circular fluorescent tubes or PL or SL miniature fluorescents.

A floodlighting set from Lotus, intended for large fountain displays. The coloured lenses produce a spectacular tricolour effect, but they can be removed for more restrained displays. ▶

A well-made bridge type light from Brillantleuchten, designed to take an 18-watt fluorescent tube. ▶

A bollard fitting from Concord. The pole is black aluminium. The clear glass lens offers all-round illumination from a tungsten bulb. ▲

A cluster of spike-mounted globe lights from i Guzzini. The covers are vandal-proof. ▶

▶ A wall-mounted carriage-style light from Chelsom, suitable for adding a touch of grandeur to entrances.

A plinth-mounted exterior light in the antique style typical of Chelsom.

▶ A clear globe light from Staff. Clear globes are less conspicuous during the daytime.

"Tap Giardino", Piuluce. A double light which takes two 60-watt tungsten bulbs. Two different heights are shown here – 100cm (40 inches) and 50cm (20 inches).

▶

◀ "Roof I", Brillantleuchten. An antique-style wall light that takes a 100-watt bulb.

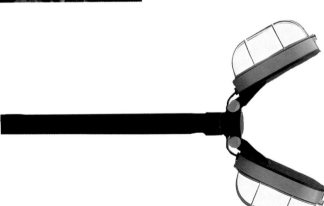

▲ A Lotus fountain light. This low-voltage fitting is used with a remote transformer. The water jet is channelled right through the centre of the fitting.

▶ A double pole-mounted fitting from Goccia. The heads can be angled downward for path lighting.

The Art of Lighting

Professional lighting designers use a repertoire of tried and tested techniques from which we can all draw lessons to apply to our own homes. For example, there are special strategies for washing a wall with light, or for accentuating a favourite painting. With most of these approaches, the secret is to get two things right – the choice of fitting (from both a functional and a stylistic point of view) and its positioning.

The basic skills that together make up the art of lighting are described in the following section of the book. As well as ground rules for background, task and display lighting, these pages offer sound advice on planning a lighting scheme from scratch. There is also a helpful section for tenants on how to revitalize lighting without rewiring.

Writing a letter, chopping vegetables, darning, reading a book or using a home computer are among the wide range of activities that demand special lighting, to provide a localized area of brighter illumination than the general level of light within the room. This is the province of task lighting. Its aim is to allow a specific task to be carried out in comfort, without risk of straining the eyes.

There is more to task lighting than simply delivering sufficient light to enable us to see what we are doing — although this is a vital criterion for success. Equally importantly, the light must fall onto the task without casting troublesome shadows or causing glare. Positioning of the fitting is critical in this respect. If you are planning a desk light in a study, you need to consider whether a right-handed or a left-handed person will use the light. If right-handed, the lamp should be placed to the left, to prevent the user's arm from casting a shadow over the papers as he writes. In some exceptional circumstances, though, shadows are a help rather than a hindrance; for example, when you are ironing you need an oblique light to reveal creases.

A general rule is that the shade should be at eye level. Any higher and there will be a risk of glare from the bulb or from the shade's inside surface; any lower and the light will be too close for comfort, increasing the likelihood of glare by reflection from a shiny page or from the desk surface.

Whatever the task, an adjustable desk light offers the easiest way to get the positioning right, and is especially convenient if the work area has more than one user, each with different requirements. However, it is also possible to use other fittings, such as a pendant (preferably, the rise-and-fall type) positioned low over the surface, or a wall-mounted spot.

The colour-rendering properties of the light source are not absolutely critical for most tasks, with the notable exception of painting. This means that you have a broad range of light sources to choose from. Tubular fluorescent sources are eminently suitable for lighting a kitchen worktop or workshop bench, while circular or miniature

1

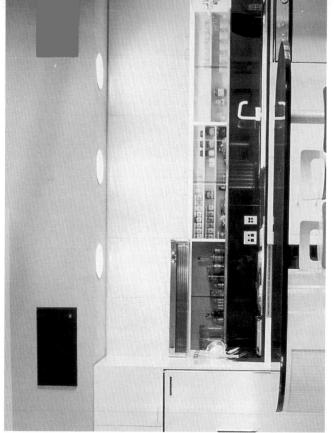

2

1 Fluorescent tubes give a broad spread of light that is useful for tasks requiring a sizeable area of a work surface — for example, a architectural drawing. Here, a tube is tamed for domestic use by an attractive tubular fitting with built-in diffuser.

2 Large recessed downlighters with diffusing covers provide even task lighting for kitchen chores. In areas where you need to use a knife, such as a kitchen worktop, good lighting is essential for safety.

3 For a kitchen table which doubles as a desk, a spun-aluminium photographer's lamp has been imaginatively recycled for task lighting. The clip-on attachment means that the light can easily be removed and used elsewhere in the flat as required. You could easily use a clip-on desk light to serve the same function.

fluorescents, or the shorter kinds of tube, are suited for tasks concentrated on a smaller area. Tungsten lamps have many uses, but you should avoid high-wattage bulbs, which are too bulky and tend to heat up a fitting to the point where it is uncomfortable to manipulate. Tungsten-halogen lighting is increasingly popular for task lighting, particularly when high-level illumination is demanded.

Different tasks call for different amounts of light, depending on the degree of detail you need to see. For example, needlework requires a greater light output than mounting photographs in an album. Reading does not require as much light as we might expect, because of the high contrast between print and page, which aids legibility. Avoid overlighting. Take the time factor into account: if you plan to spend five hours on one kind of task, you will need more light than you would for a half-hour session. Remember too that lighting requirements increase with age; a 60-year-old may need twice as much light as a 30-year-old for the same task.

It is vital to strike a shrewd balance of brightness between the work surface and its surroundings. If the contrast is too great, eyestrain will almost inevitably result. A useful rule of thumb is to keep the surroundings at no less than one third the brightness of the work surface. Some types of task light achieve this effect by permitting some of the light they give off to spread out into the room. However, most fittings will need to be deployed in conjunction with supplementary light sources.

The light you need for a task

Task	Average illuminance needed in lux/footcandles
Sewing and darning	300 lux/ 30 footcandles
Household accounts	
Prolonged reading	
Preparing food	
Work bench activities	
Casual reading	150 lux/ 15 footcandles
Household accounts	
Using stairs	100 lux/ 10 footcandles
Washing and other bathroom activities	
General bedroom or living room activities	50 lux/ 5 footcandles

103

Background lighting is desirable in all interiors for reasons of safety and comfort. Its primary function is to allow for ease of circulation, so that you can move safely from one brightly lit area to another through potentially hazardous pools of comparative darkness. Because the level of background light is relatively low, it is very restful to the eyes. If correctly positioned, it prevents glare problems by reducing the contrast when there is a bright task light in the room. Background light also has a role to play in bringing out the visual characteristics of the interior, revealing the details of fittings and furnishings as well as the architecture.

The main feature of background lighting is that it is indirect. Although some of the light may radiate directly from the source (for example, the light cast downward from a shaded table lamp), most of the illumination comes from diffusion or from light bouncing off walls, ceiling and floor – perhaps more than once, in a complex pattern of interpenetrating reflections. This creates a soft illumination that is flattering to people's faces.

For indirect, bounced light to be effective, the walls and ceiling must be of high reflectance (see page 15). White or pale painted surfaces will reflect more light than, say, cork tiles or hessian. Light acting upon a pale-coloured surface to produce background light will affect the

apparent size of the room. For example, a small room will appear more spacious if the walls are efficient reflectors than it will if the walls have a dark, matt surface that soaks up light. In large rooms, the ceiling and the floor take on most of the burden of reflecting background light, while in small rooms the walls play a bigger part. But if you give a ceiling a white gloss finish to spread more light into a room, it is important to choose the floor covering carefully: with a vividly coloured carpet, the ceiling may pick up an unwanted colour cast by reflection. For this reason, and to avoid reflections of light sources, matt surfaces are preferable.

Some fittings are designed specifically to provide indirect light – for example, the torchère-style uplighter, which directs light onto the ceiling from a powerful tungsten-halogen lamp concealed within an opaque bowl. Other sources of background lighting include diffusing pendants, portable standard lamps and bowl-shaped wall lights. You can also deploy an adjustable task light for background lighting by redirecting it toward the walls or ceiling.

Concealed lighting

Concealing the light source is a popular approach particularly favoured for fluorescent lights, which tend to obtrude upon the eye if they are allowed to show. By lowering the ceiling, you can recess the lights and cover them with diffusing panels. Lamps, control gear and fittings may also be hidden beneath shelves or on a cornice ledge. Cornice lighting looks best when the room is tall. Both walls and ceiling should have a high reflectance factor. The ceiling finish must be absolutely smooth, or the

1

1 Tungsten strip lights concealed above a coving shelf provide a gentle frieze of light that supplements natural daylight and stresses the architectural form of the room. When the light fades, this background lighting needs to be reinforced by task lighting for the specific musical activities the room is designed to accommodate.

2 Three suspended ceiling panels hide the overhead light sources in this bedroom. Balancing this arrangement are concealed strips set into shallow steps: these lights highlight the steps for safety reasons as well as for aesthetic effect. A pair of bedside table lights constitutes yet a third source of background lighting.

strongly angled light will throw any irregularities, cracks or burrs into prominence.

A pelmet board over a curtain or wall is another way to conceal tube lighting. By painting or wallpapering the pelmet board, you can make it blend with the wall. The inner faces should be painted matt white. Ideally, you should position the tube between five and eight inches (13–20cm) from the vertical surface of the pelmet, which must be deep enough to mask the tube even from someone standing quite close to the same wall. Of course, it is essential that the tube is far enough away from curtain fabric to avoid scorching.

3 Built-in lighting recesses flank a fine Greek-revival marble fireplace to provide a low level of background light. Ground-glass covers diffuse and soften the concealed tungsten strips.

Lighting can be used in a way that is frankly decorative, rather than purely functional. There are various possible approaches. One is to employ the colour or shape of the bulb conspicuously and ornamentally in a room scheme – for example, you could use a crown-silvered bulb to add a touch of sparkle, a low-wattage spherical bulb for a pleasing geometrical profile, or a row of different-coloured standard tungsten bulbs to give a fairground effect in a child's bedroom. In all these cases, a decorative role is filled regardless of whether the light is on or off.

A more traditional instance of the decorative strategy is the chandelier, whose glass surfaces break up light into sparkling multiple images. At the opposite end of the scale are exotic light sources made available by advanced technology. These include holograms (3D-effect photographs, commercially available in a framed form to hang on a wall) and lasers (extremely narrow beams of concentrated light, which still require

installation by specialists). It remains to be seen whether the craze for these exotics will prove any more lasting than the vogue for neon in the 1970s.

Some of the most satisfactory decorative lighting schemes are those that remain firmly rooted in the practicalities of functional lighting, but with a parallel decorative impact. For example, a Tiffany glass shade functions perfectly well as a shade-cum-diffuser fitting for delivering light into a room, but is also a thing of beauty in its own right. Indeed, a lighting layout planned to work *exclusively* from a functional point of view is unlikely to satisfy us: the decorative dimension is important because we *need* interest and contrast, even when concentrating on specific tasks rather than merely lounging or talking. Few people can concentrate on an activity without pausing occasionally to look around the room – perhaps as they seek inspiration, or to rest the eyes. It is at these times, as well as in sociable gatherings, that discreet "accent lighting" has its role to play. For

1

2

3

1 **Coloured glass beads hang from the engraved glass shade of a table lamp, adding a touch of old-style opulence. The shade is as decorative as the other objects in this table arrangement.**

2 **Light fittings are here used as surreal sculptures, in a scheme very much inspired by the new wave of Milanese designers. The neon tubes slashing across the attic diagonally are custom-made. However, the portable fluorescent fittings, which plug into a wall socket, are readily available from specialist retailers.**

3 **A bold feature of this room is the quartet of desk lights artfully twisted into unusual shapes that punctuate the wall surface. The track-mounted spotlights also serve a decorative function by contributing sparkle.**

4 **Lighting at its most whimsical. The plastic goose sheds little useful light, but certainly makes a powerful decorative impact, with a wry look back toward childhood.**

example, many people like to have table lights dotted around a room as visual punctuation marks.

Spotlighting offers one possible example of the dual role that lights can perform. Clearly, spotlights are functional lights: they illuminate specific areas of a room, making particular objects or surfaces visible. But if they are carefully positioned so as to avoid glare, a row of spots can also contribute a pleasing sparkle to an interior, particularly if they are the type with a faceted reflector. The decorative impact is all the more effective because we can introduce it or remove it at will. This means that it need never pall. If we have planned the total lighting scheme flexibly, switching off the spots will not plunge the room into darkness, but will simply alter its mood in a constructive way. And in daylight there is the added bonus that the spotlights' reflectors may scintillate occasionally when they catch the sun. If you wish, you can enhance the ornamental aspects of the spots by adding special accessories, such as coloured reflectors.

Whenever you want to draw special attention to a wall, perhaps because of a special finish or feature, you can employ one of two lighting methods: wall washing or wall grazing. Wall washing is the technique of using a whole row of lights carefully positioned and angled to produce smooth, flat illumination over the full extent of one wall, or over a selected part of it. This allows you to emphasize a wall full of pictures or book-lined shelves, or simply create a restful expanse of reflected background light. Wall grazing is a variation on this theme. The effect is normally produced by slightly stronger, more directional lighting, which picks out texture by casting a pattern of shadows and highlights. This approach is particularly effective for displaying brick or stonework surfaces or textile hangings. Neither method is suitable when the wall is broken up into subdivisions by doors or small windows. Glossy surfaces and walls covered in mirrors or large expanses of glass are also inappropriate, because of their high reflectance and the

consequent problem of glare. You should bear in mind that an illuminated feature wall can affect the apparent dimensions of the room. As a rule, the room will seem larger, but if it is unusually proportioned a single well-lit wall may exaggerate the visual imbalance.

Washing a wall

The neatest and most elegant way to wash a wall with light is with downlighters recessed into the ceiling. This results in an almost invisible light source and a ceiling that remains dark in comparison with the wall itself. You should install the fittings a minimum of 12 inches (30cm) from the wall: any closer and the steeply angled beams will reveal surface irregularities that are better disguised. Increasing the distance gives a greater spread of light on the surface.

The spacing between each downlighter is of critical importance if you want to illuminate the wall evenly. A symmetrical arrangement is essential. The optimum distance will vary according to the characteristics of the

fittings and the lamps. Consult the manufacturer's catalogue to find out the beam profile, and work out the ideal positioning on a room plan before you begin installation. If the spacing is too far apart, there will be a noticeable scalloped effect along the top of the illuminated area, where the beam from one light arches into the beam from its neighbour. In some installations this can be a desirable decorative feature. But if you want to avoid the effect, choose fittings and lamps that produce a widespread beam. For soft, low-level wall washing, choose 40-watt reflector lamps.

Setting up ceiling-mounted downlighters is a major operation. A simpler alternative, especially suitable for renters, is to use track-mounted versions which offer more flexibility. More convenient still is a row of small portable uplighters; these stand on the floor and connect to skirting board outlets via ordinary flex and plug. A different track altogether is to install a fluorescent cornice light. This is useful for walls that meet a sloping ceiling, but only if the wall height is uniform.

1

2

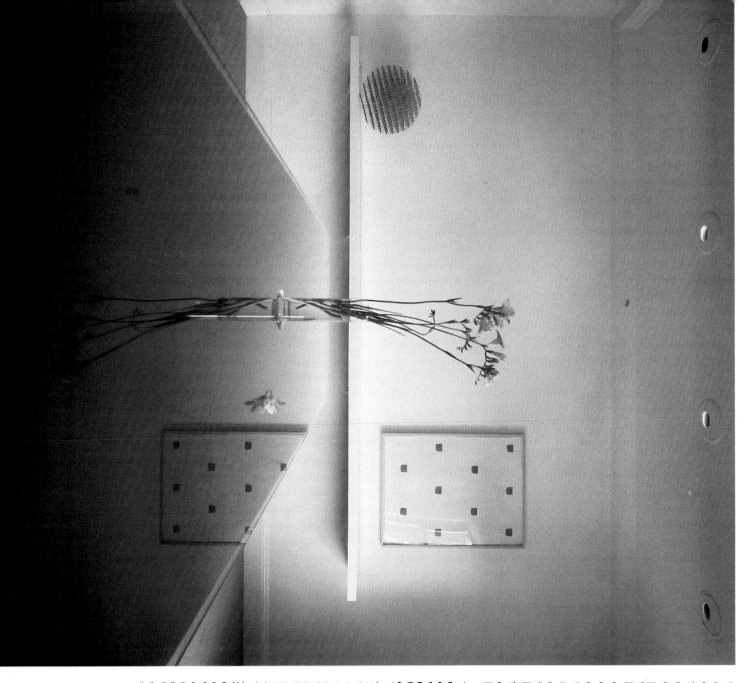

Grazing

Most of the basic techniques described opposite apply also to grazing, except that the fittings must be placed much closer to the wall. The best lamps to use are tungsten reflectors: standard bulbs produce too diffuse a light, while fluorescents create a flat, shadowless lighting that subdues texture instead of accentuating it. The higher the wattage of the lamps, the more emphatic the effect. You will need stronger bulbs if the surface is dark-toned, or the shadows will not be conspicuous enough. Dimming tungsten lights makes them redder, which may enhance red brick walls. Cornice lighting behind a fascia (painted matt white inside) is especially effective if you use a row of bare silvered spotlamps.

1 A series of small uplighters disguised in specially built cavities are used to wash the walls of a stairway, giving it a monumental feel. The technique recalls the glamour of Hollywood cinemas of the 1930s.

2 An unconventional use of wall-mounted spotlights equipped with wide-beam reflector bulbs. The low-level positioning prevents the light-washed wall from being too dominant and spoiling the low-key mood. Cut off by the right-hand edge of the picture is a goose-necked fitting that casts soft tree shadows onto the darker half of the wall.

3 Individually switched downlighters recessed into a ceiling can be used either to wash a whole wall, or to pick out specific areas. Special reflectors inside the fittings shown here angle the light toward the wall instead of allowing it to flood symmetrically downward.

The style in which we decorate our homes is one of the ways in which we express our personalities. By means of colour, pattern and texture, and possessions such as fittings and furniture, we make statements about the kind of people we are and the way we live. Sometimes, if we are sufficiently individualistic, we create our own style. But most of us borrow from pre-existing styles to create a look that suits us or pleases us – within the inevitable constraints of cost.

It is possible to identify a whole spectrum of stylistic approaches in domestic interior design. These range from the cool purism of the current monochrome, minimalist look to the nostalgic charm of the country house style. In between these extremes are the jokey decorativeness of post-modernism, the formal elegance of the traditional town house style, and the slick, glossy "decorator" look. Those who are of an eclectic persuasion, or who have inherited a hotch-potch of possessions, mix styles freely, often creating strange hybrids.

Lighting has an important part to play in supporting a style. This is not just a matter of the fittings themselves, although these make a conspicuous impact. Equally significant is the quality of light they produce, which should be appropriate to the style and period of the room. If you want to create an authentic period flavour in an 18th- or early 19th-century home, you can achieve this more effectively by choosing fairly low lighting levels than by dotting the interior with ostentatious period light fittings. Any electric fitting disguised as a gas fitting or candle bracket is, of course, an anachronism, which may or may not offend our sense of history. In period interiors, the choice of switches and other controls is also important. Modern switches look incongruous and unsightly, especially when their plastic contrasts with antique panelling. Concealment is usually the best policy. In rooms with a strongly Victorian character, reproduction antique switches, or better still, original brass plates adapted to electricity, can be appropriate.

Some kinds of fittings are strongly evocative. A conical shade of thick green glass can create something of the ambience of a smoky Edwardian billiard room. An Art Nouveau Tiffany shade will bring with it a hint of turn-of-the-century frivolity. Thick frilled-glass gas-mantle shades (whether real or reproduction) also conjure up the past, but remember that they will give off a quite unauthentic type of light when equipped with modern bulbs. Because of the flexibility of electric light, there is

2

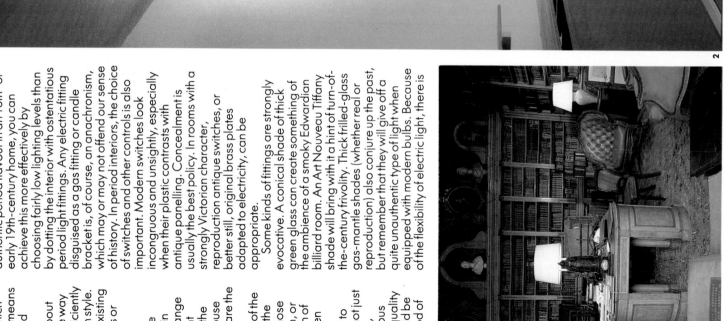

1

1 The mellow, clublike atmosphere of this library is underscored by quiet, soft, diffuse lighting from fittings with traditional fabric shades. The lights provide just enough general light to give polished wood a glint or two, but leave most of the room in picturesque shade.

2 A cool, calm, monochrome modern interior. Low-voltage tungsten-halogen lights on neatly positioned ceiling tracks add high-tech sparkle, and cast shadows that offer a substitute for colour in an all-white room.

also a temptation to put such shades to work in positions that would have been impossible in the age of gas. It is very common, for example, to find bell-shaped gas-fitting shades deployed upside down, with the open end at the bottom instead of the top. Again, it is a matter of taste whether this is admissible.

Contemporary styles

Post-war lighting design has been firmly tied to the oscillations of fashion. For example, during the 1960s, when both light fittings and the character of the lighting preferred became correspondingly brash and bright. Lighting technology was enjoyed for its own sake, the shinier the better. Rows of chrome-finished spotlights became a hallmark of style. These are now beginning to look rather dated, whereas 1950s-style interiors are moving back into vogue.

The reaction against pop technology took various forms, most notably a leaning toward the whimsical. Light fittings jokingly took on the forms of other objects, or even animals. Geese became particularly popular. The German lighting designer, Ingo Maurer, produced a much-copied shade in the shape of a giant tungsten bulb. This reaction against

bright, primary colours were the trend, shaped architecturally with their surroundings. Another fashionable modern trend is minimalism—a style which strips things down to bare essentials. Minimalist interiors have at their disposal a wide range of stark, sculptural fittings. Because of their stylistic neutrality, these fittings can also be appropriate in rooms decorated in other styles. This is especially true of uplighters, whose slim lines and elegant proportions make them perfectly in keeping even with flamboyantly historical settings.

technological modernism was most extreme in Italy, where the Memphis group produced influential fittings in eccentric shapes and colours.

A more restrained response is represented by the current revival of interest in classicism (for example, as shown by floor lights disguised as classical columns) and in fittings **that** blend architecturally with their

3 Most of the light fittings in this cheerfully eclectic room are in the 1950s revival style: only the low-hung pendant strikes a different note. The light output is reflected back into the room off white walls and ceiling – not the way they did things in the 50s, but the essential look is there.

Lighting can be used as a kind of signpost, to draw attention to favourite objects. However, casually aiming a spotlight at a print, Victorian bust or porcelain or cut-glass vase will do little to enhance aesthetic appeal. Instead, you need to follow a more considered approach, taking into account the special qualities of the object on display. Apart from showing off prized possessions in all their glory, successful display lighting has certain advantageous side effects. For example, it can balance light from other sources to reduce the level of contrast in the room or it can dispel gloom from dark corners or sidewalls.

Picture lighting

Pictures are the most difficult of objects to light properly. Even art galleries often get it wrong, and to add to the confusion curators disagree with each other about what constitutes good lighting and how to achieve it.

The first problem is choosing the right wall for the picture. If you want to see fine detail, and get the most out of brushwork and colour, do not hang a painting on a wall that has windows in it: the glare from daylight outside will sabotage appreciation – at least until nightfall when the curtains are drawn. Indeed, rooms that receive direct sunlight are best avoided altogether by those who are serious about their collections.

You can use a wide range of different light sources to show off pictures, from tungsten-filament strip lights and fluorescent tubes to low-voltage spots. A tungsten light source close to a delicate pastel or watercolour, however, can cause heat damage. Incandescent sources can also distort the colours of a picture or wall hanging, suppressing the blues and greens. If colour rendering is critical, it is preferable to choose a fluorescent light source with a colour temperature matched to that of north light from a window. Most fluorescent sources contain a high proportion of UV radiation, which may damage a painting in time; but you can solve this by using a UV filter over the lamp.

There are two basic problems common to most light source options

for picture lighting. One is the tendency of the picture frame to cast unwelcome shadows over the picture's surface (not a worry with fluorescents). The other is the way in which glass covers over pictures, and even some types of glossy oil paint, reflect light sources or bright objects within the room, causing inevitable distraction to the viewer. Careful positioning of the light source is the best answer to both these difficulties. Normally, an illumination angle of around 45°–60° to the perpendicular will cut down reflective glare, although a slightly steeper angle, up to 70°, may be required for very shiny surfaces. If reflections remain obtrusive, you can often minimize them by tilting the picture very slightly toward the floor. With watercolours, posters, prints, drawings and photographs, you can also use non-reflective glass, which must be in direct contact with the picture surface; however, this is not a satisfactory method with oils.

The classic way to light a picture is with a special fitting (usually with a brass or silvered finish) mounted on the frame itself or on the wall just above. This fitting takes a tungsten strip light and can be angled to an optimum position to overcome glare. The method effectively eliminates shadows from the frame, although you have to ensure that the fitting itself does not cast a shadow from another light source in the same room – for example, a central pendant. To illuminate the whole picture and not just part of it, choose a light that is at least two-thirds the picture's width. The greater the distance from the surface, the wider the beam will stretch.

Many people prefer spotlights (especially minispots), which can be used at a more discreet distance from the picture. The light may be either surface-mounted on the ceiling, or track-mounted for greater flexibility. A spotlight will certainly make a picture look attractive as a piece of decoration, but unless deployed with great care will not display the work to best advantage artistically. The most suitable type of spot lamp is a low-voltage tungsten-halogen bulb.

"Framing projector" spots can be

focussed to provide a tight rectangle of light corresponding exactly to the picture area – that is, excluding the frame. However, many would deem this overly dramatic. You can achieve a similar squared-off effect using a ceiling-mounted spotlight equipped with four adjustable metal leaves (known as "barndoors") to shape the light output.

Wall-washing techniques are also appropriate for picture lighting, particularly when you have a whole group of pictures on one wall. Use either a fluorescent strip concealed inside a coving unit, or a row of recessed downlighters or small, portable uplighters. As a simpler or

possibly an interim solution, try a table lamp with an opaque open-top shade, positioned just below the picture.

Avoid overlighting paintings as this may cause fading. The maximum recommended limit for oils is 150 lux (15 footcandles), but more sensitive media, such as watercolours, should not receive more than 50 lux (5 foot-candles). Dark paintings need more lighting than delicately coloured ones.

Collectibles

Most three-dimensional objects exhibited in the home are placed on some kind of shelf – either unenclosed against a wall or in a freestanding unit, or protected within a cabinet. When

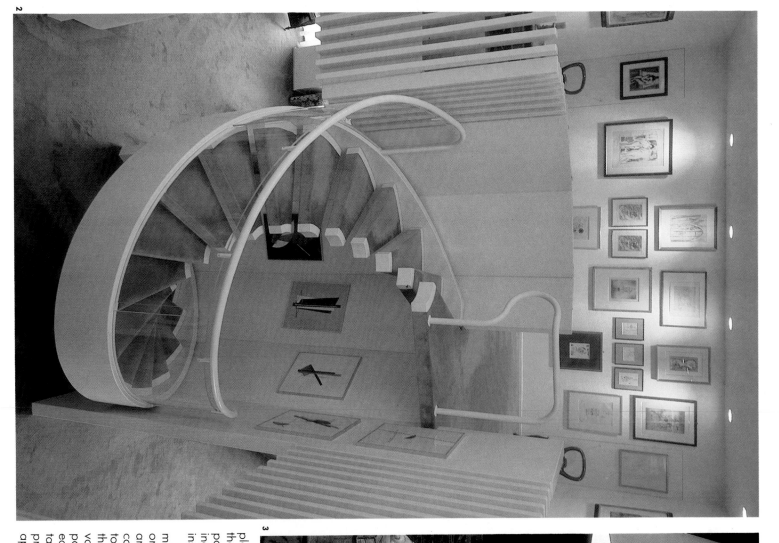

planning shelving, it is important to take the illumination into account. If possible, the wiring should be incorporated in a shelving unit at the installation stage.

One common technique is to use miniature strip lighting – either tungsten or fluorescent. Provided that the shelves are sufficiently wide apart, you can conceal the tube behind a batten fixed to the leading edge of the shelf above the object. There are numerous variations on this approach. If you possess basic carpentry skills, you can easily devise your own method, tailoring the solution precisely to the problem. One relatively ambitious approach is to build a special shelf as a

1 The grander the collection, the more important lighting becomes. Here, daylight is the main source, filtered through translucent blinds. It is supplemented by bracketed picture lights. Note the two types – twin box-like fittings, and the familiar tubular type.

2 Downlighters provide broad brushstrokes of light, which do not illuminate the pictures evenly but instead create a pleasing effect overall, with a decorative scallop where the beams intersect.

3 The circle of light beneath a table lamp is a good place to display favourite objects.

113

1

lightbox, consisting of lighting tubes sandwiched between two glass sheets (clear or opal): this setup will transmit light up and down. Less elaborately, you can use glass shelves with a single light source above or below to ensure minimum wastage of watts. For alcove lighting, it is easy to hide the lighting tube behind a fascia at cornice level.

Tungsten sources have the advantage of enhancing the appearance of natural woods, but against this you need to weigh their poor rendering of blues and greens and the danger of harming non-durable items such as leatherwork. Tungsten strips accent objects most effectively from the front. They are used in most display cabinets that are sold with built-in lighting, but it is not too difficult a job to substitute fluorescents. Minispots on tracks can also be used for shelf lighting, although it can be tricky to avoid distracting shadows. Toplighting or angled frontal lighting solves the problem, as shadows cast on the shelf surface are less noticeable than shadows on the wall behind.

Different materials demand different kinds of lighting to bring out their inherent qualities. For example, glass objects glow brilliantly when lit from above or below (especially against a dark background), whereas ceramics, wood and leather respond to frontal or toplighting to exhibit colour, texture or grain. Narrow-beam spotlights on silver, jewelry or cut glass will cause facets and bevels to sparkle.

With most kinds of sculptural object the important quality, almost by definition, is form. As explained on pages 18–19, form is revealed by the interplay of light and shadow. The light source must be direct and powerful. You can intensify the effect by opting for a narrow-beam **spot**. This creates drama, though **at the expense of detail**. For weaker, softer-edged shadows and more detail you can move the light source farther from the object, use a lamp with a wider beam, or add supplementary lighting. Do not be afraid to experiment with two or three spots of different wattage to create a more dynamic effect. Do not position the spot where it will cause you to cross the beam as you walk around the room.

114

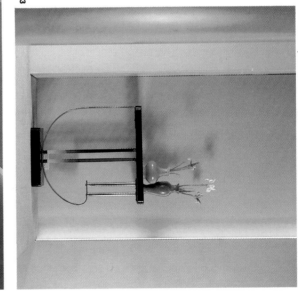

1 A single recessed downlighter shows off an unusual modern chair in a stark way that complements the chair's design. The effect is all the more impressive because of the juxtaposition with the moulded plaster wall light.

2 A pair of traditional table lamps illuminates wall-mounted blue-and-white china. Being positioned beneath the collection, the lights cast elongated shadows that fill the gaps between the pieces in an interesting way. The glazed surfaces pick up reflections of the bulbs, again adding to the total impact.

3 An Art Deco table and a pair of lustre vases receive asymmetrical lighting in a manner that evokes their period. The source is a vertical fluorescent tube covered by a diffuser panel.

4 Perspex shelves appear dramatically fringed with light, thanks to concealed fluorescent tubes whose light catches the shelves' edges. This is an effective way of drawing attention to a book collection.

1 An ancient font filled with ferns makes an eyecatching centrepiece. Lamps inside the font highlight the rich green of the plants, but are far enough away to prevent scorching. A ring of underfloor lighting hidden by a diffuser completes the effect.

2 Dried flowers need to be lit with care to bring out their textures and colours. Here, a pair of tall, slender fittings (evocative of classic candlesticks) flatter an arrangement with warm yellowish tungsten light. The lights and the flowers complement each other, creating an attractive sideboard group. The mirror duplicates the effect.

A rtificial lighting is an invaluable tool for the indoor gardener. It can be used to grow plants in the gloomier corners of the home, or even in rooms without windows. As a supplement to natural light in winter, it can keep some plants (such as African violets) unseasonably in bloom to provide year-round pleasure. An alternative approach, undoubtedly more common, is to use artificial lighting not to foster growth but purely for display purposes, highlighting greenery or flowers to bring a breath of outdoors into any room of the house.

into chemical energy and uses this to produce growth-inducing nutrients from the surrounding air, soil and water. The quantity of light required varies from one species to another. Some plants need to soak up large quantities of direct light, while others are much happier when positioned in the shade.

Few non-gardeners realize that natural sunlight is not always an essential part of a house plant's regimen. Many species can survive just as well under artificial light. Indeed, gardening under lights is becoming an increasingly popular activity. Of course, the light source must be carefully regulated. To maintain growth, at least 12 hours of light are needed daily.

Light and growth
Light is essential for the healthy development of plants. By the process of photosynthesis, a plant converts light

Scientific research has pinpointed those bands of electromagnetic radiation that promote plant health. Red light is known to help flowering, while blue light stimulates foliage. A suitable mixture of these colours can be provided by combining two kinds of fluorescent tube – a 40-watt cool white tube alongside a 40-watt daylight tube, both placed 18 to 30 inches (45–75cm) above the plant tops. If the leaves begin to curl, the light source is too close. On the other hand, if the plants start to grow tall and lanky, the tubes are too far away. Plants will suffer in the fading light of a tube that is past its prime. You should therefore take the precaution of changing each tube annually. However, do not change them both at once, or the sudden surge of brighter

light may cause dar... units with fluoresc... commercially av... fairly easy to m... tubes themse'... wooden fas...

Special... been dev... growth... radia'... exa... 30...

...it seem to glow with ...here the beam catches ...leaves. Alternatively, shiny- ...nts pick up attractive ...rts from spotlighting. A ...onal light source will cast an ...guing tangle of shadows over the ...ls or ceiling. Try using two lights ...ngled from different directions to ...duplicate this effect.

A word of warning: you must always make sure that tungsten lights are far enough away from a plant to prevent scorching. Carry out a simple test by placing your hand on the part of the plant nearest the bulb: if you can feel the warmth of the lamp, you should move the plant and the light source further apart. It may be advisable to use a cool beam PAR lamp (see page 30).

...ogether ...on a ...d plant,

bo... tungste...

3. Beautiful flowers such as lilies deserve all the lighting subtlety you can bring to bear. In this picture, two spots equipped with dimpled reflectors accentuate the flowers in a dramatic arrangement. The shadow patterns emphasize their decorative importance.

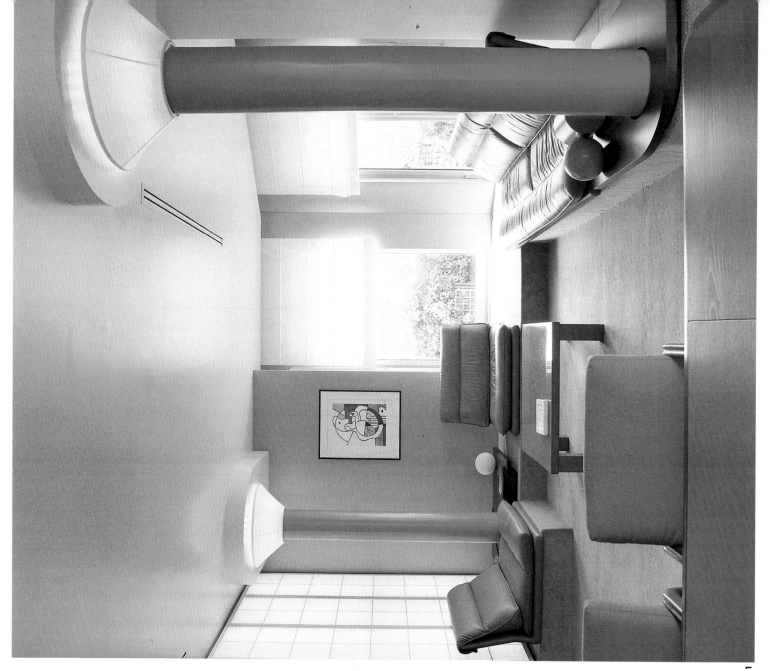

1

Some light fittings, such as mini spots, are relatively inconspicuous elements in a room, especially if they are ceiling-mounted, above the level where our eyes are likely to come to rest. But other fittings are major visual elements, occupying space on the same scale as the furniture – or even as major architectural features. Just like furniture itself, these larger fittings play a role beyond the merely functional. In addition to delivering light, they can be used territorially (whether on or off), to map out areas within a room or help to link or divide adjoining spaces. The sheer mass of some of the larger units can create a dominant presence within the room, filling up space with eyecatching shapes and textures. One of the most monumental of all such fittings, intended for halls, is a cylindrical column, 10 inches (26cm) in girth, with a ring of coathooks around the top, from the Italian firm Stilnovo.

1 Specially designed lighting towers with stretched paper shades are the most adventurous of all the decorative features in this room. Notice how their blue finish has been precisely matched to the chairs in the foreground. This is lighting on a truly monumental scale.

2 These bedside lights have a strong presence. Observe how the light they give off defines their own ribbed texture, and the way in which the shades pick up the colours of the bedhead. The owner has avoided total symmetry by placing the lights on different levels and at different distances from the bed.

Of all fittings, it is floor lights that make the greatest demands on space. Even those with a slender stem seem to claim a circle of space around them, and refuse to be crowded. The more distinctive and modern the design, the larger the area demanded, especially if the rest of the furniture is more traditional.

The most obvious way to exploit the strongly vertical emphasis of floor-standing uplighters is to echo the lines of high rooms or long, thin windows. However, this is not necessarily the best strategy. Sometimes it may be better to create a counterpoint. With low-slung furniture, a slender uplighter shifts the emphasis from the horizontal and provides a visual full-stop for the eye.

Defining space

Even quite small light fittings can be used to define spaces when deployed in pairs or groups. For example, identical lights either side of a fireplace establish a potent sense of symmetry, which can emphasize the character of a formal room.

Groups of pendants, particularly, are useful for demarcation purposes. The lower the position of the shade, the more definitely the space is separated off. If you exploit pendants to highlight seating areas, avoid placing them directly over sofas, as they can create unpleasant shadows, cause glare and sometimes appear a threat to the occupants, even when there is no real danger of banged heads.

3 Four identical desk lights with conical pendant-style shades are deployed here to mark the boundaries of an intimate, relaxing seating area, as well as to provide light for conversation or reading. The symmetrical arrangement of the fittings, echoing the tent above, makes them a distinctive design element, with an important role to play even when switched off.

This view of a restored country home highlights some of the options you should consider when planning improvements to your existing lighting.

Walls and ceilings.
Plan your lighting to work in harmony with the rest of the interior design. To spread the light adequately, you may have to redecorate the walls and/or ceiling in paler colours.

Stairways and corridors.
Adequate lighting in these areas can prevent accidents. Two-way switching is essential.

Daylight. Take daylight into account when planning the location of artificial lighting. If the windows are small, as in this room, you will probably need supplementary lighting during the daytime.

Built-in task lighting. This is particularly suitable for kitchens and bathrooms, and can serve a decorative as well as a practical function. Consider using energy-saving fluorescent tubes, which today can give perfectly acceptable colour rendering.

Display lighting. This is worth thinking about even if you are not a collector. Simple flower arrangements or humble pottery can look stunning if sensitively lit.

Many modern light fittings are so seductively attractive that it is always a temptation to start with the fittings themselves when you are planning a new lighting scheme. In other words, you might persuade yourself to buy one or two fittings that take your eye in a shop, then take them back home to work out precisely where to put them. This approach is emphatically the wrong way around. The starting point in any lighting plan should be the characteristics of the room itself and the uses to which the room will be put. From there you should proceed to work out the appropriate lighting strategy, taking mood lighting and task lighting into account and weighing colour-rendering and energy-saving requirements. The proportions of the room will play a part in formulating this broad plan. Choosing and installing the actual fittings is the last thing you do, not the first.

Ideally, a lighting scheme should be developed at the same time that the rest of the interior design is worked out. By choosing colours, finishes, light sources and fittings according to a coordinated scheme, you can ensure that these aspects of a room will work in harmony, instead of clashing or cancelling each other out. Of course, any kind of major refurbishing causes disruption and mess. All the more important, then, to make sure that you follow a meticulously worked out plan of action, leaving nothing to chance. An error or omission – for example, failing to install sufficient outlets for plug-in task lighting – will cause you another wave of disruption when, sooner or later, you decide to put the mistake right.

A common oversight by do-it-yourself lighting designers is to leave daylight out of account. You must ask yourself right at the beginning whether a room will be used primarily during the day or after dark. Rooms used in daylight generally demand a careful attempt to make the best of available sunlight, with pale-coloured, high-reflectance finishes on the walls and ceiling. At night, such rooms lend themselves well to indirect lighting – from uplighters, for example –

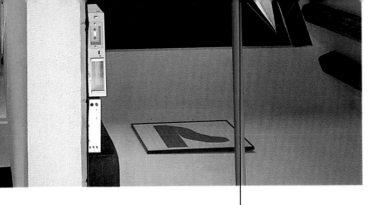

Plug-in lights. These lights have the advantage of versatility, but you must make sure that your socket outlets are in the right place. If necessary, add more. In this illustration, a plug-in light has been temporarily suspended from a ceiling hook; the owner was understandably reluctant to disfigure the antique beamed ceiling with a permanently wired-in fitting.

Recessed downlighters. Their unobtrusiveness makes them attractive for a variety of uses: here, a single downlighter provides light at the kitchen entrance. However, before buying such fittings, measure the ceiling space carefully to check that there is enough room.

Switches. Inadequate switching arrangements can spoil an otherwise excellent scheme. Plan switch locations along main circulation routes in your home.

although you also have the choice of using direct lighting. Dark walls, on the other hand, tend to be appropriate mainly for night rooms. In this case, the emphasis tends to be thrown onto the occupants and contents rather than on the setting. In this kind of room, one of the approaches you should consider is to use glossy paint finishes or metallic surfaces to catch reflective sparkle off narrow-beam spotlights. A pale-

coloured scheme will not require the same lighting levels as will a dark scheme; take this factor into account when selecting the number of fittings and the bulb wattages.

The uses of a room

Having made a preliminary choice between direct and indirect lighting, or a combination of these options, it is well worth writing down a list of activities that will take place in each room. Will it be principally a place for relaxed conversation, or for tasks requiring close attention to visual detail? Will activities always be carried out in the same position in the room, or are they likely to shift around (perhaps with the furniture) and thus require adjustable or plug-in lighting? Remember that even a seemingly undemanding activity such as watching television has special lighting requirements.

Display lighting is another aspect to consider. Is the room going to be used for exhibiting objects such as pictures or ceramics? If so, will the display remain constant, or will it grow as your collection expands or change shape as you buy and sell?

While pondering these questions, bear in mind that versatility is the hallmark of a successful lighting scheme. This point may sound familiar, but such is its importance that there need be no apologies for reiterating it. It is essential to anticipate future requirements – for example, the possible conversion of a secondary living room to a bedroom when a relative comes for a long-term stay.

The wiring plan

Once you have given thought to these matters and worked out broadly the kind of lighting you need – it is time to start roughing out your wiring plan. The most fundamental question at this stage is whether you can make use of existing wiring, or whether you need to extend it or even have it completely replaced. Electrical safety is a factor that enters this decision: if the system does not conform to modern safety standards, it *must* be renewed. Tell-tale signs of an outdated

system include pendant flex of the fabric-covered, double-twist variety, metal sockets, cracked bakelite sockets, or metal wall-mounted switches. Call in a reliable electrician to check whether these surface symptoms point to hidden dangers. Faulty wiring is among the most common causes of domestic fires.

Comprehensive rewiring gives you a good opportunity to re-plan the number and positions of fixed lighting points and socket outlets for plug-in wiring. However, to minimize the extent of the rewiring while retaining a large measure of flexibility, a track system is an attractive idea – although you may reject this for aesthetic reasons. At the same time, you should think about the switching options you need for each light; for example, if a room has two doors, you will need a switch at each of them. Dimmers are virtually essential to enlarge the range of lighting options.

You are now ready to draw a lighting plan for each room. Use squared paper, and draw the plan on a 1:50 scale. After you have carefully drawn the room outlines, mark in the windows, doors and any built-in features, such as fitted shelving units. Then trace the plan, retaining the master copy so that if you have any second thoughts from this stage on you do not have to re-do the outline. On the tracing, mark in the movable furniture where you plan to put it. Then, mark each fitting type at the requisite position, together with the lamp type you plan to use with it. On the same plan, indicate the control positions and the circuits, and key the latter to individual lighting positions.

This is a good time to check the costing to make sure that you are keeping within your budget. After making a generous estimate for rewiring and redecorating, you can work out how much money you have left for the fittings.

Consult manufacturers' catalogues and price lists. For downlighters and spotlights, use manufacturers' beam profiles to work out which fittings are suitable for your particular needs, and to calculate the optimum spacing. If you need to make a saving, it is sensible to economize on the fittings

1

matter of graphic convention. You can easily devise your own symbols to indicate switches, socket outlets and different types of fitting. Provided that you follow the symbols consistently, provide a clear key, and keep everything to scale, your plan will serve its purpose – as a basis either for doing the installation yourself or for talking over your requirements with a professional consultant.

Living room/dining area

The first room scheme shown here (this page) is an unusually shaped living/ dining room in a Miami residence designed by Juan Montoya Design Corporation (New York). The dining section is raised on a platform, and is further emphasized by a custom-built ceiling fitting over the table. To highlight the platform edge (for safety as well as aesthetic reasons) and to provide subdued lighting for relaxation, a series of tungsten lights has been built into the platform. In the

themselves rather than the rewiring; this way, you can easily upgrade the fittings at some future date with minimum disturbance to the home.

Sample schemes

These two pages feature two rooms with contrasting lighting schemes, each one designed in harmony with the room's character and with the uses for which the room is intended. Both schemes were planned by professionals. Alongside the photographs is a plan of each room based on a simplified version of the architect's original drawing.

There are various conventional symbols used on lighting plans, but these are not rigidly standardized. The system used here is by no means universal. For example, some designers use a small black semicircle to indicate a switch, instead of the S symbol adopted here. If you wish to plan your own lighting scheme, you should not be intimidated by this

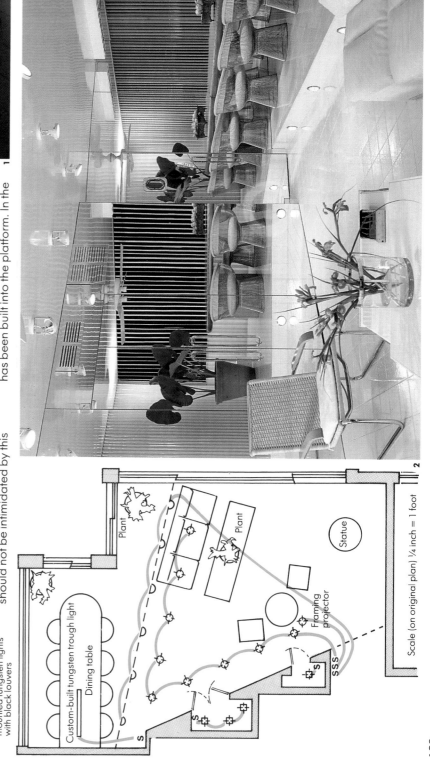

2

1 and 2 These views of a Miami living/dining room eloquently show the flexibility offered by dimmer switches – a low-key mood for late-night relaxation, a brighter mood for activities. In the picture below, observe how light from the downlighters reflects on chromium and other shiny surfaces to create attractive sparkle. In the plan, note the useful cupboard lights. The switching arrangements in the room itself allow 16 different lighting permutations.

Key

S   Switch

Built-in platform lights

Adjustable surface-mounted downlighters

Custom-built surface-mounted tungsten lights with black louvers

Custom-built tungsten trough light

Dining table

Plant

Plant

Statue

Framing projector

S S S

Scale (on original plan) ¼ inch = 1 foot

living area, downlighting is provided by a V-shaped arrangement of adjustable fittings, with a separately switched framing projector focussed on a piece of sculpture (shown in the plan but not in the photographs). Mirror walls spread the light and create a sense of spaciousness.

Library

A more reticent lighting scheme was wanted for the library/study on this page—part of an imposing Llewellyn Park, New Jersey, residence designed by Robert A.M. Stern Architects, who worked with Incorporated Consultants Ltd on the lighting. The lynchpins of the scheme are concealed tungsten reflector lamps above the windows and a pair of bowl-shaped wall lights. Together, these supply a background for individual plug-in lights (table and floor-standing) which provide task lighting, as well as adding a traditional touch that blends in well with the classic simplicity of the interior design.

3 and 4 These two views of a spacious library/study are from opposite sides of the room. The keynote of all aspects of the interior design, including the lighting, is a subtle blend of modernity and traditionalism—the latter provided by the open fireplace, desk and floor lights, leather-topped table and classical-style wall mouldings. A pair of "Quarto" wall lights give indirect lighting off the ceiling as well as decorative halos on the wall surfaces. A fascia over each window hides a string of bare tungsten bulbs; at night (3) this arrangement gives an attractive emphasis to the alcove accommodating the sofa.

3

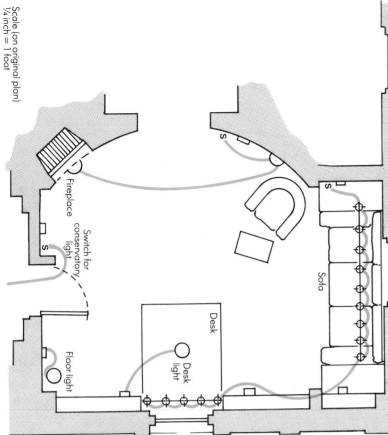

Scale (on original plan)
¼ inch = 1 foot

Fireplace

Switch for conservatory light

Floor light

Desk

Desk light

Sofa

4

Key

S   Switch
□   Socket outlets
▱   Flos "Quarto" lights
○   Plug-in lights
✦   R 20 Reflector lamps (30 watts) concealed by fascias

1 A decorative floor light gives a visual lift to this bedroom corner. If cost is a major problem, you could obtain a very similar effect to this by using a tungsten bulb behind a paper parasol.

2 This clip-on spot (known as the "Hot Dog") from the German company Brillantleuchten has many different decorative and task applications. For example, you can attach it to a bedhead for nighttime reading. Here, the light is used in a child's room, illuminating a toy drawer.

First-aid ideas

If you are unhappy with your present lighting system, the first thing to do is

N ot everyone is able to plan a lighting scheme from scratch. Costs may be prohibitive, or a tenancy agreement may limit what alterations are possible. But if you are faced with such restrictions, there are still various ways to improve the quality of your lighting, without structural alterations or substantial rewiring. Such improvements may be desirable even in a newly built home, as architects and builders rarely pay any attention to the lighting system beyond installing the bare minimum number of ceiling fittings. They assume, of course, that people will make their own lighting arrangements, designed to suit particular needs or tastes. In fact, few people do this. Yet most householders are left dissatisfied with the way their homes are lit, often without quite knowing why.

examine the types of light source in each fitting, and check whether an improvement could be made by substituting a more appropriate lamp. For example, a bulb might be too bright for its fitting or for its surroundings, causing discomfort glare. On the other hand, a higher wattage could go some way toward brightening gloomy corners. If you have inherited spotlights from a previous occupier, you may find they have standard tungsten bulbs instead of the more appropriate reflector lamps, which will put out more light. You should familiarize yourself with the different kinds of reflector lamp available (including PAR lamps), so that you are equipped to make the optimum choice for any fitting or situation (see pages 30–31). As well as the bulbs, you should also cast a critical eye over your shades. A diffusing shade, for example, might be preferable to an opaque conical one. Dimmers can also greatly improve a scheme: they are available for both fixed lighting and plug-in

lighting, and are very easy to install. To enlarge the range of options with minimum difficulty, investigate the possibilities of a track system. When the time comes to move on, you can unscrew and remove the track with minimal damage to surfaces. Lighting track is mostly used for spotlighting (see page 52), but with the help of a special adaptor it can also take pendants. The power can be supplied from an existing ceiling installation, or alternatively you could use a flex-and-plug fitting. The drawback of the latter method is that a length of flex is left visible, stretching along ceiling and walls from the track to the outlet. To ensure that flex is as unobtrusive as possible, run it across the ceiling to the nearest wall, then along the wall-ceiling corner, then down to floor level along a corner between two walls, and finally along the skirting board to the power point. At ceiling level, it is a good idea to disguise the flex inside special coving. Or to reduce flex length, consider the option

of a wall-mounted track. There are various other ways to exploit the convenience of skirting board power outlets. One of the most effective is to invest in a floor-standing uplighter to provide indirect light bounced off the ceiling. To get the best service from this type of fitting, you may have to paint the ceiling a paler colour. Other useful fittings that can be run off a wall outlet include clip-on spots and, of course, task lights. If you are planning to buy a desk light, select one that can be adjusted to a wide range of positions, so that you can bounce the beam off any area of the walls or ceiling, as an alternative to using it for tasks.

The pendant problem

Centrally placed pendants are the major cause of poor lighting. The light they give is usually unsympathetic (and certainly far from intimate), and casts troublesome shadows that can get in the way of activities in the peripheral

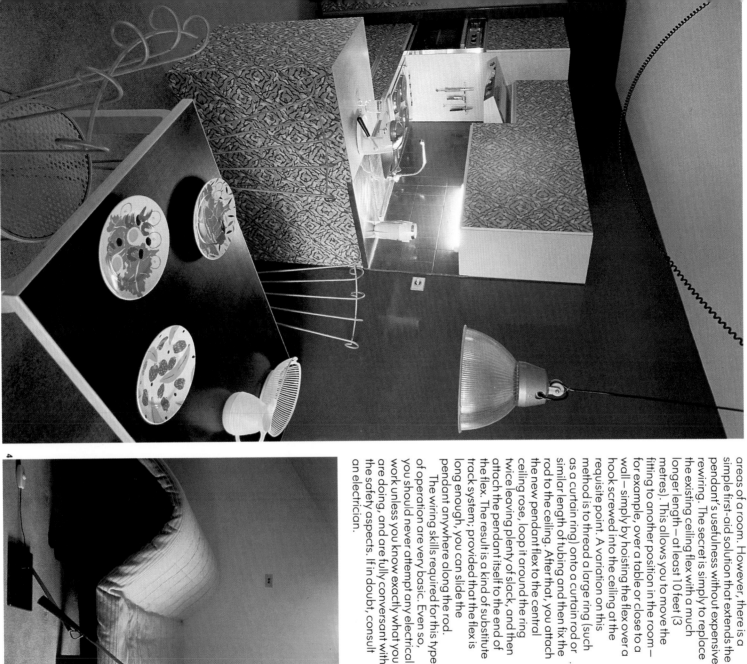

areas of a room. However, there is a simple first-aid solution that extends the pendant's usefulness without expensive rewiring. The secret is simply to replace the existing ceiling flex with a much longer length – at least 10 feet (3 metres). This allows you to move the fitting to another position in the room – for example, over a table or close to a wall – simply by hoisting the flex over a hook screwed into the ceiling at the requisite point. A variation on this method is to thread a large ring (such as a curtain ring) onto a curtain rod or similar length of tubing and then fix the rod to the ceiling. After that, you attach the new pendant flex to the central ceiling rose, loop it around the ring twice leaving plenty of slack, and then attach the pendant itself to the end of the flex. The result is a kind of substitute track system; provided that the flex is long enough, you can slide the pendant anywhere along the rod.

The wiring skills required for this type of operation are very basic. Even so, you should never attempt any electrical work unless you know exactly what you are doing, and are fully conversant with the safety aspects. If in doubt, consult an electrician.

3 A hook in the ceiling, screwed into one of the joists, enabled the owner of this kitchen to reposition the pendant over the breakfast table.

4 An elegant floor light is always a worthwhile investment, provided that it is sufficiently versatile. This one, from Arteluce, has adjustable elbows and is made of coloured fibreglass. It is also available in a clamp-on version, for use on a shelf edge.

Room by Room

Every room in the home has its own special lighting requirements, which vary according to the activities in which we engage there and the range of moods we deem appropriate. For example, the atmosphere of clinical efficiency we might welcome from kitchen lighting would normally seem quite unsuitable in a living room, bedroom or entrance hall.

The following pages take each major area of the home in turn and examine the most feasible lighting options, covering background, decorative, task and display applications. Among the many photographs showing well-planned lighting schemes, some have been singled out for special analysis, using annotation to identify the features that add up to overall success.

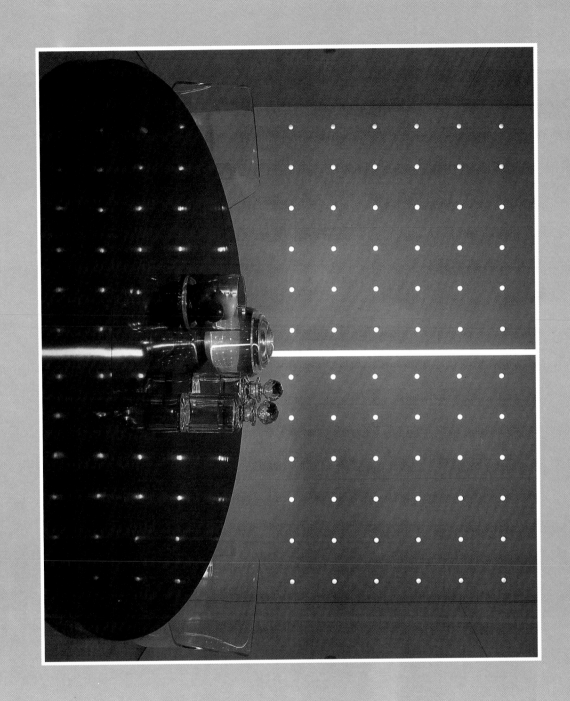

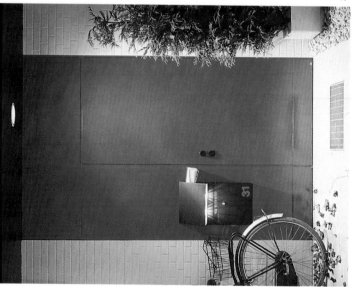

Lighting at the front door and in the entrance hall has two special requirements: to create an instantly welcoming first impression, and to help ensure the safety of the home. If there is a street frontage, the way in which the front door is lit can be of primary importance in establishing the style and character of a home. It is essential to look at things from the viewpoint of visitors, who should not be submitted to harsh glare, as if from a searchlight. Tungsten lights look warm and inviting, but must be housed in fittings that will stand up to outdoor use — in particular to rain. Fluorescent lights, which must also be weatherproof, have the advantage of lower running costs — a crucial factor if you plan to leave a light on all night or most of the night.

On a practical level, there must be sufficient light for members of the household to find their keys and locate the lock. Visitors unfamiliar with the property will need enough light to properly prevent them from stumbling over the threshold. The other side of the coin is that the occupiers looking through a security spy-hole or a front window

1 A concealed strip light above an alcove draws the eye to a simple flower arrangement in a beautifully proportioned circular hallway.

2 The rich, inviting red of this front door is given even more emphasis by the well-positioned porch light — a recessed downlighter. Additional light from a mailbox unit illuminates the house number and family name.

3 A view of a book-lined hallway, showing the impact of wall-mounted uplighters used to supplement daylight. At night, the white ceiling reflects sufficient light for browsing among the volumes.

4 Downlighters with spot lamps conspicuously announce the use of a corridor as a picture gallery as well as a passageway. The lighting track emphasizes the passage's length, as well as drawing visitors in.

4

should be able to identify night callers. When no-one is at home, external lighting should also have the function of enabling neighbours or passers-by to see any intruder who is tampering with the lock.

A pair of matching fittings on each side of the door, or a globe light above, may answer these various requirements. However, if you have a deep porch, avoid laterally placed fittings, as they will leave the front door in darkness. Other methods of lighting a front door include special fittings which combine the light source with a house number, or even a security camera.

Beyond the threshold

An entrance hall does not have to be a simple workaday place in which you store coats and boots. It can be a theatrical setting to show off pictures or pieces of furniture, lit in a way that will give a pleasurable sense of anticipation, like a curtain-raiser to a dramatic performance. Because no-one spends much time in a hall, lighting effects can be more dramatic than in

adjacent living rooms. For example, a row of sparkling spotlights can make an attractive first impression, or you could install recessed eyeball spots trained on pictures or plants. Alternatively, you may want to choose fittings which establish a strong directional sense, such as a row of pendants that seem to lead you into the rest of the home. Remember, though, that the hall is a place of transition in which our eyes should be able to adapt from night to indoor lighting, and vice versa. To avoid excessive contrast between outdoors and indoors, the overall level of illumination needs to be judiciously thought out. A dimmer gives you more control.

As with front-door lighting, there is a practical dimension to consider. Because this is a circulation area it is no place for free-standing uplighters, unless they are reliably stable. The output of light must be such that people with failing eyesight can move around without fear of stumbling. This is even more important on staircases, where a fall can have tragic consequences. A good way to make steps safer is to

avoid flat, shadowless lighting and instead go for strongly directional light that will accentuate the contrast between vertical risers and horizontal stair treads. The best arrangement is a fitting at the top of the flight balanced by a weaker light at the bottom; this throws the risers into comparative shadow. Landing lights should be shaded carefully so that they are never too glaring for people using the staircase. Wall brackets can be useful as a source of additional stair lighting.

Long, narrow passageways can severely test our lighting skills. A common fault is to space the fittings too far apart, creating alternating sectors of brighter and dimmer light; however, sometimes this works as a deliberate effect. Circular or miniature fluorescents, not too distantly spaced, offer a cost-effective solution, although many people prefer the convenience of track-mounted spots. Pale-coloured wall surfaces will help spread the light more efficiently.

1 Diffuse lighting from a bowl-shaped wall fitting flatters this hallway by softening shadows and adding tonal variety to the monochrome colour scheme. The subdued decoration on the fitting is in keeping with the rest of the room.

2 Judicious use of paintings, furniture and, above all, lighting brings a lived-in feel to a country house hallway. The picture lights not only highlight individual canvases but also improve the overall picture quality. Any modern fitting other than this recessed downlighter would probably have struck a jarring note at ceiling level. The candles add a vitality that less successful hall schemes tend to lack.

3 This stately room is one of the remarkable features of the London home of architectural critic Charles Jencks. Although it was designed to be lived in, the classical-style pillars, which conceal light fittings, deliberately conjure up the grand entrance halls of the past. Low-voltage downlighters set in special reflective ceiling panels marry new technology to an impression of aristocratic grandeur.

4 Strings of miniature low-wattage tungsten lights define the edges of a high-level walkway, providing visual reassurance: without them, this bridge to one of the bedrooms might appear somewhat dangerous.

131

Lighting in the kitchen offers a clear demonstration of the dual nature of artificial lighting, which must generally play both an aesthetic role and a functional one. A kitchen lighting scheme must obviously facilitate food preparation – a task which can be visually very demanding. Yet it is also important that the food looks appetizing as it is being prepared and served. And because many people spend a great deal of time in their kitchens, the lighting must be congenial and attractive, or the most devoted cook will quickly lose heart.

Much more happens in kitchens than cooking. This is often the effective headquarters or nerve-centre of the home, used for meals and as an informal living room, where members of the household gather and spend much of the day. Typically, kitchens are used extensively after dark, as well as during the daytime. Therefore, kitchen lighting has heavy duties to fulfil. Versatility is the keynote of a successful lighting plot. There are two possible approaches: either you provide a number of different kinds of lighting systems within the room, or you choose fittings that are suited to a multiple role.

Good natural daylight is a huge asset, which should never be underestimated. Unless you are contemplating a wholesale remodelling of your home, the availability of daylight will be difficult to alter. However, if your present kitchen is dark and gloomy, it makes sense to relocate it elsewhere in the home, assuming that a more suitable space suggests itself. For example, a sunny but underused dining room could make a better kitchen than a stygian basement. In some circumstances you may be able to enlarge existing windows, or demolish a lean-to shed or other projection that poaches the room's entitlement of direct sunlight. Where there is no possibility of increasing the natural light in any of these ways, it is essential to supplement it with sympathetic and useful light from artificial sources.

Safety and efficiency

The kitchen is a place of potential hazards. Most domestic accidents take place here – especially those involving cuts, scalds, grazes and burns. Poor lighting is often to blame for these mishaps, either directly or as a contributory factor. Without adequate light, people can all too easily burn themselves on hot pans or cut themselves on sharp edges. Chopping, grinding, grating, blending and opening cans can become dangerous operations.

A single, central pendant fitting will not do. Even if glare is not a problem with this arrangement, you will cast your own shadow over tasks you attempt on work surfaces around the edges of the room, and the corners of the room will be dimly lit. Two diffusing globe pendants or a fluorescent tube are an improvement, but you will still need additional lights.

A kitchen runs a little like an industrial production line. You often need to carry out a wide variety of tasks in sequence in different parts of the room. One way to enable the workflow to proceed smoothly is to provide localized light sources focussed on each task area. Provided that these are all of similar brightness and the eye does not have to face excessive contrast, this is a feasible approach. However, the best strategy is to supply a general level of shadow-free lighting from an indirect or diffuse source and supplement this with special task lighting in selected parts of the kitchen.

For food preparation, it is the horizontal surfaces that are important. However, when using kitchen appliances, vertical surfaces require careful lighting – for example, the control panels on cookers, washing machines and dishwashers.

Planning in detail

When assessing your needs for a kitchen lighting scheme, it is useful to make a list of the tasks you regularly carry out, and the various movements they involve – for example, from store cupboard, to book shelf (for a recipe), to worktop, to oven, to sink. Remember that you will need enough light at the sink to distinguish between clean and dirty dishes, and that you will need to see into cupboards.

In a fully fitted kitchen, built-in lights

A suave table lamp with a turned wooden base marks the transition between living and working areas and enriches the colours of fruit in a basket.

A decorative wall light with a pleated shade of synthetic fabric gives useful light for dishwashing.

An attractive modern pendant slung from the original central ceiling rose. Used on its own, this light would leave the corners of the room in shadow and be totally unsuitable for kitchen tasks. However, it plays a useful supplementary role.

Hanging baskets pick up the theme of the pendant, preventing it from looking too isolated.

Wall-mounted spotlights illuminate the cooking area. From this viewpoint they are attractively diffused by a glass screen that marks off the cooking space.

Pine panelling looks much richer in tungsten lighting than in the colder light given out by fluorescent tubes.

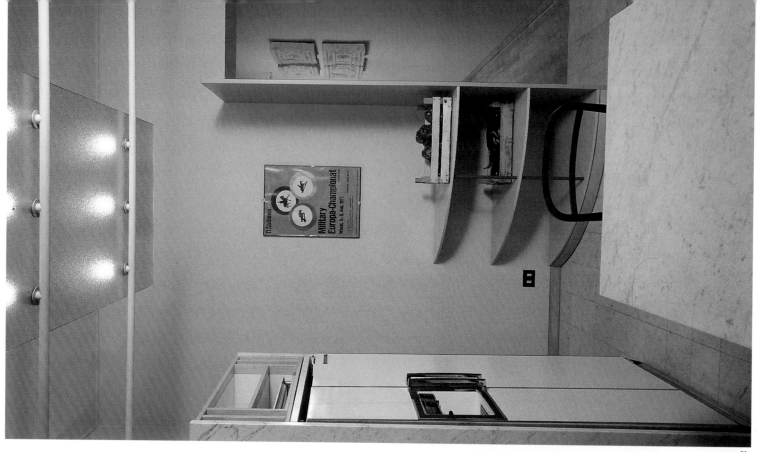

2

1

may already give enough illumination for many of these basic activities. They most commonly take the form of concealed fluorescents (or tungsten strip lights) positioned in wall-mounted storage units over work surfaces. If you do not have these already, it is relatively easy to fit your own. Attach the fittings to the underside of the units, and conceal them with a wooden batten. The ideal position is along the front of the cupboards, but you can successfully place them at the back if the wall beneath is not glossy and if the wall and ceiling surfaces are pale.

Concealed fluorescents also serve a useful role on top of storage units: their output bounces off the ceiling and the upper part of the walls to provide a diffuse, indirect light throughout the room. If you have no storage units, an alternative method of producing general lighting is from a luminous ceiling, which is excellent for small windowless kitchens. Whatever the lighting scheme you choose, a good rule to follow is that the general lighting in the kitchen should be dimmer than worktop lighting under storage units.

When choosing fluorescents for a kitchen, be sure to opt for a product with suitable colour-rendering qualities. "Warm" tubes will enhance the look of food and blend in satisfactorily with tungsten lighting. On the other hand, "cool" tubes will tend to make red meat and fresh green vegetables look greyish.

Tungsten versus fluorescent

Fluorescent lights have gained widespread acceptance in kitchens not only because of their low running costs

but also because during the 1960s and 70s we became accustomed to the idea of the kitchen as a clean, clinical environment. However, this look is now falling out of favour, and a warmer, more domestic character is preferred in many households. Access to this is provided by tungsten lighting. The problems of glare, harsh shadows and reflections from metallic surfaces make spotlights less than ideal – although they are good for throwing light into cupboards. A safer method is to make judicious use of pendants, particularly over a table or peninsula-style counter. Pendants have a softening effect in a kitchen, and cater well for non-cooking activities, such as eating a late-night snack or reading an evening newspaper. If you want to combine an intimate pool of light with a relatively high-tech fitting, look at the enamelled steel pendants originally designed for industrial settings. A group of pendants over a worktop looks attractive, but they will have to be spaced close enough together to provide a uniform level of light. Rise-and-fall fittings have the advantage of maximum versatility.

1 Discreet flush-mounted lights over the sink area are supplemented here by frankly decorative bare bulbs at cornice height, giving a warm effect to the ceiling, which appears mottled with light.

2 An inventive way of lighting a kitchen amply justifies any rewiring involved. Here, the impact of spherical tungsten bulbs is tempered by a thick sheet of glass with a rippled finish. The steel tubes that support the glass also carry the current.

3 A row of enamelled-steel industrial-style pendants are a major design element in this kitchen, as important for their repeated geometric shapes as for the light they distribute over the work surface. The dining area beyond picks up the same theme, the strongly linear effect of both ranks of fittings helping to unify the two spaces into one.

4 Fluorescent tubes hidden beneath storage cupboards emit high-intensity task lighting that contrasts with the dark-painted woodwork. A spotlight aimed at the highly reflective floor provides background lighting, while another casts a sharp-edged beam over the cooker; although none of these three fittings are visible in the photograph, their effects are clearly apparent.

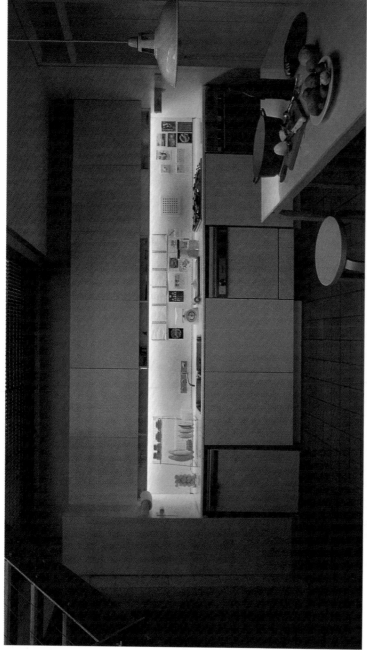

1

2

1 The rear part of the lower shelf of these kitchen storage units is recessed to shield a row of tungsten strip lights. Because each strip is positioned very close to its neighbours, the lighting is even. Note also the white enamelled pendant over the breakfast bar, positioned low enough to avoid glare.

2 Attractive globe lights provide a twin point of interest on a serving surface in a well-planned kitchen. The plant is precisely placed to soften the symmetrical arrangement of the light fittings.

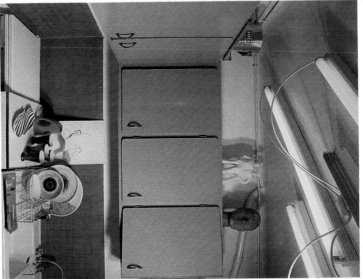

3 Spotlights can look very good in kitchens when used to light a wall or a high-level shelf. In this case, the owner has wisely fitted clip-on baffles and shades to prevent dazzle. The lighting track, slotted flush into the ceiling, has a neatness that is well worth emulating.

4 The revolt against kitchens that resemble scientific laboratories takes many forms. Here, the dissenting voice comes from the playful use of coloured celluloid to give a decorative appearance to fluorescent tubes.

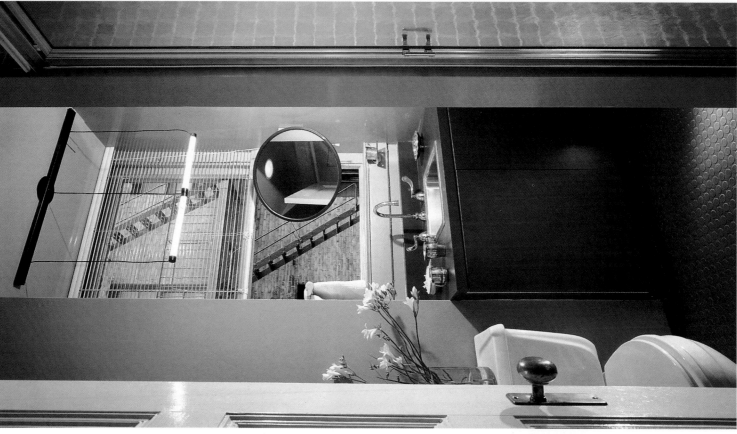

2

E lectricity and water make a dangerous combination, as many of us know from schoolday physics. Even a small amount of moisture will conduct electricity, bringing the danger of a potentially fatal shock. This is why no electrical appliance run off the mains supply should ever be handled with wet or even damp hands. It is also the reason that in some countries special regulations govern the provision of electricity in bathrooms. For example, in Britain the rules are stringent: switched electrical sockets (except double-insulated ones for shavers) are banned; open lampholders need a special skirt to shield the metal bulb cap so that you cannot touch it accidentally while replacing a bulb (and are preferably used with enclosed, steamproof fittings); flexible-drop pendants are prohibited; and lights must be operated either by a cord-pull switch or a switch outside the room.

In some other countries, such as the United States, the regulations are more lenient, but that is no justification to lower your guard. There are basic safety guidelines that apply universally. When replacing lamps, switch off the mains or the appropriate circuit breaker; this is especially important if you have a pull-cord switch, because when the lamp has failed there is no way of telling whether the circuit is switched on. Never position lights where they are likely to get splashed by a shower. If in doubt about whether a particular lighting arrangement is potentially dangerous, always err on the safe side until you have consulted a qualified electrician.

Creative options

Safety factors by no means rule out the possibility of creating attractive lighting in bathrooms. You can make them appealing and relaxing places to be by

1 Surface-mounted downlighters strike the only modern note in this period-style bathroom with a Victorian claw-foot bath. They bring out the rich tones of the walls and timber floor, and give a lift to the plants.

2 A modest but attractive bathroom in a renovated tenement block, with two simple light sources — a downlighter (in the mirror) for background lighting, and a pair of tungsten strips for washing and shaving.

"Pinhole" downlighters set into a dark-toned ceiling stand out as decorative foci of light. Steamproof lenses cover the mouths of the fittings, which are operated from a pull-cord switch near the door (not visible in the photograph).

Broad expanses of mirror spread the light more efficiently, as well as multiplying the visual impact of the light sources.

A flamboyant wall light projecting from a mirror acquires the appearance of a chandelier, minus its chain. The fitting adds an ingredient of grandeur not often found in bathrooms.

A mirror with a built-in light source is a useful addition to any bathroom. This table mirror is double-insulated for safety and equipped with an annular opalescent diffuser to eliminate glare.

treating them as rooms like any other – that is, by introducing furniture, plants and pictures on the walls. Lighting, as with any other room, plays a big part in such metamorphoses. Indeed, bathrooms without windows – as so many of them are – positively demand that you give careful thought to the aesthetics of the lighting, in order to humanize what would otherwise be a bleak and claustrophobic atmosphere. There is no reason to treat the room simply as a utilitarian capsule.

There are two schools of thought about bathroom lighting. Some people prefer it to be bright and stimulating, whereas others like a more cocooned, intimate feel, with lower levels of illumination. If you run the lighting on a dimmer, you can choose either approach according to your mood.

The basis for most bathroom schemes is a central ceiling fitting, which may be a tungsten light enclosed by a glass or plastic diffuser or a fluorescent fitting (either for a tube or a circular lamp). Stylish tungsten bulkhead lights are available in a range of colours. If your bathroom is low-ceilinged, it is a sound idea to choose recessed fittings to avoid the risk of knocking them with a towel or hand while you are drying yourself. If you like reading in the bath, a ceiling-recessed downlighter with a lens attachment will help to ensure that you receive enough light where you want it.

So far, the options described might seem somewhat uninspiring. However, you can turn a very simple lighting arrangement into something much more impressive by making use of mirrors in a calculated way. Mirrors not only spread daylight and artificial light super-efficiently, but can also be exploited to create a feeling of wide-open space. Large wall mirrors strategically placed at right angles or on opposite walls can make one or two fittings the source of a long series of diminishing visual echoes. Used in moderation, this effect can be quite stunning, especially with fittings that are boldly coloured or distinctively shaped.

At the washbasin

In conjunction with a washbasin and mirror, a task light of some kind is vital for shaving, facial care, teeth inspection and applying or removing makeup. For all these activities, the illumination must be shadow-free. A strip light over the mirror (either tungsten or fluorescent), or one at either side, are the usual alternatives. Some mirrors and mirrored bathroom cabinets have their own built-in light. Strip fittings with integral shaver sockets are also popular.

A more decorative method is to use low-wattage pearl bulbs arranged in ranks down both sides of the mirror, and perhaps along the top as well. This gives a Hollywood-style star dressing-room look, and is not only glamorous but also very practical. Moreover, the warm-coloured tungsten bulbs flatter skin tones.

Much less effective as a task light, but highly dramatic in its visual impact, is a fluorescent lamp concealed directly behind a mirror to create a halo of light around the mirror edges. In practical terms, this will usually involve mounting the mirror on a simple, home-made timber frame.

Large mirrors that run all the way across a vanity unit generally demand some kind of built-in lighting. One effective method is to conceal a fluorescent tube behind a pelmet positioned above the mirror, so that the light bounces off the mirror onto the face. To scatter the illumination, there should preferably be a diffusing cover.

1 A sunny bathroom, in which the lights serve a purely decorative role during the daytime. In addition to the trio of tungsten bulbs in steamproof fittings and the recessed downlighters (only one of which can be seen here), a neon strip, used discreetly for once, underscores the relaxing pastel colour scheme.

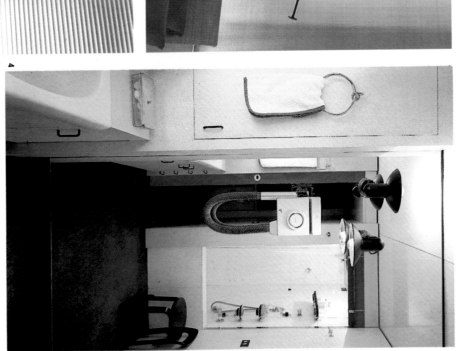

2 An unconventional bathroom, with a decorative, domesticated feel that is strengthened by the "Tizio" desk light and the strip light on the mantelpiece. Using plug-in fittings in a bathroom in this way is permitted in some countries, including the USA.

3 Suspended basin mirrors with built-in fittings for tungsten bulbs add a note of glamour to a well-equipped bathroom. A third mirror in the same style (seen here as a reflection) completes the effect.

4 Two spotlights projecting from a giant bathroom mirror appear twinned and floating in space. The crown-silvered bulbs cut down glare, as well as supplying a decorative touch.

So many different kinds of activity take place in living rooms that it would be pointless to attempt an exhaustive list. Convivial conversation, reading, watching television, listening to music, playing with children and crafts such as knitting and sewing are perhaps the most common. For such a versatile room, the lighting must be flexible in both quantity and quality.

Used either individually or in various combinations, the fittings should be able to provide appropriate lighting for any of the activities you are likely to

engage in – whether alone, with other members of the household or with guests. Your fittings should also provide different kinds of light to suit a whole spectrum of moods, and on overcast days should give you the option of using artificial light to supplement daylight effectively – either to facilitate a task or just to add a touch of cheerfulness.

It is unwise to be too dogmatic about optimum lighting schemes for a living room, as so much depends on personal taste. Sweeping statements about the

need to combine "general" with "supplementary" lighting have a satisfying theoretical neatness, but are not very useful in practice. In many living rooms, especially those without any kind of pendant, individual fittings do not fall unambiguously into either of these broad categories. Instead of being supplied from one or two main fittings, the general lighting might come from a combination of fittings, which individually serve also as task, display or decorative "accent" lights.

However, one generalization that

can be made safely is that many people have an insufficient number of fittings for a wholly successful living room scheme. Even in a moderately sized room, a half-dozen or more light sources is not necessarily excessive. For example, a room might have six recessed downlighters, a pair of table lights, a concealed light inside a shelving unit, and an individual spot trained on a work of art. Of course, this is just one of an infinite number of permutations; some other ideas are shown here and on the following pages.

Adjustable eyeball fittings take up less space above the ceiling than downlighters that are completely recessed. Diffusing covers prevent glare.

Dark walls do not steal too much light if there is a large, pale-coloured ceiling.

A white minimalist painting reflects light back into the room.

This adjustable light shows off another painting but if desired can be repositioned for other tasks.

A classic table light helps to provide background lighting.

Creating a mood

In the days before gas lighting, portable oil lamps or candles created pools of light that marked out clearly defined territories. This effect, which we can re-create with table lights, task lights or floor lights, is generally perceived as relaxing, and also tends to appeal to our sense of nostalgia. Its allure is perhaps all the more potent by contrast with the monotonous lighting often experienced in work environments, such as offices, stores and factories.

The atmosphere generated by localized pools of light is most obviously appropriate to traditional interiors – for example, in cottages, or in rooms decorated in a rural or farmhouse style. In this kind of setting, it might even be appropriate to use an authentic oil light for special occasions (doubling as an emergency light source

in the event of power failure). In a starker, modern interior, such an emphatic note of traditionalism might jar. However, there is no reason why modern interiors should be restricted to bright, uniform lighting. Even in the most minimalist, modernist room, it is desirable to provide a wide range of lighting options, including shadow areas to vary the tones in the room and rest our eyes.

Remember that the mood in a living room depends not just on the lights themselves but also on their interaction with the room's decorative appearance and contents. For example, by placing a table light close to a curtain, you can emphasize the folds of drapery and conjure up a mood of romantic opulence: the deeper the shadows in the folds, the richer and more suggestive will be the effect, with overtones of the pre-electric age.

1 Shaded floor lights and table lights have stylistic similarities that reinforce their role as luminous "boundary posts". Close to the walls, they encourage free use of space.

2 A flamboyant torchère adds Empire-style luxury and atmospheric lighting to a traditional living room.

3 An adjustable wall light, craning far into this room, provides ideal lighting for after-dinner conversation.

1 To get the best out of a spectacular nighttime panorama, you need subdued lighting. In this New York apartment, the table fitting, "Mezzaluna" uplighter and concealed display fitting provide just enough light for relaxation. A brighter effect is easily obtained by turning up the dimmer on the uplighter.

2 Eileen Gray designed a series of classic pieces of modern furniture in the 1920s, including the floor-standing tungsten strip fitting at the far right of this picture. An elegant object in its own right, the fitting is also an effective source of shadowless light. Notice also the unusual double table light, which casts one beam on the sofa, the other on a book.

Architecture and space

As well as contributing to atmosphere, living room lighting should be planned to accentuate architectural features, such as a hearth or alcove. Attractively textured wall surfaces, such as red brick, usually demand strongly directional light to bring out their special qualities.

When planning the lighting, take wall mirrors very carefully into account; they are useful for spreading light into dark corners, but can cause glare problems – particularly with spotlights or with other light sources that are only partially shielded.

The primary focus of a living room is often a seating area – conventionally, a pair of sofas facing each other across a low table. Use lighting to reinforce this emphasis. One approach is to position an uplighter at either end of a sofa to spread indirect light over the whole

area and provide vertical elements that signify the area's importance. If you prefer to use pendants in the same role, site them over the front or back edge of the sofa: over the middle they will cast awkward shadows over people's faces.

Watching television

Some people watch television with all the lights off, not realizing that this causes severe eyestrain. However, lights too close to the viewing position can reflect on the screen, obscuring details of the picture. A table light or floor light at the side of the TV set will usually solve the problem. Or if the set stands on a shelf, you could use tungsten strip lighting concealed behind it. Another alternative is a ceiling-mounted downlighter, which will illuminate the floor area without interfering with the screen.

3 This ritzy, high-gloss lounge is lit directly by downlighters, and indirectly by fluorescent tubes beneath the marble table. The generous provision of mirrors and shiny surfaces bounces light around the room, creating a stage-like setting for entertaining, rather than a relaxing retreat.

1

Controlling the lights

Plug-in lights have the advantage of portability: you can easily move a table light, for example, from a side table to a chest of drawers, to give yourself a completely fresh lighting option.

However, when performing this kind of change, or when planning a new position for a plug-in light, pay close attention to the problems of trailing wires. This normally means confining plug-in lighting to a sector around the edges of the room. Do not be tempted to hide the flex under a rug, as this is a potential hazard.

Dimming is a more useful method of controlling a light than merely moving it from place to place. Dimmer switch attachments on both fixed and plug-in lighting allow you more scope to ring the changes. For maximum convenience, it is also important to get the circuitry and switching right. Small groups of fittings can be individually switched on their own circuits, or alternatively they can be linked so that one switch operates a prearranged selection of lights.

Switching also has a security aspect. Leaving a living room in darkness while you go out for an evening could be an invitation to burglars. On the other hand, lights switched on prematurely are also a giveaway. You can protect your home with a time switch, which will turn lights on and off at programmed intervals, and thus make the home seem occupied. An alternative, which requires no special wiring, is a plug-in time control for use with a table light or floor light. This is available in both 24-hour and seven-day versions.

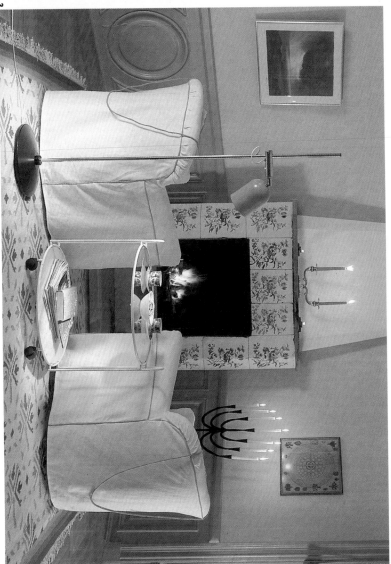

Here are three different ways of using a floor light in a living room, all equally imaginative. In the large picture (1), a makeshift uplighter fashioned from a photographer's floodlight bounces light off a ceiling. In a more purist setting (2), the floor light's translucent green shade provides an accent of colour in an all-white decorative scheme. The light it gives off is reinforced by concealed wall-washing downlighters and a picture light on the window wall. In picture 3, the modern style of a floor-standing spot creates an effective contrast with candlelight and a blazing fire.

ew bedrooms are used just for sleeping. In most homes, they function also as a dressing room and a place to store clothes. They may also be pressed into service as a study or workroom, or simply as a quiet sitting room where you can get away from the rest of the household during the day. To sustain this multiple role, and to make the bedroom a thoroughly relaxing and pleasant place to be, you need to take considerable care over the detailed design of your bedroom lighting.

Background lighting

The first priority is to create an appropriate mood. Sometimes the bedroom will need to be a romantic or seductive place, its sensual connotations enhanced by soft, caressing light. A self-consciously playboy or playgirl style, with pink light bulbs, silky fabrics and mood music, will end up looking slick, heartless and clichéd. However, an element of escapism and fantasy can be appropriate in the bedroom. Lighting is often the best way to hide the

mundane realities of the room and create an intimate atmosphere with a minimum of distractions, whether the object is romantic or simply to create a restful ambience conducive to sleep. Low lighting levels, fine-tuned with a dimmer, are part of the answer. An uplighter for indirect lighting is a good idea, provided that you are content to have a pale ceiling. A pendant fitting with a low-wattage bulb will also provide useful background light, but may cause problems (as in any other room) if sited centrally: not only will it throw the corners into gloom but it may get in the way of easy circulation and limit the possible positions where the bed may be located.

Spotlights in the bedroom are avoided by many people, as they

sometimes create a sensation of being on stage. However, miniature low-voltage spots can give off an attractive light, as can recessed downlighters. The latter can be very pleasing when set into a dark-coloured ceiling, especially if they are of narrow diameter. Remember, though, that your eyes will often be drawn upward when you are in bed, and for this reason it is essential to take special precautions against glare. One way is to fit louvers over the lights. Better still, concentrate directional downlighters along the walls, training the beams toward pictures or bookshelves.

Because we are seldom in the bedroom for long periods of time, this is a favourite area for purely decorative lighting, often of a rather

outlandish kind. Fittings in the shapes of animals, or of objects such as shopping bags, are popular. And so are "kite" wall lights, which create a soft, diffuse effect by filtering tungsten light through stretched fabric. Fittings which throw shadow patterns on the walls or ceilings are also much favoured.

A well-planned switching system is particularly important in a bedroom. We all know how intensely irritating it is when, having been lulled into a state of near slumber over a book, we have to force ourselves up again to locate a distant switch. Life becomes easier if you can operate all the lights from the bed. And if you remove a central pendant, make sure that at least one light can be switched on from the door.

1 Two matching pairs of tungsten-halogen fittings from Artemide have been chosen for this spacious room: pillar-like "Megaron" uplighters and gracefully angular "Tizio" task lights. The theme of twinned objects is wittily continued by the palms and the antique busts.

This pair of "Tizio" lights has at least three different roles to play, depending on how they are angled. In this position they can highlight the precious objects on the glass tables. They could also be angled upward to display the pictures, or to create a pool of light on the wall immediately above the bedhead. Or alternatively, in the positions shown in the photograph in the opposite page, they could be used for bedtime reading.

A table lamp ("Faccia", from Flos) uses a 100-watt bulb to provide background lighting, but also serves an important decorative purpose when the light is switched off.

A "Jill" halogen floor light provides a high level of background light (some diffused through the glass bowl, but most reflected off the ceiling) for changing or trying on clothes, packing suitcases, tidying or other bedroom activities. The switch is conveniently located near the door (just to the right of this photograph).

Task lighting

Bedside lighting can be provided in a number of different ways. The choice is broadly between portable and fixed fittings. The latter option is space-saving and convenient, eliminating dangling wires and the risk of overturning a table light while groping for a switch in the dark. However, fixed lighting may confine the bed to a particular spot, and may also be a limiting factor if you ever want to convert the bedroom to another function.

A neat approach is to conceal built-in fluorescent fittings within the bedhead, or mount them behind a pelmet fixed to the wall above. For many people, though, this comes uncomfortably close to the impersonal feel of a hotel room. Adjustable wall-mounted tungsten lights (task or decorative) may be a more attractive variation.

Even pendants can be used as bedtime reading lights, although you may find it psychologically unsettling to have one dangling overhead. To overcome this, you could try positioning one at each side of the bed at eye-level, preferably with a wall switch within easy reach.

Conventional desk lights make excellent portable lights for the bedside, especially the low-voltage halogen type with a built-in dimmer. It is worth bearing in mind that bedside fittings do not always have to stand on tables. A spotlight clipped to a wall shelf, or a special clip-on reading light for the bedhead, may suit you better. A dramatic alternative is to place a floor-standing uplighter at each end of the bed, to create an effect rather like that of a four-poster.

Shared bedrooms need to have their lighting arranged in such a way that each occupant can use the room with a minimum of disturbance to the other person. Double reading lights (perhaps two mini spotlights on a wall bar) are virtually essential.

A supplementary source of task lighting will be needed at the dressing table, particularly around the mirror (which should be placed near a window but not where it will block daylight). The basic choices here are the same as those for bathroom lighting (see pages 138–41). A fundamental principle is that a dressing-table light should be in front of your face, not behind it. Other task lights will be needed, of course, if you intend to use the room as a study.

Do not neglect to pay attention to bedroom storage lighting. The innermost recesses of walk-in cupboards will not be adequately lit by the general illumination in the room: they will need their own specific light sources. It is a sensible idea to fit the cupboard with a miniature fluorescent which will switch on automatically when the door is opened – like a refrigerator light. Where headroom is limited, you could use a small recessed downlighter.

1 The flex from these matching table lamps has been neatly concealed inside the headboard unit, which has duplicate switch and dimmer controls in a convenient position near each pillow.

2 Opalescent glass shades in this room not only emphasize the symmetry of the bed area but also function as low-key wall-washers, accentuating the four pictures.

3 This attic bedroom, made to seem more spacious by a large mirror, evokes the style of the 1950s with its authentic period fittings. The double floor light is a collector's piece. Indirect light is provided both by the wall bracket (sited near the ceiling to maximize output) and by the desk light angled to serve as a wall-washer.

1 In this bedroom two beds are separated from each other by a venetian blind, which makes the psychological division without robbing the inner section of early-morning sunlight. The matched spotlights and "Tokio" desk lights link the two halves of the room. The owner has avoided glare from the bullet-type spotlights on the ceiling by angling them toward the wall units; the mirrors aid the distribution of light.

3

2 The hybrid style of this room (exemplified by a Josef Hoffmann bentwood side chair alongside a high-tech steel-and-glass table) is matched by a similar eclecticism in the choice of light fittings — an eccentric shaded table light, a slender chrome uplighter turned toward the wall, and a bare pearl bulb in the alcove.

3 A recessed downlighter symmetrically positioned over the centre of the bed is a deliberate focal point in this view from the separate changing area, where all the lighting is indirect.

The most enjoyable evening meals are those for which an effort has been made to create a festive atmosphere. To some extent, the choice of tableware highlights the special importance of such occasions. Equally significant is the lighting setup. Indeed, these two aspects of a dinner party reinforce each other, creating by their interaction a complex effect that contributes to the mood of civilized enjoyment.

Special occasions

Traditionally, festive meals have been lit by a profusion of candles grouped to create clustered pin-points of light, either on the table itself or hanging low above it in a chandelier. It is no accident that the style of silverware and glassware used for such occasions makes the most of the special qualities of candlelight. Polished or facetted surfaces multiply the impact of flickering candle flames, creating a sumptuous impression, particularly when set against a snowy white linen tablecloth.

Although candlelight is no longer the universal light source for festive evening meals, the basic design of tableware has changed very little over the centuries. To recapture a sense of celebration at mealtimes, it is therefore a good idea to choose a lighting scheme that approximates to candlelight in its general effect. Ideally, the arrangement should include groups of small, low-intensity light sources.

The simplest and most attractive approach is to incorporate real candles in the room: imitation ones fool no-one and look pretentious. You

A "Quarto" wall light draws attention to the serving table.

1 Glass goblets are a classic way to shield candles from draughts and avoid the risk of singed sleeves as diners pass food, wine or accoutrements to each other. In this neo-classical dining alcove, additional lighting comes from a pair of portable uplighters concealed behind impressive plants.

2 In this grand dining room created by the innovative American architect Robert Stern, the different light sources are all closely related to the architecture and positioned where they create maximum impact.

An adjustable drum-type downlighter trained on the hearth adds a decorative touch to the lighting scheme. It is well-positioned to avoid dazzling diners at the table.

Light from a recessed downlighter makes silverware sparkle, as well as reflecting light off the pale green wall.

The chimney breast contains concealed fluorescent tubes.

Glass candleholders affirm a traditional theme that blends well with the elegant modern furnishings.

1 A dining alcove with a touch of fantasy provided by a galaxy of miniature tungsten lights, of the kind used for Christmas tree lighting. These are let into a wooden barrel-vaulted ceiling. The main lighting on the table comes from downlighters (not visible in this photograph).

2 Silver and glass ware catch the shimmering reflections of candles in this traditional table setting. The fake candles in the chandelier continue the theme – an acceptable contrivance, since the bulbs are above eye-level where they do not draw too much attention to themselves.

3 Architect Ricardo Bofill's dining room, housed, unlikely as it may seem, in a converted cement silo on the outskirts of Barcelona. Vertical fluorescent tubes neatly echo the lines of the architecture and provide an unusual shadow-free light for dining. Every detail of the room is subordinated to design, with no concessions made to the traditional intimacy of a dining area.

4 Five pendants illuminate a long, narrow table, their crown-silvered bulbs supplying glare-free light. The curly pendant flexes are a conscious decorative flourish. Additional accent lighting is derived from a pair of wall-mounted task lights.

could use a couple of candelabra on the table (preferably, ones that are not too ostentatious in style, unless you are aiming for ritzy grandeur); or alternatively you could choose a hanging fitting.

Candlelight on its own, quite apart from being very dim, often comes over as a rather strained, self-conscious attempt to enforce an intimate mood. For these reasons it is preferable to use it in conjunction with supplementary electric light. The two sources may be deployed in different combinations. Thus, while guests are being introduced to each other or shown their places at the table, the background lighting from electric sources will need to be relatively generous. But once everyone has settled down, you can alter the balance with a turn of the dimmer, allowing the candlelight to come more positively into its own.

Creating a focus
Whether you are entertaining or dining more humbly en famille, the focus of any dining room scheme should, of course, be the table. It is important to

choose a sympathetic arrangement that will show off an attractively laid and decorated table to best advantage, and also do the same for the food when it arrives, putting diners into a suitably expectant mood. However, it is no less crucial to pay attention to the secondary function of mealtimes – that of supplying a suitable context for relaxed conversation. The success of this aspect depends on the diners being able to see each other properly across the table, without being dazzled or thrown into gloom.

One favourite way to give a dining table its due emphasis is to concentrate direct lighting upon it, keeping light from the same source well away from other areas of the room, such as the walls or ceiling. This is best done with a pendant positioned over the table. For an intimate, enclosed effect, you should position the pendant not too high – ideally, just above the eye-level of the diners. Choose a design of fitting that will not cause glare at this height. Diffusing types tend to appear too bright and are best avoided. A better choice would be a fitting that directs most of its light output downward – perhaps with glare-preventing louvers. A long rectangular table will often require two pendants.

Normally, the light source will be a standard tungsten bulb, although with some kinds of fitting a crown-silvered bulb is more appropriate. Miniature fluorescents are less suitable, as they cannot be conveniently dimmed. Dimming is an important facility, as it allows you to suit the lighting to the occasion: casual relaxed family suppers are normally suited to higher levels of illumination than formal dinner parties where you are aiming to impress.

A rise-and-fall pendant is especially useful in dining rooms that also serve for additional activities. Moving the table aside and raising the pendant creates an area of free circulation, where a fixed, low pendant might get in the way. Even in rooms used exclusively for meals, a rise-and-fall fitting is advantageous, as it allows you more scope to adjust the lighting for cleaning and other tasks.

Spotlights are not generally recommended for the dining table, as it is very difficult to get the angles exactly right: usually, at least one diner will be at risk of being dazzled. A better arrangement would be a group of downlighters over the table, or even a framing projector. The latter, strategically located, can cover the surface of the table with a precise rectangle of light, making it seem

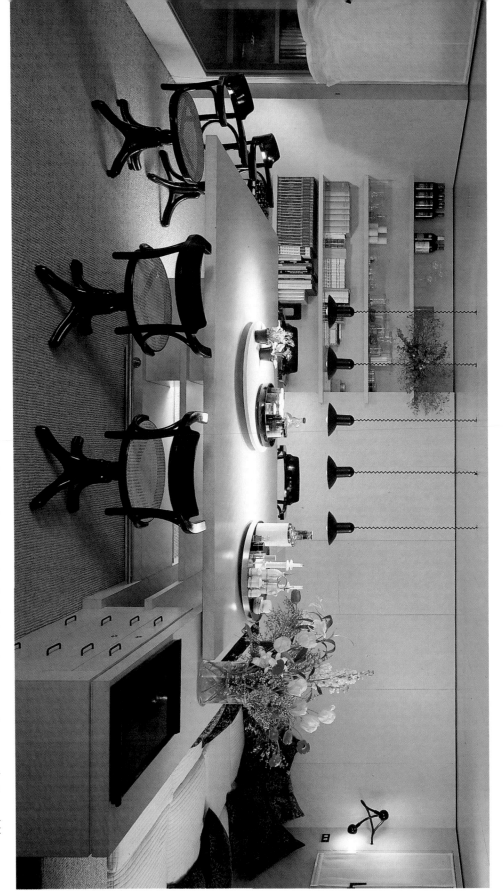

almost to levitate within the darkened room.

Supplementary lights

Despite the desirability of emphasizing the table, it is usually advisable to provide supplementary lighting in a dining room. You might wish to install wall-washing downlighters to highlight the colour, pattern or texture of a wall or a pair of floor-length curtains. Or alternatively, you could use display lights to accentuate paintings or other collectibles. Additional lighting of this kind has the merit of reducing overall contrast. However, it is important to judge the lighting proportions correctly. To keep the dining table isolated, additional areas of localized light should preferably be at some distance away: for example, it would be a mistake to concentrate light on a wall adjacent to the eating area.

Dining rooms often double as studies, and indeed many people use the table itself as a work surface, especially when they need to spread work out over a large area. If you keep a desk light permanently in the dining room with this purpose in mind, you can also give it a function at mealtimes – either to provide indirect background light (bounced off one of the walls) or to illuminate a serving table.

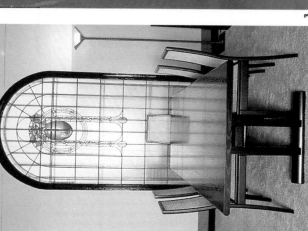

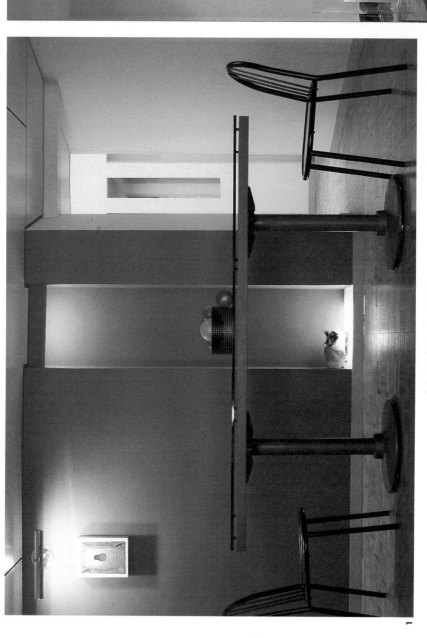

1 Not a dining room in the traditional sense, but a corner of a sophisticated apartment. Concealed fittings at the top and bottom of an alcove emit indirect lighting, dimly reflected back into the room off dark walls. A picture light completes the effect. During an evening meal, candles could be used to provide subdued table lighting.

2 Another arrangement in which candles would probably be brought out for evening meals. Supplementary lighting is provided by the "Scarpa" halogen uplighter, made by Flos.

3 An example of open-plan living with two distinct areas for eating – a central glass-topped dining table and a more casual breakfast table (foreground). Each table has a rise-and-fall pendant, whose institutional style counterpoints the cool, sleek finishes elsewhere in the room. The sideboard area is lit separately with a combination of recessed downlighters, a trio of matched wall lights and a pair of candles. The Memphis wheel light on the floor adds a purely decorative touch.

4 A spacious dining room with an opaque-shaded pendant hanging only a foot or so above the table. This is supported by a pair of spotlights put to decorative use in other parts of the room. A mirror on the wall helps to boost the overall lighting level, making up for the low-reflectance green walls.

Safety is a primary criterion for judging lighting in children's rooms. Of course, every type of light in the home should be safe, but because young children cannot be expected to treat electrical fittings with the same healthy regard as adults, special precautions are necessary. This is true not only in children's bedrooms but also in other areas of the home where children can reach light fittings.

Safety

A serious potential hazard is the use of poorly engineered, shoddily constructed fittings. For example, if the electrical insulation is inadequate, the metal parts of a fitting can become live. The best safeguard against such risks is to select products that display an authorized safety symbol. Steer clear of cheap imports, and avoid using old fittings, unless they have been checked or overhauled by an electrician.

Another danger to watch out for is the possibility of a curious child probing inside a fitting with his or her fingers. The safest defence against this risk is to use lights in which the source is sealed inside some kind of enclosure. The bulkhead style of design falls into this category, and is the basis of many nursery lights.

To protect against fire, scorching or burns from hot lamps, adhere to the fitting manufacturer's specified maximum wattage. If the fittings are within reach of young fingers, use sources that give off little heat, such as miniature fluorescents. Portable lights should have moulded plugs (resistant to experiments with screwdrivers and other pointed instruments) and should be used with special childproof sockets.

Lighting for the growing child

A child's room tends to change in the ways in which it is used far more rapidly than any other room in the home, as the occupant grows and develops new interests and skills.

During the earliest years of life, the lighting should be arranged to suit the convenience of the parents, but with the child's safety as the paramount factor. A dimmer switch is particularly useful, allowing fairly bright light for nappy-changing and other tasks and low-level light for late feeds and general reassurance.

As children grow older, more active and less dependent, the lighting requirements become more complex. You should anticipate future needs when wiring up the room. Flexibility is the keynote of a successful scheme.

1 **A pair of children's bunk beds, each with a separately switched, functional-looking wall light. The eyeball spot is suitable for games, or simply to provide a low-key mood for nighttime conversations.**

2 **Cloud and star lights (from Brillantleuchten) make an attractive cotside feature. The wall sockets are safely out of reach of infant fingers.**

3

Background lighting should be supplemented by adequate localized light in places where a child reads, draws, makes models or plays with toys. Remember that young eyes soon feel the strain. A bedlight is essential for looking at picture books, even before reading age. If you have two children in a pair of bunk beds, be sure to provide independently switched fittings at each level: all too often, the child in the lower bunk receives insufficient light. If possible, position the main light switches in the room at a child's level so that the child will feel in control of his or her own environment.

Children who bring home schoolwork need their own work surface. An adjustable task light concentrated on this area will help to prevent their attention from straying, and, equally important, will help to build their self-esteem.

Special fittings

There is an ever-growing range of novelty lights designed with young children in mind. Many of these take the form of wall or table lights with plastic diffusers moulded into recognizable shapes, such as balloons, airplanes, clouds, stars, ice cream cornets and characters from cartoon stories and nursery rhymes. The West German company Brillantleuchten has a large range of fittings in this category. Such lights not only supply attractive background illumination but also are very reassuring to children who are afraid of the dark. Virtually all children need the comfort of a night light at some point in their lives, whether to dispel anxieties or nightmares or to serve during the long nights of childhood illnesses. Non-decorative low-wattage night lights are specially made for this

purpose: although your child is unlikely to grow specially fond of them, they are less expensive to run than the more decorative kind of fitting.

For the youngster who needs the security of lighting during the brief period of settling down to sleep, a time-delay dimmer wall switch is a good idea. Once activated, this fades out the main light in the room to absolute darkness over a period of time (usually from five to twenty minutes).

3 This well-equipped child's room has a lighting scheme that takes future requirements into account. The suspended fluorescent fitting will one day be useful for homework and other tasks. The spotlights offer versatile display lighting to cope with the fickleness of youthful enthusiasms.

A study may be a room elaborately equipped to serve the needs of someone who works from home, with a desk, filing cabinet, shelving system, electric typewriter – even a home computer. Or alternatively, it may be just a corner of a living room, bedroom or kitchen, set aside for letter writing or to cope with household bills or accounts. Either way, it is a place of quiet concentration, whose lighting should be arranged to encourage maximum efficiency and comfort. Atmosphere is also important, particularly for desk workers who rigorously exercise their imagination: if the mood is off-key, the creative flow can easily be impeded.

The standard ingredient for typing, writing or reading is a plug-in adjustable task light, angled to provide relatively shadow-free illumination. Space may be an important factor in the precise choice of fitting, especially for people who need to spread themselves out (because either their work or their temperament demands it), or those who have a bureau-style drop-front desk rather than a spacious flat-topped table. There are various space-saving strategies. For example, you could choose a clip-on task light, or a fitting with a heavy base that can be placed several feet away from the work surface with the shade in the normal position over the object of study. Another approach is to use a wall-mounted task light, such as the "265" in the Arteluce range (see page 75). Choose a fitting that responds to finger-tip pressure, rather than one that needs two-handed screw-turning manoeuvres. The light source may be tungsten, low-voltage halogen or fluorescent. The latter gives a broad area of shadowless light that is suitable for draughtsmanship.

There are various alternatives to the orthodox task light. One popular choice is a floor light with a reflector and bulb that can be adjusted to give direct, downward illumination. Alternatively, you could use a rise-and-fall pendant fitting with a diffusing cover. Another feasible option is a ceiling-mounted downlighter, although the height of the fitting will prevent you from fine-tuning the lighting direction

easily. A downlighter should be fitted with a lens, or the light will be too harsh for performing tasks.

A temptation when using a study lamp alone at night is to rely on the desk light alone. Working in a distinct pool of light isolated from the surrounding darkness, we have the impression of being cut off from distractions – like a writer in a garret. However seductive this kind of lighting, it is undoubtedly bad for the eyes. A localized task light should not be used as the only source of illumination in a room, but should be supplemented by additional lighting – for example, from a standard lamp – to reduce the contrast level between the task area and the immediate surroundings.

Some studies and libraries have a strongly traditional feel, however modern the rest of the house. This is entirely appropriate, because books can be a repository of the past. A good way to strengthen the historical dimension is to use traditional shaded table lights or standard lamps. Dimmers will allow you to maintain low lighting levels for relaxation, casual browsing and listening to music: for many people, the study is also a music room. Playing a musical instrument from a score requires, of course, much higher lighting levels, depending on the score's complexity. A portable light clipped to the music rack is less satisfactory than a directional floor-standing fitting.

Books furnish any room, but they are especially prominent in a study and the *raison d'être* of the library. They should be lit in a way that makes them look attractive, but also facilitates a search for a particular volume. An ideal approach is to use a row of dimmable downlighters positioned a little way in front of the shelves, on the same principle as wall washing (see pages 108–9).

Increasingly, home computers are coming into the study. They present similar lighting problems to TV screens. The contrast between the VDU and its surroundings should not be too great, but on the other hand direct sources of light should be kept away from the screen, as they cause reflected glare.

1 Restricted headroom in this mezzanine-level library made pendants scarcely feasible. Instead, the owner has used luminous glass globes built into the shelving units. These provide useful background light and help to define the shape of the central island of shelves.

2 A row of makeshift plug-in pendants makes an unusual source of illumination over a work surface. The lights consist of reflector bulbs inside aluminium shades which are suspended on strong wires arching out, with flex attached, from the bookshelves.

3 A study area with a traditional flavour. The desk is equipped with a simple conically-shaped table light that dispels any atmosphere of the office. A modern tungsten-halogen floor light is angled downward to keep the emphasis of the lighting in the lower half of the room.

Garden lighting is primarily a matter of effect, very much like stage lighting in its scope and style. You can use it to create a spectacular environment for night walks on warm evenings, or as a way to tempt party guests outdoors. Even in cold weather, garden lights serve a key purpose, extending space by creating a pleasing view through a living room window. Whether the lights highlight flowers or greenery or sparkle on frost or snow, the visual impact is equally powerful.

The secret of garden lighting is to avoid uniformity, instead creating well-planned accents of illumination. This approach allows you to suppress the least attractive areas of the garden and highlight its special features – for example, flowerbeds, trees, pools and architectural features such as summer houses and pergolas.

If you prefer to flood the whole garden with light, the best way is to set up an asymmetrical arrangement of

fittings mounted on the outer wall of the house – perhaps a 500-watt tungsten-halogen floodlight mounted centrally beside a first floor window (for ease of adjustment and maintenance) and a 300-watt flood at the house corner, so that the weaker beam crosses the main, central beam. This will yield a pleasingly graduated effect.

The variety of creative options available may be illustrated by the simple example of trees. You can use a strongly angled spotlight to emphasize the texture of gnarled bark, or alternatively you can use a spotlight close to the tree and angled directly upward into the foliage – a strategy that creates a leafy patchwork of light and shade. Other options are to festoon a tree with coloured bulbs, or to wallwash a white-painted wall so that the tree stands out against it in bold silhouette. All these effects look even more dramatic when a breeze stirs the leaves or a boisterous wind

1 Two powerful Bega floodlights bring out the copper colours of autumn foliage, as well as usefully illuminating a patch of lawn.

2 A procession of weatherproof beacon lights guides the visitor to the porch of an imposing modern house in East Hampton, New York.

makes branches sway.

Vine-clad pergolas or weeping willows benefit from an upward-angled spotlight placed right in the middle of the greenery, making it glow like a tent of green light.

Paths need to be punctuated with light to lead a way through the garden safely. Make sure that you light dangerous steps, changes of level or patches of rough terrain. The lights should illuminate the path, not the person walking on it: dazzling lights could be just as dangerous as no lights at all.

Many outdoor lights are finished in green, to make them less obvious during the day. However, carefully unobtrusive siting is usually more effective than camouflaging paint. In most gardens, it is not too difficult to find a bush, hedge, low wall, flower tub or other feature that will serve to disguise the fitting. Some fittings, of course, are deliberately decorative. When choosing a fitting that is meant

to be seen, make sure that its style is not at odds with the architecture of the house.

Sensitively lit patios provide a delightful area for barbecues and outdoor dining. Broad, bright floodlights, however, will dispel the romance. A better choice would be a group of fittings that integrate into the architectural features — for example, eaves-hung pendants, newel-post lights or wall brackets, with accent lighting on special features. One or two lights some distance off in the garden will create a sense of depth, dispelling the feeling that black, unfathomable night extends right up to the patio's edge.

To pick out the house frontage with light, avoid using wall-mounted fittings; they cast shadows that distort architectural features. Instead, it is better to use a pair of spotlights angled onto the house from different directions, so that the shadows cancel each other out. Angle the lights in such

3 A trio of spotlights mark the peaks of gabled eaves in this one-storey dwelling. Two of the fittings wash the patio area with light, while a third, angled sideways, picks out a display of mock flamingos with a narrow-beam lamp.

4 A covered patio receives general illumination from weatherproof downlighters. Outside the covered area, the three clear globe lights at different levels soften the transition between patio and garden.

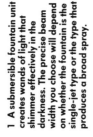

a way that they are not glaring to people inside looking out.

Water

Pools and streams in the garden can be magically transformed by a judicious lighting scheme. A spotlamp used above water level will cause a pleasing sparkle, especially if the water is in motion. Many submersible fittings are sold with optional coloured glass covers, which are well worth experimenting with. Single-jet fountains look particularly effective if you can angle the light right along the line of the jet.

In swimming pools, submersible fittings will make a midnight swim more tempting, as well as helping to define the pool's edge to prevent anyone falling in. A lighting level of 500 lumens per square metre is sufficient for most private pools. Make sure that any underwater fittings are easily removable for regular maintenance. Most pool fittings are unsuitable for use in sea water.

1 A submersible fountain unit creates wands of light that shimmer effectively in the darkness. The precise beam width you choose will depend on whether the fountain is the single-jet type or the type that produces a broad spray.

2 Flower tubs can be used to create a spectacular nighttime showpiece. In this example, the light comes from an L-shaped low-voltage fitting securely embedded in the soil of the tub. Additional interest is supplied by a string of waterproof lights ("Sunset Strip") along a fence-post. (Both fittings are produced by Peter Burian Associates.)

3 Two spotlights, wisely hidden from view to prevent glare, dramatize a Japanese-style garden in a view from inside looking out. Notice how the strongly directional lighting accentuates the raked troughs of soil and defines the forms of the rocks.

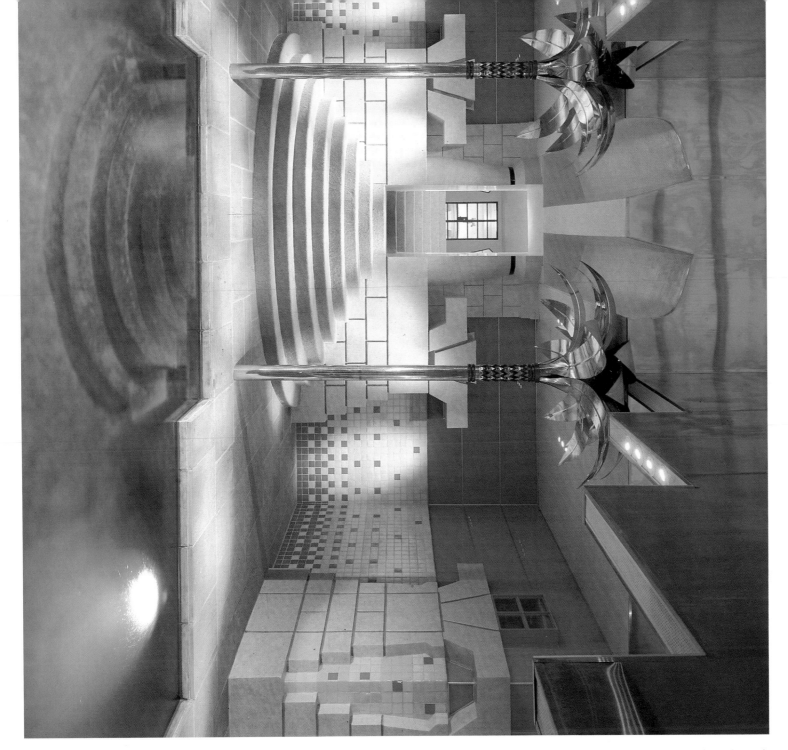

4 An exotic, luxury swimming pool with subtly atmospheric lighting from recessed downlighters. The pool itself is illuminated by underwater fittings that house low-voltage PAR 56 reflector lamps.

Practicalities

There are various possible approaches you can take to putting new lighting in your home. One way is to place the whole operation into professional hands. Another is to employ a consultant to work out the design, then do the installation yourself. Or you could hire an electrician to follow a scheme of your own devising. Adventurous souls may even wish to take a do-it-yourself approach from start to finish. The decision depends on your aptitude, the time and money you have available, and the complexity of the work required.

Whichever line you take, this final section of the book will answer some of your basic questions: how do you put in a new switch or socket outlet or a new wall light or pendant? what precautions must you take when dealing with electricity? how do you find an expert to do the whole or part of the job? The section has a list of useful addresses (including designers, retailers and manufacturers), a glossary of technical terms and a chart of common lamp types.

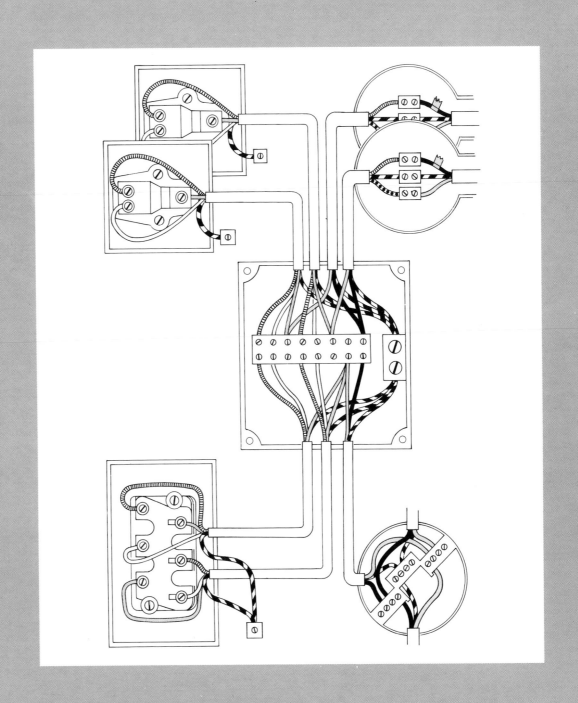

The electricity supply to your home arrives via an underground or overhead cable. Immediately after it enters the house, the cable runs into the Electricity Board's main service fuse; this is usually rated at 60 or 80amps, and governs the maximum current your house can draw from the system. The cable then runs on to your electricity meter, and from there to your fusebox or consumer unit. All equipment up to and including the meter is the property of the Electricity Board, and must never be tampered with.

Whatever type of fusebox or consumer unit you have, it is important to know how it controls the various lighting and power circuits. In a home wired to modern standards you will find a one-piece consumer unit containing the house supply's main on-off switch and a number of circuit fuses or miniature circuit breakers (MCBs). Each will be labelled (and probably colour-coded) to indicate what type of circuit it protects – 5amp (white) for lighting, 30amp (red) for power circuits, plus 15amp (yellow) and 20amp (blue) for special circuits to individual appliances. Inside the unit should be a chart identifying each circuit – "upstairs lighting", "kitchen ring main circuit" and so on.

In an older installation you may find a number of separate smaller units, each containing one or more fuses and with its own on/off switch; all these will then be linked to one main on/off switch unit. Again, the fuse ratings will help you to identify each circuit; make sure each box is clearly labelled. A system of this type is probably

Your fusebox or consumer unit may contain old-fashioned rewirable fuses, cartridge fuses or miniature circuit breakers (MCBs). In the first type a length of fuse wire of the appropriate rating links the two terminals of the fuseholder, and melts in the event of overloading or a circuit fault. The second type works the same way but the fuse wire is contained in a small cartridge; there are different sizes for each circuit rating. MCBs are electro-mechanical switches that trip to off if overloading or a fault occurs.

thoroughly out of date and unable to cope with present-day wiring needs; if it is wired up in old rubber-sheathed cable, you should have it inspected at once by a qualified electrician, and you should certainly be contemplating having the whole system rewired.

Once you have identified each circuit in the house and know how to isolate it from the mains, you can begin to plan any alterations or extensions you want to carry out.

Safety guidelines

Whatever electrical work you carry out, here are a number of sensible rules and precautions to follow in order to eliminate risks – either to yourself as you carry out the work, or to anyone else using the system after you have finished.

1 Never tackle any electrical work unless you are absolutely sure how to carry it out properly.
2 Turn off the main isolating switch before starting the job. If you are working on only one circuit, remove the appropriate circuit fuse (or switch off the MCB) before turning the main switch back on to restore power to the rest of the house. Check that the circuit you have isolated is dead before working on it.
3 Double-check all connections you make to ensure that the cores are connected to the correct terminals, that they are secure and that no bare conductor is visible.
4 Always unplug plug-in lights before attempting to work on them.
5 Never omit the earth conductor if one is needed; any fitting with metal

parts should have an earth terminal on it, and should be wired up with three-core flex.
6 Avoid long trailing flexes and overloaded adaptors. If you have insufficient outlets, install more (see page 175).

Wiring regulations

The IEE (Institution of Electrical Engineers) Wiring Regulations contain many requirements for house wiring practice. As far as lighting is concerned, note the following points:
● Each lighting circuit should feed a maximum of eight lighting points.
● 1.0mm² two-core and earth cable should be used for all extension work on existing circuits.
● Heat-resistant flex is recommended for connections between the lamp and the circuit cables in enclosed fittings.
● Lampholders within 2.5m (8ft 6in) of a bath or shower must be fitted with a protective skirt to prevent the metal parts from being touched, unless the fitting is the totally enclosed type.

Tools for electrical work

Even if you are likely to do no more than extend a flex or change a plug, you will need a small electrical screwdriver with a sheathed blade, a sharp trimming knife and a pair of wire strippers. For more comprehensive electrical work you will require:
● A pair of pliers with insulated handles.
● A mains tester for checking connections and circuit continuity.
● A brick bolster (wide masonry chisel), cold chisel (narrow masonry chisel) and club hammer for chopping out cable runs in walls.
● A power drill with extension lead and a selection of wood and masonry bits.
● A floorboard saw or circular saw for cutting through floorboards.
● A number of everyday DIY tools such as hammers, screwdrivers, chisels, saws.

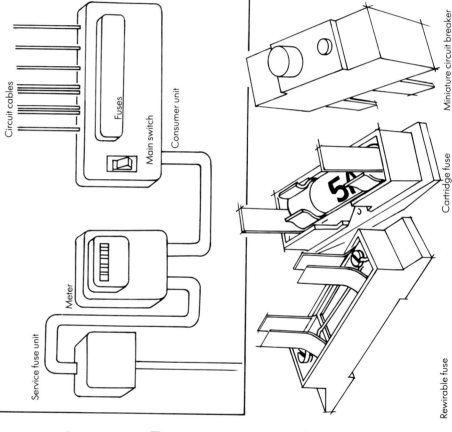

Circuit cables

Fuses

Main switch

Consumer unit

Meter

Service fuse unit

Rewirable fuse

Cartridge fuse

Miniature circuit breaker

a
A lighting circuit junction box links the two circuit cables (or, at the last box on the circuit, just one cable) to the switch and light cables.

b
A light switch has two terminals (three if used for two-way switching). Up to six switches can be incorporated in one switch box.

c
A loop-in ceiling rose contains three banks of terminals and links the circuit cables, switch cable and flex to the pendant.

d
A socket outlet on a ring circuit provides power to a plug-in light. It can also be the connection point for a spur cable to a fused connection unit for wall lights.

e
A fused connection unit allows a lighting sub-circuit to be connected to a power circuit. For lighting it must be fitted with a 5amp fuse.

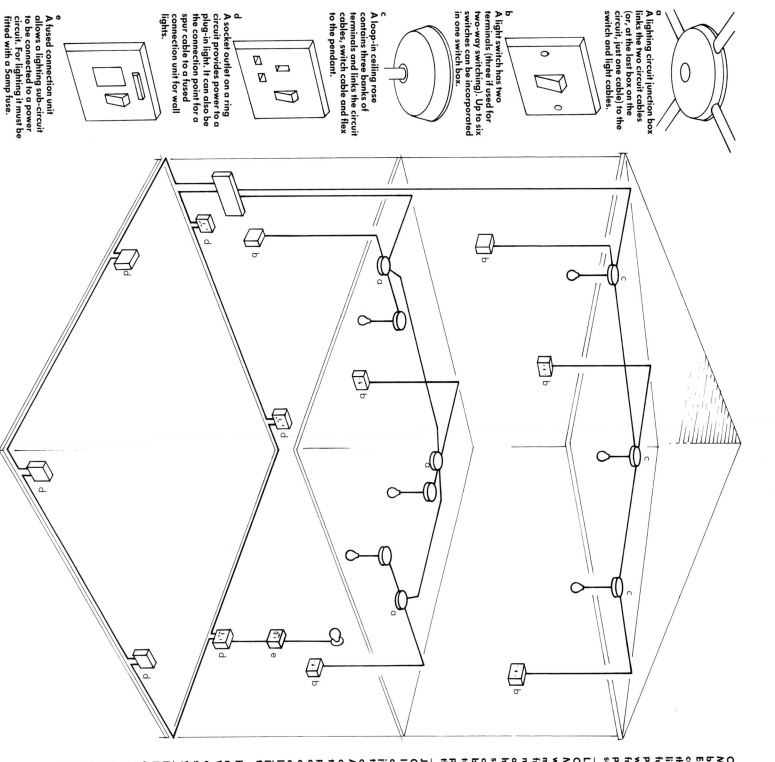

CIRCUITS FOR LIGHTING
Most lights in your home will be wired into lighting circuits. Each circuit is run in 1.0mm² cable from a 5amp fuseway in the consumer unit. Some fixed lighting may be wired as fused spurs from one of your power circuits. Plug-in lights will, of course, take current from a power circuit via a plug (with a 5amp fuse) and socket outlet.

LOOP-IN LIGHTING CIRCUITS
Most modern homes are wired using the loop-in method. The circuit cable runs from one light position to the next, looping out of one rose and on to another. Each rose has three banks of terminals so that the cable to the switch controlling the light can also be connected in. The circuit terminates at the light position most remote from the fusebox.

JUNCTION-BOX LIGHTING CIRCUITS
In older homes lighting circuits are wired up by the junction-box method. Here, the circuit cable runs from one junction box to another. At the junction box two other cables are connected in – one to take power to the light position, the other running down to the wall switch controlling the light. The circuit terminates at the last junction box. Each junction box contains four terminals.

In practice, many modern homes are wired using a mixture of the two systems. When extending a lighting circuit, by all means mix the systems yourself if this gives you a saving on cable.

POWER CIRCUITS
Fixed lighting may be connected to power circuits via a fused spur – a branch of 2.5mm² cable taken off a ring circuit and run to a fused connection unit containing a 5amp fuse. From here 1.0mm² cable is run to the light fitting(s). This method is common with wall lights.

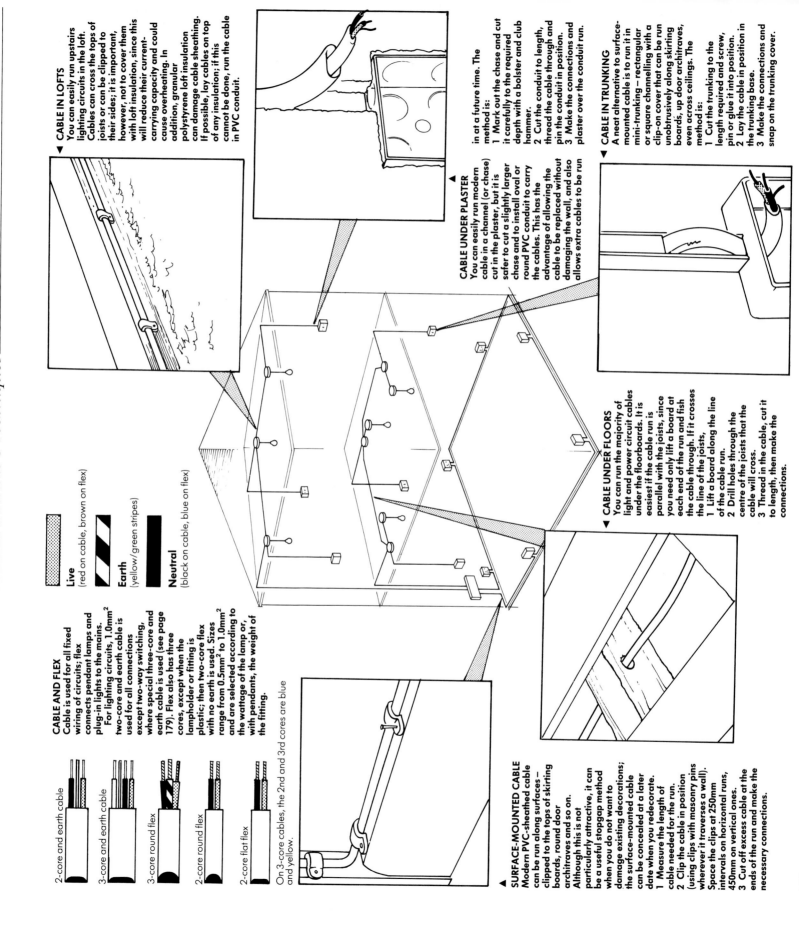

CABLE IN LOFTS
You can easily run upstairs lighting circuits in the loft. Cables can cross the tops of joists or can be clipped to their sides; it is important, however, not to cover them with loft insulation, since this will reduce their current-carrying capacity and could cause overheating. In addition, granular polystyrene loft insulation can damage cable sheathing. If possible, lay cables on top of any insulation; if this cannot be done, run the cable in PVC conduit.

CABLE UNDER PLASTER
You can easily run modern cable in a channel (or chase) cut in the plaster, but it is safer to cut a slightly larger chase and to install oval or round PVC conduit to carry the cables. This has the advantage of allowing the cable to be replaced without damaging the wall, and also allows extra cables to be run in at a future time. The method is:
1 Mark out the chase and cut it carefully to the required depth with a bolster and club hammer.
2 Cut the conduit to length, thread the cable through and pin the conduit in position.
3 Make the connections and plaster over the conduit run.

CABLE IN TRUNKING
A neat alternative to surface-mounted cable is to run it in mini-trunking — rectangular or square channelling with a clip-on cover that can be run unobtrusively along skirting boards, up door architraves, even across ceilings. The method is:
1 Cut the trunking to the length required and screw, pin or glue it into position.
2 Lay the cable in position in the trunking base.
3 Make the connections and snap on the trunking cover.

CABLE UNDER FLOORS
You can run the majority of light and power circuit cables under the floorboards. It is easiest if the cable run is parallel with the joists, since you need only lift a board at each end of the run and fish the cable through. If it crosses the line of the joists,
1 Lift a board along the line of the cable run.
2 Drill holes through the centre of the joists that the cable will cross.
3 Thread in the cable, cut it to length, then make the connections.

CABLE AND FLEX
Cable is used for all fixed wiring of circuits; flex connects pendant lamps and plug-in lights to the mains.
For lighting circuits, 1.0mm² two-core and earth cable is used for all connections except two-way switching, where special three-core and earth cable is used (see page 179). Flex also has three cores, except when the lampholder or fitting is plastic; then two-core flex with no earth is used. Sizes range from 0.5mm² to 1.0mm² and are selected according to the wattage of the lamp or, with pendants, the weight of the fitting.

Live (red on cable, brown on flex)
Earth (yellow/green stripes)
Neutral (black on cable, blue on flex)

2-core and earth cable
3-core and earth cable
3-core round flex
2-core round flex
2-core flat flex

On 3-core cables, the 2nd and 3rd cores are blue and yellow.

SURFACE-MOUNTED CABLE
Modern PVC-sheathed cable can be run along surfaces — clipped to the tops of skirting boards, round door architraves and so on. Although this is not particularly attractive, it can be a useful stopgap method when you do not want to damage existing decorations; the surface-mounted cable can be concealed at a later date when you redecorate.
1 Measure the length of cable needed for the run.
2 Clip the cable in position (using clips with masonry pins wherever it traverses a wall). Space the clips at 250mm intervals on horizontal runs, 450mm on vertical ones.
3 Cut off excess cable at the ends of the run and make the necessary connections.

Mounting electrical fittings

Wall-mounted electrical fittings can be installed in two ways – surface-mounted, or set in flush with the wall surface. The latter method is neater, and is usually used in conjunction with concealed wiring under the plaster surface. However, it is easier to fit surface-mounted accessories, and this method may be favoured if new cable runs are being fixed on the wall surface as well.

Flush mounting

With flush-mounted accessories – switches, socket outlets or fused connection units – the faceplate of the accessory is screwed to the lugs of a metal mounting box that is recessed into the wall. The recessed cable enters the box through a hole knocked out of the side or base of the box; a rubber grommet prevents the cable from chafing on the metal edges. The box

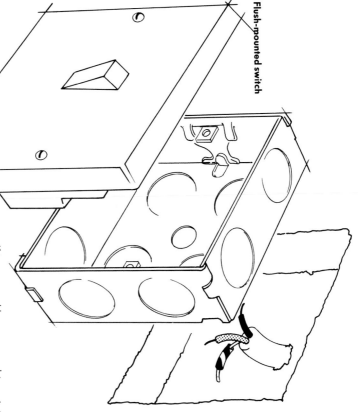

Surface-mounted switch

Flush-mounted switch

itself is secured by screws driven into wall plugs in the masonry behind.

Flush boxes for light switches are 16mm deep, while those for socket outlets and fused connection units are 25mm or 35mm deep.

Surface mounting

With surface-mounted accessories the faceplate is fixed to a plastic mounting box that is simply screwed to the wall in the required position. The cable can be concealed, entering through the back of the box, or surface-mounted, either clipped or run in trunking and entering through the side. As with flush-mounted accessories, the box depth depends on the type of accessory you plan to fit.

Ceiling fittings

Whatever type of ceiling fitting you choose, it must have a secure fixing – it is not enough to drive screws directly into the ceiling.

Ceiling roses are surface-mounted, so it is generally possible to fix them directly beneath a joist. The cable leading to the rose can then enter through the knockout hole in the

baseplate. If this is not possible, a batten is nailed between the joists above the ceiling surface, and the rose is screwed to the ceiling surface, and the cable is fed to the batten from beneath (as shown in the diagram below). Of course, to fix the batten in place you will have to lift a few floorboards in the room above or, alternatively, climb up into the loft.

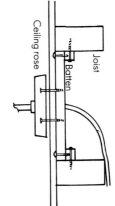

Ceiling rose

With close-mounted pendants, a special round box called a conduit box or BESA box has to be set into a hole cut in the ceiling, its lip flush with the ceiling surface. Here, a variation on the batten method mentioned above is used, with the batten set a little way above the ceiling surface. The box is screwed to the underside of the batten, the cable is fed into it from above and the fitting itself is either secured to the box if it has a matching circular baseplate, or otherwise to the batten. The connections between the circuit cable and the flex leading to the fitting are then made using small terminal connector blocks that are concealed within the box when the fitting is finally positioned.

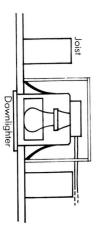

Joist

Downlighter

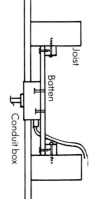

Joist

Batten

Conduit box

Recessed light fittings are installed in much the same way, with the addition of a heat-resistant pad above the light to protect floorboards above it from excess heat build-up.

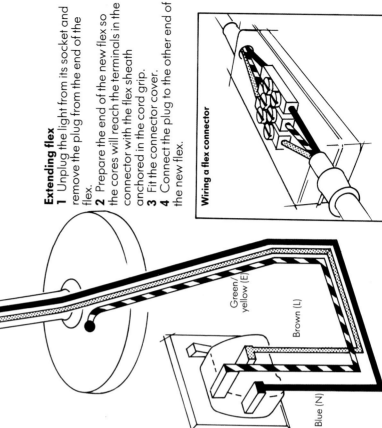

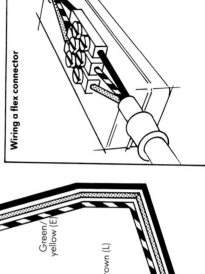

Wiring a flex connector

Extending flex
1 Unplug the light from its socket and remove the plug from the end of the flex.
2 Prepare the end of the new flex so the cores will reach the terminals in the connector with the flex sheath anchored in the cord grip.
3 Fit the connector cover.
4 Connect the plug to the other end of the new flex.

Green/yellow (E)

Brown (L)

Blue (N)

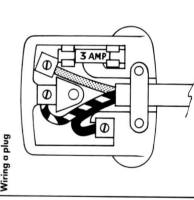

Wiring a plug

3 AMP

Plug-in lights
It is still rare in the UK to be able to buy a plug-in light with a plug attached. When you unpack the fitting you will probably find that the end of the flex has been stripped back ready to receive the plug. You may also find a label attached to the flex telling you how to wire it up. This is broadly applicable to old-fashioned round-pin plugs as well as more recent rectangular-pin plugs.

Choose plugs with care. The best quality rectangular-pin plugs have captive (non-removable) pins, a captive centre screw, and a cord grip consisting of two nylon jaws. The harder you pull on the flex, the more tightly the jaws hold it. This is an important safety feature; without it anyone tripping over a flex trailing across the floor could tear it out of the terminals, causing a short circuit next time the light is switched on.

When buying a new plug, either select one fitted with a 3amp fuse, or buy a supply of 3amp fuses to replace the 13amp one which is often fitted as standard. Use the surplus 3amp fuses to replace any 13amp fuses in plugs on any other light fittings that you own.

Lights with no metallic parts are fitted with two-core flex; there is no earth core, since there is no metalwork that could become live in the event of a fault. Fittings with any metal parts — even just a metal lampholder — must be fitted with three-core flex: live, neutral and earth.

Each fitting you wire up should have its own plug. Never be tempted to connect two (or more) flexes into the same plug just because you do not have enough socket outlets. You can use adaptors to connect up to three plugs to one socket outlet; however, this is not good practice as the leads can get tangled and there is a risk that the combined weight of adaptor and plugs will pull the assembly out of the socket, leading to poor electrical contact. It is better to increase the number of socket outlets, either by converting existing single sockets into double (or even triple) ones, or by adding completely new sockets as spurs from your existing power circuit, as described and illustrated on the

opposite page.

Many plug-in lights are sold with only a comparatively short length of flex attached. Even in a home with ample power points, the lead may not be long enough to reach to the nearest socket. In this case you need to extend the flex. The best way of doing this is to remove the existing flex and replace it completely with a new piece of the required length (and of the same type and current rating). On some light fittings this may be difficult, and you will have to extend the flex instead. Use a special flex connector for this (shown below right) — either a one-piece connector, or a two-piece one with the "female" part connected to the flex that runs to the plug. The latter method ensures that if the connector is pulled apart while the flex is still plugged in, accidental contact with live pins cannot occur.

Wiring a plug
To wire a plug for a plug-in light:
1 Open the plug and lay the flex in it, with the sheathing over the cord grip, to check that the flex cores will reach the terminals with 12mm extra for making the connections. Trim the cores if necessary, or cut back the sheath to expose more core.
2 Connect the brown core to the live (L) terminal, the blue core to the neutral (N) terminal and the green/yellow core if present to the earth (E) terminal.
3 Secure the flex in the cord grip.
4 Fit a 3amp fuse and then replace the plug top.

Gaining more socket outlets

There is no restriction on the number of socket outlets that can be part of a modern ring or radial power circuit. As well as adding sockets on the circuit cable itself, you can also add branch lines (or spurs) from the circuit to feed extra sockets, provided that the number of spurs taken from a circuit does not exceed the number of sockets on the main circuit.

The simplest approach is to convert all your existing single sockets into double (or triple) ones. What you do depends on whether your existing outlets are flush- or surface-mounted and on whether you want your new sockets to be flush or surface fittings. The options are diagrammed below.

Options

Recessed single

Surface single

Surface double

Recessed double

The easiest changeover is to exchange a surface single for a surface double socket. This involves turning off the power at the mains, disconnecting the existing faceplate, removing the old mounting box, fitting a new double one in its place and connecting up the new double faceplate. From a single flush to a double surface-mounted fitting is also an easy progression: you simply screw the new double box to the lugs of the old single box using the original faceplate fixing screws, then connect up the new faceplate.

There is a little more work involved if you want your new double socket to be flush-fitting. If your existing single socket is flush-mounted, you have to remove the old faceplate and box, enlarge the hole in the wall to take a new double box and connect up the new faceplate. If the existing single socket is surface-mounted, you have to cut out a new double-sized hole in the wall.

If you want outlets in other locations, you must extend your existing circuits with spur cables to feed new sockets. There are two methods: you can either connect a spur cable into the back of an existing socket, or you can cut the existing circuit cable at a convenient point and connect in the spur using a three-terminal junction box.

The only drawback with the former method is the danger of contravening IEE Wiring Regulations. The socket you want to connect your spur cable into may not be on the main circuit; if it is itself a spur you are not allowed to extend it. To be sure of keeping within the safety regulations, follow these guidelines:

● If the existing socket has only one cable entering its box, it is on a spur and you cannot connect in a spur cable.

● If the existing socket has three cables entering its box, a spur has already been run from it and you may not add another.

● If two cables are present, the socket is probably on the main circuit and so you can run a spur from it. However, it may be an intermediate socket on a now prohibited two-socket spur. The only way to be sure is to call in an electrician to check the circuit.

Adding a spur: junction-box method

You can connect into the existing power circuit at any convenient point on its run using a 30amp three-terminal junction box. There are two types: a circular one used for connections within ceiling voids or under floors, where the box is screwed to the side of a joist; and a rectangular one used for installations where the circuit cables are run on the surface.

To fit a junction box, the first step is to cut off the power to the circuit: to do this, remove the appropriate circuit fuse or switch off the circuit MCB. Then screw the box base in position, cut the circuit cable, prepare the cut ends and connect the cores to the terminals – lives to the first terminal, neutrals to the second, earths to the third. Prepare the end of the branch cable and connect its cores to the box terminals too. Then screw on the junction box cover.

Wiring a socket outlet

Whatever changeover job you are tackling, you will be reconnecting the existing circuit cable (or cables) to the terminals of your new double socket faceplate. Do not disconnect any cable cores that have been twisted together; simply reconnect them to the new faceplate as they are, taking the red cores to the live (L) terminal, the black cores to the neutral (N) terminal and the earth cores to the earth (E) terminal. If the earth cores are bare, slip on a length of green/yellow striped PVC sleeving before connecting them up. Then fold the cable neatly back into the mounting box and screw on the faceplate.

Adding a spur from a socket outlet

Unscrew the socket faceplate (again with the power off), and connect in the new spur cable to the faceplate terminals. It is usually easy to feed the new cable into the existing box along the same route that the circuit cables take.

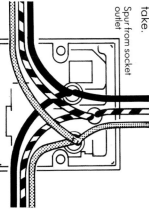

Spur from socket outlet

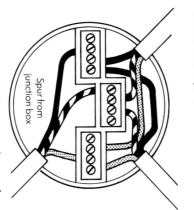

Spur from junction box

Green/yellow (E)

Black (N)

Red (L)

Wiring a double socket outlet

175

Replacing a pendant

Fitting a new pendant will usually involve removing the existing ceiling rose and its flex.

Before you start, isolate the circuit you will be working on by removing the circuit fuse or turning off the MCB at its fusebox. It is not enough simply to turn off the light switch, as the circuit cables at the rose will still be live.

Begin by removing the existing shade (if there is one) from the lampholder. Then unscrew the ceiling rose cover. You may need to cut round the cover with a sharp handyman's knife to free it from the paint that successive redecorations have left around its edge. Slide the cover down the flex; then, holding the flex with one hand, use a small screwdriver in the other hand to disconnect the flex from the rose terminals.

The next step is to unscrew the cable terminal screws. If there are two or more cables present, make a note of which cables went where before disconnecting them. Do not untwist any cables that are twisted together. You can now undo the woodscrews that hold the rose in place, and lift the rose away.

You will now be left with the circuit cables protruding through a small hole in the ceiling. What you do next depends on the type of fitting you are planning to install.

With close-fitting bowl pendants, fluorescent fittings and some types of track lighting system, the circuit cables connect directly into a small terminal block within the fitting. Thus, all you have to do is connect up the wires and attach the fitting's backplate securely to the ceiling, ready to receive the bowl, diffuser or cover. You will see flex cores within the fitting leading to the terminal block; link red cable cores with the brown flex core, black cable cores with the blue flex core and the cable earth cores with the green/yellow flex core. If the cable earth core(s) is (are) bare, cover it (them) with green/yellow PVC sleeving. With spotlights and many other types of ceiling fitting, the cable/flex connections are made within a special terminal box that has to be recessed into the ceiling.

Removing a ceiling rose

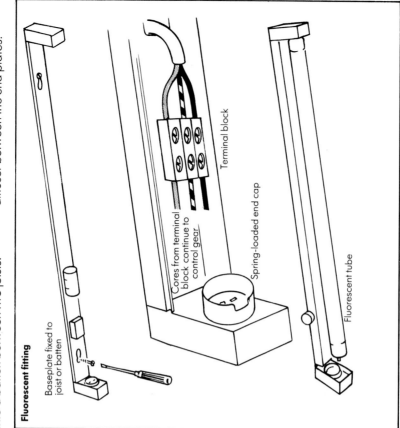

Ceiling rose

Flex supporting fitting

Cable

Bowl lights

Close-fitting bowl lights have a terminal block on the upper surface of the baseplate. Screw the fixing bar to the ceiling, make the connections, attach the baseplate.

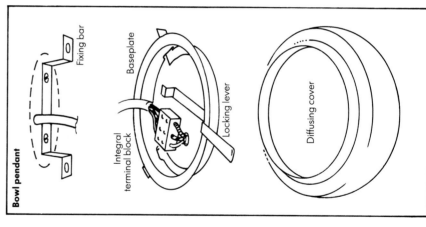

Bowl pendant

Fixing bar

Baseplate

Integral terminal block

Locking lever

Diffusing cover

Fluorescent fittings

Fluorescent fittings are easier to install than you might imagine. Thread the cable through the baseplate of the fitting and attach this to the ceiling — screwing it into a joist or alternatively into a batten between two joists.

Connect up the wiring. This varies according to the fitting type, so follow the manufacturer's instructions carefully. Slot on the cover plate, then snap in the fluorescent tube. Fit the diffuser between the end plates.

Fluorescent fitting

Baseplate fixed to joist or batten

Cores from terminal block continue to control gear

Terminal block

Spring-loaded end cap

Fluorescent tube

Wiring a terminal block

Exactly how you link the circuit cable and fitting flex depends on the wiring at the original ceiling rose. If it was a junction-box rose with only one circuit cable present, you need a three-terminal block. Link red cable core to brown flex core, black cable core to blue flex core and cable earth core to green/yellow flex core. Sleeve the cable earth first if it is just a bare wire.

If it was a loop-in rose, with two or three cables present, you need a four-terminal block. All the cable live cores go to one terminal, all the cable earth cores go to another. The return core (black) goes to the third, the mains neutral core(s) to the fourth, as shown in the diagram (right).

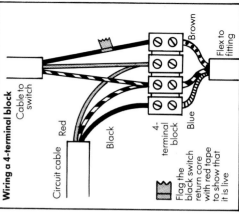

Wiring a 4-terminal block

Cable to switch

Brown

Circuit cable

Red

Black

Blue

Flex to fitting

4-terminal block

Flag the black switch return core with red tape to show that it is live

Recessed downlighters

With a recessed downlighter, the connections are made at a terminal block on the fitting. You have to cut a hole in the ceiling to accept the fitting. Check before you buy the light that there is enough height available.

Installing a recessed downlighter

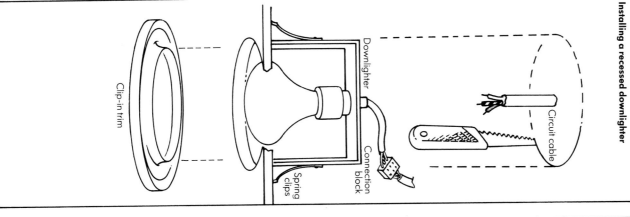

Downlighter

Connection block

Spring clips

Clip-in trim

Circuit cable

Installing a conduit box

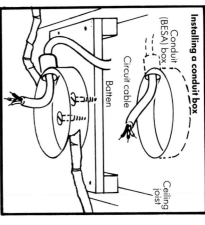

Conduit (BESA) box

Circuit cable

Batten

Ceiling joist

Conduit box method

Fittings with a small circular baseplate are mounted over a conduit (BESA) box recessed into the ceiling and screwed to a batten between the joists, as shown above. Screw the baseplate to the box with machine screws.

Installing a spotlight

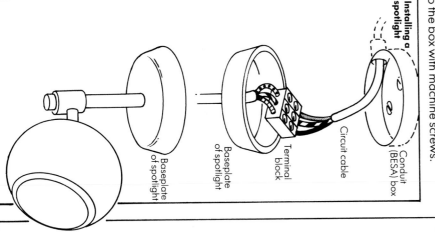

Baseplate of spotlight

Baseplate of spotlight

Terminal block

Circuit cable

Conduit (BESA) box

Rise-and-fall fittings

Rise-and-fall fittings also need a conduit box. The fixing bar and hook are screwed to the box to support the rise-and-fall mechanism, which is covered by a conical plastic or metal cover.

Installing a rise-and-fall pendant

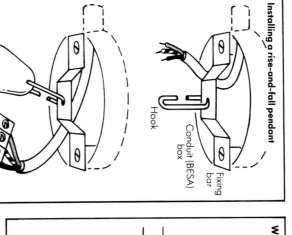

Fixing bar

Conduit (BESA) box

Hook

Connection block

Canopy

Track lighting

With some types of track lighting, the connections are made directly within the track (as shown below). With others the track can be connected into the terminals of an existing ceiling rose, which need not therefore be removed.

Wiring a track

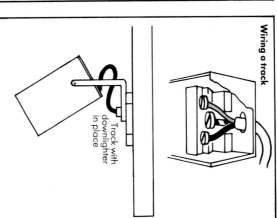

Track with downlighter in place

The importance of earthing

The Wiring Regulations now require lighting circuits to be earthed. If, when you expose your cables, you find that there is no earth core, you have a choice of two courses of action, depending on the state of the wiring. If it is in good condition, with no signs of perishing, you can run in a single-core earth cable to link the new light position with the main earth terminal at your fusebox (ideally, linking this terminal to all other light positions on the circuit at the same time). If the cable shows signs of deterioration, you should completely rewire the lighting circuit with new PVC-sheathed two-core and earth cable. Never take chances with an old installation; if you are in any doubt about its safety, call in a qualified electrician to check it.

Remember that all bare earth cores should be covered with slip-on green/yellow sleeving where they are exposed for making connections within a fitting or conduit box.

Installing new circuit cables

If you want to install new lights where no lights exist at the moment, you will have to extend existing circuit cables – or even run in a new circuit. In theory, a lighting circuit fused at 5 amps can supply 5 × 240 = 1200 watts of power; each light is nominally rated at 100 watts, so you can have a maximum of 12 lights on each circuit. In practice this is restricted to eight lights to cater for high-wattage bulbs or multi-bulb fittings. If your new lights will cause you to exceed this limit, you will need a spare fuseway in your consumer unit to wire in a new circuit; or alternatively you will have to add a separate switchfuse unit alongside the consumer unit. It is best to call in an electrician for this.

If you can extend the existing circuits, there are several options. With loop-in wiring, you can connect a spur cable into the terminals of the rose, run this to the new light position and install a new rose (or conduit box) there. The switch can then be connected into the new rose. (A, a, d, e)

Alternatively, you can take a spur cable from any convenient point on the main lighting circuit cable. With the power off, cut the cable, insert a three-terminal junction box and run your spur from here to the new light position. (B, b)

It may save cable to use junction box wiring instead. In this case you cut into the circuit cable at a convenient point and insert a four-terminal junction box. From this, one cable is run to the new light position, another to the new switch. (C, c, e, f)

You can also feed your new lights from a power circuit by running a spur in 2.5mm² cable from a 30 amp junction box or socket outlet to a fused connection unit fitted with a 5 amp fuse. (D, g, j) The rest of the wiring beyond the connection unit is in 1.0mm² cable.

Where your new light is fitted over a conduit (BESA) box, the terminal connections within the box will vary according to the type of switching. (E, h, F, i)

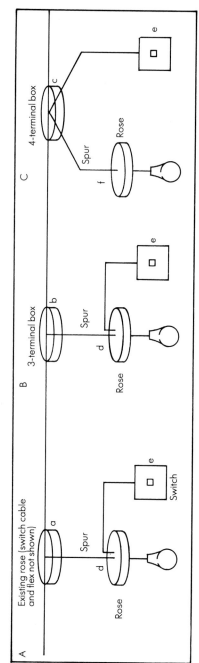

A
Existing rose (switch cable and flex not shown)
Spur
Rose
a
d
Spur
e
Switch

B
3-terminal box
Spur
b
Rose
d
Spur
e

C
4-terminal box
c
Spur
Rose
f
e

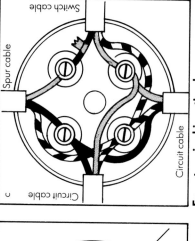

Switch cable
Four-terminal junction box
Spur cable
Circuit cable
Circuit cable
c

Four-terminal junction box
It may be more convenient to cut a four-terminal junction box into the circuit cable, and to run the switch cable from here rather than from the rose.

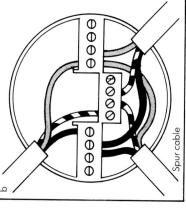

b
Spur cable
Spur cable

Three-terminal junction box
An alternative way to add a spur to an existing circuit is to cut in a 5 amp three-terminal junction box at a convenient point.

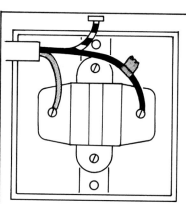

f

New loop-in ceiling rose (2)
If the switch cable for the new light is run from a four-terminal junction box, there will be only the spur cable to connect into the new rose.

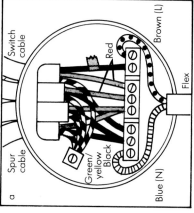

a
Spur cable
Switch cable
Red
Green/yellow
Black
Brown (L)
Flex
Blue (N)

Existing loop-in ceiling rose
A loop-in ceiling rose can be used to connect in a spur cable. A maximum of four cables can be accommodated inside the rose.

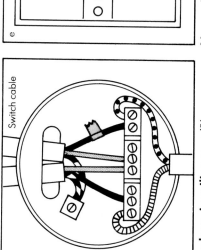

e

New switch
At the switch position, connect one core to the upper terminal, the other to the lower. Take the earth to the terminal on the mounting box.

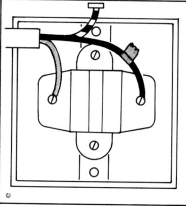

d
Switch cable

New loop-in ceiling rose (1)
If you have taken the spur from a rose or three-terminal box, connect the switch cable into the new rose and add the pendant flex.

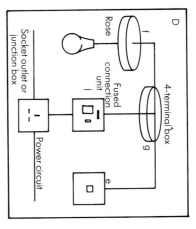

D

Socket outlet or junction box

Rose

f

Fused connection unit

i

4-terminal box

g

Power circuit

e

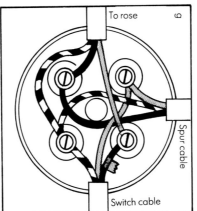

g

To rose

Spur cable

Switch cable

Spur from ring circuit

You can also take a spur from a ring circuit – either from the back of a socket outlet or from a 30 amp three-terminal junction box.

Fused connection unit

Run the spur to a switched fused (5 amp) connection unit, then take the circuit cable on to a four-terminal junction box (g) or loop-in rose.

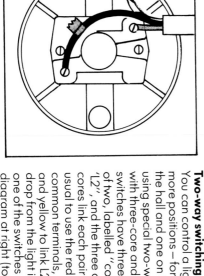

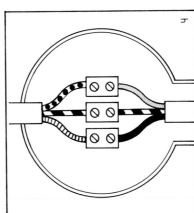

E

Close-fitting light

h

Conduit box

Spur

4-terminal box

c

Cord switch

k

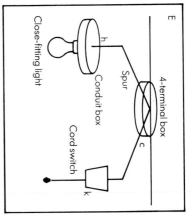

h

Conduit box (1)

If your new light is mounted on a conduit box and is fed from a four-terminal junction box, you need a three-terminal block for the connections.

Ceiling switch

Sometimes you may want a ceiling-mounted switch. As with a wall switch, you should "flag" the black core to show it is live.

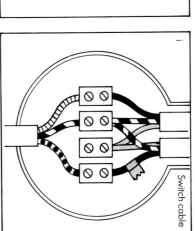

F

Close-fitting light

Conduit box

i

3-terminal box

b

e

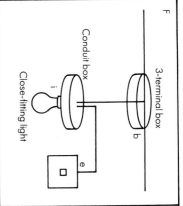

i

Switch cable

Conduit box (2)

If your new light is mounted on a conduit box and is fed from a rose or three-terminal junction box, you need four blocks for the connections.

Two-way switching

You can control a light from two or more positions – for example, one in the hall and one on the landing – by using special two-way switches linked with three-core and earth cable. The switches have three terminals instead of two, labelled "common", "L1" and "L2", and the three colour-coded cable cores link each pair of terminals. It is usual to use the red core to link the common terminals, blue to link L1 to L1 and yellow to link L2 to L2. The switch drop from the light is connected into one of the switches as shown in the diagram at right (top switch).

You can also control the light from a third position if you wish. The circuit is wired up as for two-way switching, but the third switch is an intermediate switch with four terminals, connected up as shown in the diagram.

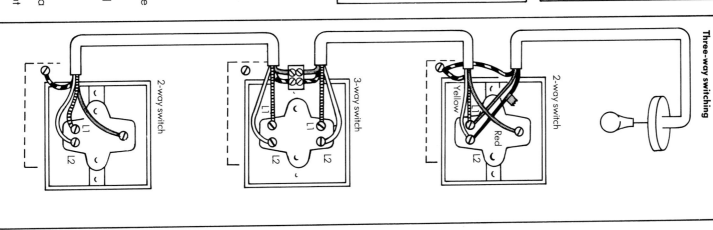

Three-way switching

2-way switch

L1

L2

3-way switch

L1

L2

L1

L2

2-way switch

Yellow

L1

Red

L2

Two-way circuits

As already described (page 179), simple two-way switching of a single light involves adding a new switch linked to the existing one by three-core and earth cable. However, you may want a more complicated switching arrangement – for example, to control a pair of bedside wall lights from beside the bed and at the bedroom door. In this case you will save cable and avoid confusion by using a multi-terminal junction box to make all the connections.

The power supply to the junction box is provided as a spur from the existing lighting circuit via a three-terminal junction box (or a loop-in rose). Cables are then run from the box to each wall light and corresponding bedside switch; these cables are connected up within the main box as shown in the diagram (below). Two further cables are run from the main box to a new two-gang two-way switch by the door to provide complete two-way control of each light from either switch position.

If you already have a light in the room controlled by a switch at the

In order to avoid confusion when wiring up a multi-terminal junction box, label each cable as you run it in – either by writing on the sheathing or by attaching a self-adhesive label to it. Then strip off a generous amount of sheathing to allow you to make the connections within the box, checking as you work that each core is connected up correctly according to the diagram. Mount the box on a plywood or chipboard backing secured on battens nailed to the sides of the ceiling joists.

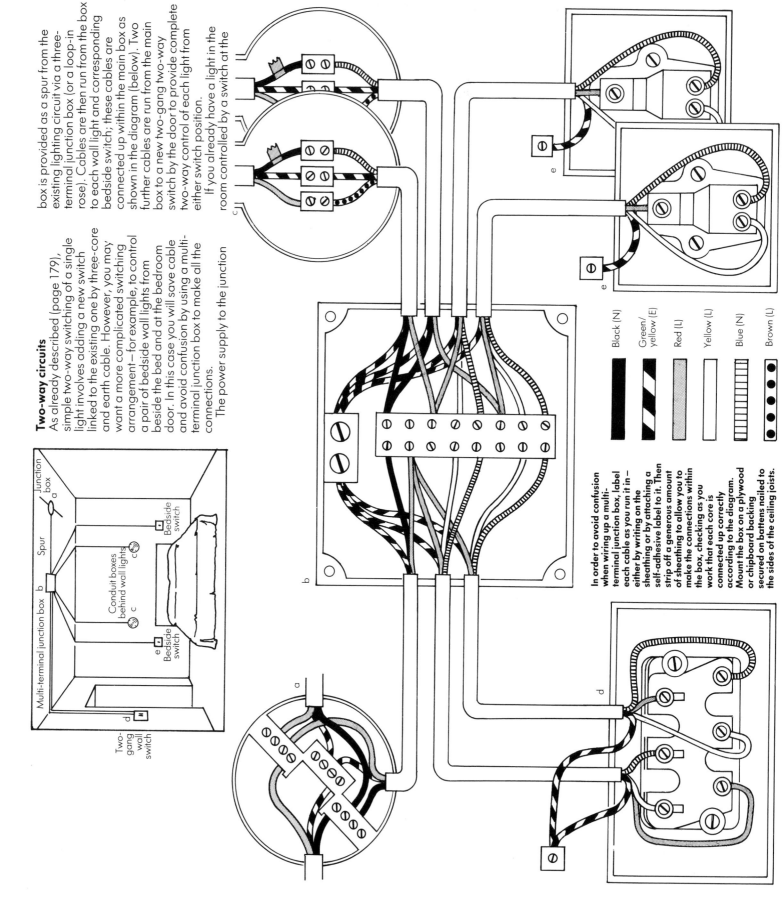

Black (N)

Green/yellow (E)

Red (L)

Yellow (L)

Blue (N)

Brown (L)

Junction box

Spur

Multi-terminal junction box

Conduit boxes behind wall lights

Bedside switch

Bedside switch

Two-gang wall switch

door, fit a three-gang switch at this point and connect the switch cable from the centre light into the third gang of the switch.

Stairwell switching

Two-way switching is particularly useful in a stairwell, so you can turn off the hall light from upstairs or turn on the landing light from the hall. Many homes have partial two-way switching which allows only the landing light to be controlled from both positions; the hall light is switched only in the hall. It is simple to convert this arrangement to full two-way switching.

To do this you need to run in a second three-core and earth cable between the two switch positions. If any conduit was used for the original installation it may be easy to feed the new cable through alongside the existing one. Then the existing two-gang two-way switch is used to connect up the bottom end of the new cable as shown below. On the landing the existing one-gang two-way switch is replaced by a new two-gang two-way switch, and the two three-core and earth cables plus the switch drop cable from the landing light are connected in as shown to complete the installation.

The same wiring arrangements can be used to provide two-way control of any pair of lights from two positions — for example, living room lights with switches at each end of the room.

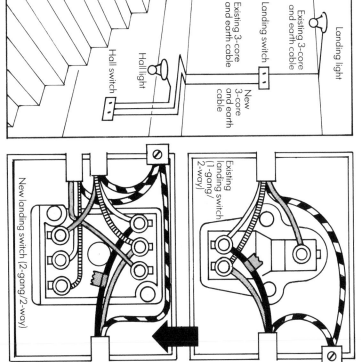

Landing light · Hall light · Hall switch · New 3-core and earth cable · Existing 3-core and earth cable

Stairwell switching — Existing hall switch (2-gang/2-way) · Existing 3-core and earth cable · Landing switch · Existing 3-core and earth cable · New hall switch (2-gang/2-way) · New landing switch (2-gang/2-way) · Existing landing switch (1-gang/2-way)

Exterior lighting

Exterior lighting must be wired up properly if it is to be both safe and permanent. What you have to do depends on the type of lights you want to install and where you want to fit them.

The easiest option of all is to use low-voltage lights, which are usually mounted on a spike or a simple wall bracket for easy installation. These are linked with special multi-strand two-core low-voltage cable which can be run on the surface of walls or simply laid across flower beds; there is no need to bury it underground in conduit. The lights are then connected in series to the cable by laying the cable in position over the terminals within each fitting and pressing it down firmly; spikes pierce the insulation and make the electrical connection.

The power for a low-voltage circuit of this type is provided by a transformer which can simply be plugged into a convenient socket outlet inside the house (or in an outbuilding with a power supply — it must be under cover and protected from the elements).

If you want to use mains-voltage lights, the wiring must be a permanent installation: you are not allowed to have leads snaking about across the garden. Lights mounted on the wall of the house to illuminate a patio, path or drive can be wired up as extensions of the house wiring. Make sure that the fittings and any outdoor switches are weatherproof, and use ordinary PVC-sheathed cable clipped to the wall to make the connections. Where cable passes through the house walls, drill holes that run slightly uphill from the outside so there is no risk of water penetration, and then seal the holes thoroughly with some non-setting mastic.

For lighting remote from the house, you will have to install a separate lighting circuit, supplied from its own 5 amp fuseway — either in your consumer unit, if you have a spare fuseway, or otherwise by means of a separate switchfuse unit installed alongside the existing consumer unit. How the circuit cable is run depends on whether the lights are to be fixed at ground level or on posts or walls. For ground-level lights you should run the cable underground, protected in rigid PVC conduit buried at least 450mm (18in) under the soil surface.

If the lights are to be mounted on posts or walls, you may still wish to run the cable underground. However, it may involve less upheaval to install it above ground. You can fix it to walls with cable clips, but you must never attach it to a fence (which might blow down and rupture the cable). Otherwise, you can run it from post to post down the garden — unsupported, if the span is less than 3.5m (11ft) between posts, or otherwise using a supporting wire. The cable must be at least 3.5m (11ft) above the ground (5.2m/17ft if it crosses a driveway).

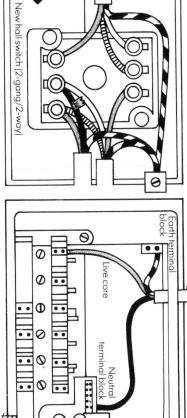

Earth terminal block · Live core · Neutral terminal block · Meter tails

ADDING A NEW CIRCUIT
This diagram shows a new 5 amp exterior lighting circuit wired into a consumer unit. For the sake of simplicity, the wiring for all other circuits is omitted.

Fittings and shades

Cleaning your light fittings should be part of your regular household routine: it keeps the fittings looking good, and if their light output depends on reflection, helps to ensure that they continue to operate efficiently. Cleaning is especially important if there are smokers in the household, as tobacco smoke soon coats shades, fittings and reflectors in a dulling, sticky film. Pendants, bowl-type wall lights and uplighters need regular attention, as they collect fluff and dead insects.

Shades attract dust because of the lamp's heat. To clean a shade it is easiest to remove it from the fitting; switch off the light first. Fabric shades are not usually washable, but you can brush them gently to remove dust. Paper shades should be lightly dusted with a vacuum cleaner attachment or feather duster. Acrylic shades can be washed in warm soapy water. When rubbed dry, they quickly attract dust, but you can cut down the static by giving a final wipe with a cloth damped in detergent and water or by using a special anti-static Perspex polish; the latter should be used sparingly and thinned with water if necessary.

Anyone who cleans a light fitting should be thoroughly aware of the electrical safety aspects. Before removing a fixed light for cleaning, it is essential to isolate the appropriate circuit. Any fitting should be allowed to dry thoroughly before you replace it. Aluminium reflectors can be cleaned with a damp cloth or sponge.

If you use a detergent, rinse this away and dry the surface with a soft cloth. Staining can be tackled beforehand with a metal polish.

For glass surfaces, use commercially available cleaning or polishing products. Avoid oily substances; they will create unwanted rainbow effects.

Flex, plugs and accessories

Any faults to the flex or plug of plug-in fittings should be repaired as soon as they become apparent.

When reconnecting flex to a plug, leave a little slack on the earth core, so that if the flex is pulled slightly the earth core will not become disconnected from its terminal before the live or neutral. Remember, the plug must have a 3-amp fuse.

You can repair damaged flex using a flex connector (see page 174) but it is better to replace the flex entirely. With the fitting unplugged, loosen the lampholder from its mounting and ease the old flex through the body of the fitting until you can lift off the lampholder sufficiently to disconnect the cores from their terminals. If the flex path through the fitting is unobstructed, simply draw it out and thread in the new flex; this, of course, must be of the appropriate type and rating (see page 172). If the flex follows a tortuous path through a tubular channel, twist the cores of the old and new flex tightly together and use the old flex to draw the new one through. Then thread the new flex through any grommets in the fitting and remake the connections at the plug and lampholder. With three-core flex, make sure the earth core is connected to a terminal on the lampholder or the fitting.

It is equally important to replace any electrical wiring accessory – a switch, socket outlet, ceiling rose or lampholder – that has been cracked or broken. You may also want to replace old-fashioned fittings, and you must replace ones that are obviously faulty – a light switch that sparks when operated, or a socket that overheats because its terminals are loose and do not grip the plug pins properly.

As a first step, isolate the circuit you are working on by removing the circuit fuse or switching off the MCB. Then unscrew the accessory from its mounting box or baseplate, lift it away carefully and disconnect the cable cores from their terminals after making a note of which one goes where. Do not untwist any pairs of cables you find. Then reconnect the cores to the terminals on the new accessory and mount this on the original mounting box. It is a good idea to retain the original fixing screws for this: new accessories will have screws with metric threads, and these may not marry up with the lugs on the mounting box. Of course, if the new accessory is a different shape or size to the existing one, you will have to fit a new mounting box as well. If you find rubber-sheathed cable with crumbling insulation, be sure not to fit the new accessory until you have had the wiring checked (and, if necessary, replaced) by a qualified electrician.

Fluorescent tubes

Fluorescent tubes fail gradually rather than suddenly. The first sign of trouble may be flickering, poor starting or an incomplete discharge. The fault may be in the control gear rather than in the tube itself. Use the chart (left) to track down the cause of the trouble.

Employing an electrician

However confident you are of your ability to carry out basic electrical jobs, there will be occasions when you need to call in an electrician. The difficulty is to find one whom you can trust to do the work properly. Sadly, there are many fly-by-night electricians, whose workmanship can be downright dangerous and who can never be traced again if something goes wrong.

Personal recommendation is the best criterion of choice. Failing this, make sure that anyone you contact is a member of the National Inspection Council for Electrical Installation Contracting (NICEIC) or the Electrical Contractors' Association (ECA). Both these bodies insist that their members carry out work in accordance with the Institution of Electrical Engineers' (IEE) Wiring Regulations, and will investigate complaints about members' work. Local Electricity Board showrooms display lists of registered electricians, so finding a local firm should be relatively easy.

It is worth asking at least two electricians to submit a detailed estimate for the job. This should specify exactly what is to be fitted where, and should itemize materials and labour separately. It should show clearly whether VAT is included.

It is important that you are given a satisfactory guarantee. The ECA has a Guarantee of Work scheme; this undertakes to put right faulty work, and also specifies that if a member goes out of business any unfinished work will be completed by another ECA member at the same price.

Designers, consultants and architects

If you want some expert input into your lighting system, and are prepared to pay for the privilege, you should think seriously about calling in a specialist for advice. Consultant lighting designers who will handle domestic installations are still comparatively few and far between, but they are likely to become more common as the demand for their services grows.

A lighting consultant will be able to advise you on the capabilities of particular types of lighting in the context of your own home – much more valuable than advice in the abstract! In addition, he will be able to design a lighting scheme tailored closely to your needs and, if you wish, supervise its installation, ensuring that the work is carried out to a high standard and that it meets the appropriate safety regulations.

Fluorescent tube faults

Fault	Likely causes	Action
Tube fails to light	Faulty connection	Check lampholders
	Blown circuit fuse	Replace fuse
Tube keeps trying to start	Starter not operating	Replace starter
	Old tube	Replace tube
Tube glows only at one end	Faulty connection	Check lampholder at dead end
	Broken tube electrode	Replace tube
Electrodes glow but tube will not start	Starter not operating (white glow)	Replace starter
	Old tube (red glow)	Replace tube
Blackening at tube ends	Old tube	Replace tube
Reduced light output	Old tube	Replace tube

Some people employ a lighting consultant just for the initial concept stage, and then use the consultant's proposals as the basis for carrying out the work themselves. Almost always, this is more economic than attempting the whole job yourself, from design to installation, as the expert will often be able to suggest savings.

In the lighting world, things are moving very quickly, which is another reason for using a specialist designer. He will offer you the benefit of a thorough knowledge of the many different types of fitting available, including some that may not yet be in the catalogues. And he will be able to advise on new developments in lighting technology and on products that are available only from specialist suppliers.

It can be useful to visit specialist showrooms to see the range of fittings on display. Sometimes, these showrooms employ their own lighting advisers. By all means ask their advice, but remember that to some extent they will be biased toward their own products.

When undertaking a wholesale remodelling of your home with the help of an architect or interior designer, bear in mind that not all of them are equally expert in lighting design. Try to choose one who can show you schemes they have worked on – either through photographs or, better still, a site visit. Alternatively, call in a lighting specialist to work with the architect. Many architects have lighting consultants with whom they collaborate regularly.

The first important stage of hiring an architect, interior designer or lighting consultant will be a preliminary discussion about your needs. It is important that you prepare for this meeting properly. Remember to consult the rest of the household – including any teenage children. Make a written note of any special points: it is surprisingly easy to forget the essentials. This is also the time to talk about how much you want to spend. After the initial meeting, the expert will prepare a proposal and an estimate, based on your budget. Make sure that you understand and approve the proposal before you give the go-ahead for the next stage – the detailed lighting plan; and that you understand that before going any further. Mistakes can be very expensive. If you have seen the plans, there is no excuse for a misinterpretation on your part. Do not be afraid to ask questions if there is anything you don't understand, even if you feel you are being difficult.

Lighting designers are usually paid on an hourly basis if their work is purely consultative. However, if they are also responsible for supervising the installation, the basis of payment is a percentage of the total cost of the lighting contract. Never rely on a verbal estimate alone: it is important to have it on paper.

Glossary

The glossary includes terms that are likely to be found in manufacturers' catalogues and other technical literature, as well as words used in the text of this book. SMALL CAPITAL LETTERS indicate cross-references.

Adaptation
Adjustments made by the eye to cope with a change of light levels.

Amp
Abbreviation of ampere, the SI unit of electrical current.

Apostilb
A metric, non-SI unit of LUMINANCE, now obsolete.

Apparent brightness
A subjective impression of how bright an area looks. The technical term for this is LUMINOSITY.

Arc
A luminous discharge of electricity across a gap in an electrical circuit or between two electrodes.

Background lighting
Subdued general lighting, which is usually unobtrusive, unfocussed and indirect.

Baffle
A device attached to a light fitting to prevent GLARE. In spotlights and DOWNLIGHTERS, baffles commonly take the form of concentric black grooves on the inside surface of the cowl; these are known as multigroove baffles, and their purpose is to reduce the apparent brightness of the light source and restrict SPILL LIGHT.

Ballast (choke)
A component used in the CONTROL GEAR of a DISCHARGE LAMP to regulate the current and prevent overheating.

Barndoors
Adjustable, hinged shutters or flaps (usually two or four) attached to the front of a spotlight to control the shape of the beam.

Batten fitting
A fitting with an enclosed channel designed to take a FLUORESCENT LAMP and its CONTROL GEAR.

Batten holder
A CEILING ROSE with an integral lampholder for a tungsten bulb.

Bayonet cap
A standard type of cap with two lugs for attaching a tungsten bulb to its lampholder.

Beam
The spread of direct illumination from a REFLECTOR LAMP, floodlight or spotlight. The edges of the beam are normally designated as points where the light intensity is half that of the beam's centre.

Bi-pin cap
A two-pin lamp cap, characteristic of tungsten-halogen reflector lamps, low-voltage tungsten-halogen lamps and fluorescent tubes.

Blended lamp
A light source consisting of a high-pressure mercury DISCHARGE tube and an INCANDESCENT filament contained within one bulb. The filament acts as a current control so no external CONTROL GEAR is needed. A blended lamp has a much longer life than an ordinary incandescent lamp – as long as 6,000 hours for some types.

Bulb
The lay term for an electric lamp, particularly a TUNGSTEN-FILAMENT LAMP.

Cable
A sheathed bundle of insulated wires used to carry electrical CIRCUITS around the home.

Candela
The SI unit of light intensity.

Ceiling rose
A housing, normally circular, that projects from a ceiling and contains the connection between a PENDANT light fitting and the electrical supply.

Circuit
The complete path of an electric current along the supply cables to light fittings and socket outlets.

Circuit-breaker
A switch in an electrical consumer unit that performs the same function as a fuse: that is, under abnormal or potentially dangerous conditions it cuts off the current flow to the circuit.

Colour appearance
The apparent colour of light emitted by a particular source.

Colour rendering
The effect of a particular light source on the visual appearance of coloured surfaces, usually judged by comparison with daylight. A lamp may be attributed with a colour-rendering index (CRI), which is a number between one and 100; the higher the number, the truer the colours.

Colour temperature
A measure of the relative redness or blueness of a light source, measured in kelvins.

Contrast
In lighting, the difference in brightness, experienced subjectively, between two parts of a VISUAL FIELD seen simultaneously or successively.

Control gear
The means by which the current passing through a FLUORESCENT or other DISCHARGE LAMP is controlled. The control gear may also play a part in the starting of the lamp. It consists essentially of a BALLAST (choke), but may also have a capacitor and STARTER.

Cool beam lamp
A type of PARLAMP with a DICHROIC reflector which reflects visible light but transmits infrared radiation, so that the heat in the beam is greatly reduced.

Dichroic lamp
A lamp incorporating a dichroic reflector: this has a multi-layered coating which transmits some wavelengths and reflects others to produce intensely coloured light.

Diffused lighting
Lighting that is filtered evenly through a translucent material, such as that of a fabric shade.

Diffuser
A translucent screen used to shield a light source and at the same time soften the light output and distribute it evenly.

Dimmer
A controller with a range of adjustments that allows the lighting levels of lamps to be raised or lowered.

Direct lighting
Lighting provided directly from a light fitting, without being reflected off surfaces such as walls or a ceiling.

Directional lighting
Lighting designed to illuminate a task, object or surface predominantly from a particular direction. Directional light fittings (such as spotlights and desk lights) are almost invariably adjustable.

Disability glare
GLARE that impairs our ability to see detail.

Discharge lamp
A lamp whose illumination is produced by an electric discharge through a gas, a metal vapour or a mixture of gases and vapours.

Discomfort glare
GLARE that causes visual discomfort, possibly leading to eyestrain.

Downlighter
A fitting (usually ceiling-mounted or track-mounted) that emits light vertically or steeply downward.

Earth
A connection between an electrical circuit and the earth. Its purpose is to conduct electricity out of harm's way in the event of a fault or malfunction in the wiring – for example, a break in the insulation on a circuit cable, allowing an appliance casing to become live.

Efficacy (luminous efficacy)
The ratio of the light output of a lamp to the electrical power it consumes, measured in LUMENS per watt.

Electronic starter
In some fluorescent lamp circuits, a starter that uses a solid-state component to pre-heat the cathodes.

Electromagnetic radiation
Energy emitted from a source in the form of waves. The electromagnetic spectrum includes gamma rays, X-rays, ultraviolet (UV) radiation, visible light, infrared radiation and radio waves.

Filament
In a light bulb, a thin wire (usually of the metal tungsten) which emits light when heated to incandescence by an electric current. See INCANDESCENT LAMP.

Fitting
The housing for a LAMP and LAMPHOLDER, designed to protect the light source, provide a means of connection to the electricity supply, and often to direct and control the flow of light. The technical term for a fitting is luminaire.

Flex
A flexible cord of insulated wires, used to connect a light FITTING to the power supply.

Floodlamp
A tungsten reflector lamp used in a spotlight fitting to produce a powerful, broad beam.

Fluorescent lamp
A type of DISCHARGE LAMP, in which the light is produced by the excitation of fluorescent phosphors by ultraviolet radiation.

Flux
See LUMINOUS FLUX.

Footcandle
A unit of ILLUMINANCE, equal to one lumen per square foot. Now obsolete in Britain, but still used in the USA.

Foot-lambert
An obsolete unit of LUMINANCE (still used in the USA): the flow of light from a uniform DIFFUSER emitting one lumen per square foot.

Framing projector
(Also known as a profile spot.) A spotlight with attachments that allow accurate control over the shape and focussing of the beam. This is especially useful for picture lighting.

Glare
The discomfort or impairment of vision that results when some parts of the VISUAL FIELD are much brighter than their surroundings. See also DISCOMFORT GLARE and DISABILITY GLARE.

GLS lamp
General Lighting Service lamp: the trade term for the standard TUNGSTEN-FILAMENT LAMP.

Halogen lamp
See TUNGSTEN-HALOGEN LAMP.

HID lamp
A high-intensity DISCHARGE LAMP used for exterior lighting.

Illuminance
The amount of light that falls on a surface, expressed in LUMENS per square metre, or lux.

Incandescent lamp
A light source in which the light is produced by heating a filament to the point of incandescence (that is, the point at which it gives off light) by an electric current.

Indirect lighting
Lighting in which most of the light output is received only after it has been reflected off a ceiling or one or more walls.

ISL lamp
An internally silvered lamp, more commonly known as a REFLECTOR LAMP.

Kelvin
See COLOUR TEMPERATURE.

Lamp
Strictly, an artificial light source – a light bulb or tube. The term is also used colloquially to mean a FITTING, as in "table lamp" or "standard lamp".

Lampholder
A receptacle into which a lamp is connected.

Louver
A metal, plastic or wooden slat, or system of slats, attached to a light fitting. Generally arranged in parallel, they cut off the light source from direct view at certain angles, and thus prevent GLARE.

Lumen (lm)
The SI unit of LUMINOUS FLUX.

Luminaire
The technical term for a light fitting.

Luminance
(Measured brightness.) A measure of the light leaving a surface in a particular direction, measured in CANDELAS per square metre.

Luminosity
See APPARENT BRIGHTNESS.

Luminous flux
The light emitted by a source, or received by a surface. Measured in lumens.

Lux
Lumens per square metre: the SI unit of ILLUMINANCE.

MCB
Miniature Circuit Breaker. See CIRCUIT BREAKER.

Neon lamp
A lamp containing neon (an inert gas) at low pressure, which emits a red or pink glow when voltage is applied.

Opal finish
An interior coating of silica on the glass envelope of a lamp, creating a milky appearance.

PAR lamp
(Parabolic Aluminized Reflector lamp.) A sealed-beam lamp with a front of heat-resistant glass. The back of the lamp is parabolic in cross-section and internally aluminized to reflect and spread a powerful beam of light. PAR lamps can be used without protection outdoors.

Pendant
A light fitting designed to hang or project from a ceiling.

Phosphor
A substance capable of emitting visible light when bombarded with electromagnetic radiation. Used for the inner coating of fluorescent lamps.

Polar curve
A diagram used to show the precise profile of light output from a lamp or fitting.

Quartz-halogen lamp
An alternative term for TUNGSTEN-HALOGEN LAMP, derived from the use of a heat-resistant quartz envelope around the filament.

Quickstart circuit
A type of FLUORESCENT LAMP circuit that dispenses with the STARTER.

Rated life
The number of hours at which fifty percent of incandescent lamps of a given type are expected to fail under standard test conditions.

Reflectance
A measure of how effectively a surface will reflect light – that is, the ratio of lumens reflected off a surface to LUMENS falling on it. Pale surfaces have a higher reflectance than dark ones.

Reflector
A surface of mirrored glass or polished metal, shaped to project the beam from a light source in a particular direction. Reflectors may be an integral part of a LAMP or alternatively they may be part of the FITTING.

Reflector lamp
A lamp with an internally silvered surface, used for spotlighting or floodlighting.

Refraction
The bending of light rays that pass obliquely from one medium into another – for example, from air to glass, or vice versa.

Semi-matt
A term used to describe a surface that

scatters some light (in the manner of a matt surface) but also reflects some directionally.

Shade
A device used on a light FITTING to (a) prevent GLARE by hiding the light source from direct view, (b) control light distribution and sometimes (c) diffuse (and perhaps colour) the light emitted.

SI
Système International d'Unités. An internationally agreed system of scientific measuring units.

Sidelighting
Lighting from one side, often used to emphasize the modelling or texture of an object or surface.

SON lamp
A high-pressure sodium lamp.

Specular reflection
Reflection of light from a mirror-like surface.

Spill light
Light that strays outside the main profile of a BEAM.

Spur
A CABLE used to extend a circuit in order to supply electricity to an additional fitting or to provide for an additional switch.

Starter
A device in the CONTROL GEAR of many FLUORESCENT LAMPS, used in the process of striking an ARC between the electrodes when the lamp is switched on.

Starterless circuit
An alternative to the SWITCH-START CIRCUIT commonly used for fluorescent lamps.

Switch-start circuit
The usual kind of circuit for a fluorescent lamp. It incorporates a starter, a choke and a capacitor.

Task lighting
Localized lighting designed to facilitate a particular activity.

Throw
The distance between a REFLECTOR LAMP and the farthest object it can illuminate.

Transformer
A device that can transfer current from one circuit to another, usually with either a decrease or an increase in voltage. A transformer is an essential component in the installation for any kind of low-voltage lamp.

Trunking
A system of long, box-like enclosures used mainly to conceal wiring and/or to suspend light fittings.

Tungsten-filament lamp
The familiar domestic electric bulb, so-called because it contains a filament of tungsten – a metallic element with an extremely high melting point. The glass envelope enclosing the filament contains a low-pressure inert gas (usually argon) or a vacuum.

Tungsten-halogen lamp
A special type of TUNGSTEN-FILAMENT LAMP, with a gaseous filling containing a halogen – one of a group of chemical elements that combines with tungsten in certain conditions. The halogen has a recycling effect on the evaporation of the tungsten filament, thus extending lamp life. Tungsten-halogen lamps (also known as quartz halogen lamps, or simply halogen lamps) give a brighter light than equivalent-wattage ordinary tungsten bulbs.

Ultraviolet (UV) radiation
A form of ELECTROMAGNETIC RADIATION with a WAVELENGTH shorter than that of visible light.

Uplighter
A light fitting that directs the light upward onto the ceiling or upper walls to illuminate a room by reflection.

Veiling reflections
Glaring, high-luminance reflections off a glossy surface, such as a sheet of glass. Veiling reflections usually impair task performance, because they reduce CONTRAST.

Visual acuity
The ability to distinguish fine detail when concentrating on a task.

Visual field
The area that can be seen in front of us when our head and eyes are at rest.

Voltage
The pressure difference that drives the CURRENT through an electrical circuit.

Watt
The SI unit of power (equal to the one joule per second).

Wavelength
The distance between two identical successive points of an ELECTROMAGNETIC wave.

Working plane
The horizontal, vertical or inclined plane in which a particular visual task is performed.

COMMON LAMP TYPES

The charts below and on page 186 give data for the most common lamps that are suitable for domestic use. Details may vary slightly depending on the manufacturer.

Abbreviations
BC Bayonet cap
ES Edison screw
SBC Small bayonet cap
SES Small Edison screw

TUNGSTEN LAMPS

Watts	Cap	Approx. length (mm)	Diameter (mm)	Initial lumens Single Life	Double Life	Finish
GLS, 1,000 hours or Double Life (2,000 hours), pearl or clear						
25	BC/ES	105	60	230		
40	BC/ES	105–108	60	420	375	
60	BC/ES	105–108	60	710	630	
75	BC/ES	108	60	940		
100	BC/ES	105–108	60	1360	1220	
150	BC/ES	118–128	65–69	2180	1960	
200	BC/ES	160	80	3150		
Mushroom, opal						
40	BC	103.5	60	385		
60	BC	103.5	60	660		
100	BC	103.5	60	1250		
150	BC	124.5	76	2030		
Decor Round						
40	BC/ES	144	97			Opal
Golf Ball						
25	BC/SBC/ES/SES	68.5	46			Opal, clear, crown-silvered, amber, red, green, purple
Plain Candle					Finish	
25	BC/SBC/SES	100–104	36			Pearl, clear
40	BC/SBC/SES	97–104	36			Pearl, clear
60	BC/SBC/SES	97–104/128–133	36/46			Pearl, clear
Twisted candle						
25	BC/SES	100–104	36			Opal, clear
40	BC/SBC	128/133	47			Opal, clear
60	BC/SBC	128–133	47			Opal, clear
Architectural lamps, opal				Initial lumens		
35	S14d Single base	300	30	220		
60	S14d Single base	500	30	420		
120	S14s Double-base	1000	30	840		
35	S14d Single base	300	30	240		
60	S14d Single base	500	30	420		
Tubular (striplight), clear or opal						
30	S15s Double cap	221/284	26			
60	S15s Double cap	221/284	26			
25	Single cap	85	26			
40	BC & SBC Single cap	85	26			

TUNGSTEN REFLECTOR LAMPS

	Watts	Cap	Length (mm)	Diameter (mm)	Finish
	Top-silvered reflector lamps (standard voltage)				
R16/R50	25	SES	86	50	Diffusing front
	40	SES	86	50	Diffusing front
	40	BC/ES	102.5	64	Diffusing front or lacquered blue, green, red, yellow
R20/R64	60	BC/ES	102.5	64	Diffusing front or lacquered blue, green, red, yellow
	40	BC/ES	114.5	80	Diffusing front, or lacquered blue, green, red, yellow
R080/R80	60	BC/ES	114.5	80	Diffusing front
	75	ES	112	80	Diffusing front
	100	ES	112	80	Diffusing front
R095/R95	75	BC/ES	141.5	95	Diffusing front or lacquered blue, green, red, yellow
	100	BC/ES	141.5	95	Diffusing front or lacquered blue, green, red, yellow, amber
R40/R125	150	BC/ES	183.5	125	Diffusing front
	Top-silvered reflector lamps (24 volts)				
	150	ES	183.5	125	Diffusing front
	Crown-silvered, lemon-shaped				
	40	SES	77.5	46	
	Crown-silvered, GLS-shaped				
	60	BC/ES	105	60	
	100	BC/ES/BC 3-7 pin	124.5	68	
	Crown-silvered, round				
	40	BC/ES	144	97	

Reflector lamps (dichroic), single-ended, low-voltage (12 volts)

Watts	Cap	Length (mm)	Diameter (mm)	Light output (lumens)	Beam
20 (M51)	GZ4	35	35	1760	Medium (17°)
20 (M52)	GZ4	35	35	5500	Spot (10°)
20 (M62)	GZ4	35	35	600	Flood (30°)
35 (M65)	GZ4	35	35	9000	Spot (8°)
35 (M66)	GZ4	35	35	3000	Medium (20°)
50 (M49)	GX5,3	44.5	51	10000	Spot (12°)
50 (M50)	GX5,3	44.5	51	4500	Medium (20°)
50 (M58)	GX5,3	44.5	51	1550	Flood (38°)
70 (M60)	GX5,3	44.5	51	16000	Spot (12°)
70 (M61)	GX5,3	44.5	51	2250	Flood (38°)

MINIATURE FLUORESCENTS

	Watts	Initial Lumens	Equivalent tungsten GLS bulb	Dimensions (mm)	Weight (g)
Philips SL (prismatic glass* or opal finish)	9	420*	40w	148mm lgth	430
	13	710*	60w	158mm lgth	460
	18	940*	75w	168mm lgth	560
	25	1360*	100w	178mm lgth	710
Philips PL	5	300	25w	90mm lgth	41
	7	410	40w	112mm lgth	43
	9	570	40w	144mm lgth	45
	11	890	60–75w	213mm lgth	47
Thorn 2D	16	1050	60/100w	140mm sq	65
	28	2050	150w	205mm sq	130
Toshiba Neo Ball	18	580	60w	145mm lgth 110mm dia	420
Wotan Circolux	12	700	60w	165mm dia	210
	18	1000	75w	165mm dia	210
	24	1450	2 × 60w	216mm dia	240
Wotan Dulux S	25	900	75w	165mm lgth	210
	5	250	25w	105mm lgth	10
	7	400	40w	112mm lgth	20
	9	600	60w	144mm lgth	25
	11	900	75w	212mm lgth	40
Wotan Dulux D	10	600	60w	116mm lgth	30
	13	900	75w	146mm lgth	50

FLUORESCENT TUBES/COLOURS

Colour appearance (with colour temperature in Kelvins)	Triphosphors/polyphosphors (krypton or argon), Deluxe high output	Ordinary phosphors (argon), Deluxe
COOL (4000k)	Philips Colour 84* / Thorn Polylux 4000 / Wotan Maxilux White 31 etc.	NATURAL*
INTERMEDIATE (3500k)	Thorn Polylux 3500K etc.	
WARM (3000K–2700K)	Philips Colour 83 / Thorn Polylux 2700 / Wotan Maxilux Warm White 31	Thorn Plus White etc. / WARM WHITE DELUXE

* Proprietary colour names are given in italics. Standard colour descriptions are in capital letters.

FLUORESCENT TUBES/LENGTHS AND RATINGS

Length	Watts (Krypton)	Watts (Argon)
2400mm/8ft	100	125
1800mm/6ft	70	78/85
1500mm/5ft	58	65/80
1200mm/4ft	36	40
600mm/2ft	18	20

CIRCULAR AND U-SHAPED FLUORESCENTS

	Watts	Diameter (mm)	Length (mm)
Circular	22	210	
	32	305	
	40	410	
	60	410	
U-shaped	40		525/570
	65		570/765

PAR LAMPS

	Watts	Cap	Length (mm)	Diameter (mm)	Finish	Light output (lumens)
PAR 38 spot	75	ES	138	123	Clear front	1350
	100	ES	138	123	Clear front	2100
	150	ES	138	123	Clear front or lacquered blue, green, red, yellow	
PAR 38 Cool Beam Spot	150	ES	138	123	Clear front	
PAR 38 flood	75	ES	138	125	Clear front or lacquered blue, green, red, yellow	
	100	ES	138	123	Clear front or lacquered blue, green, red, yellow	
	150	ES	138	123	Clear front	
Low-voltage (24 or 110 volts) PAR 38 Spot	150	ES	138	123	Clear front	
PAR 56 (wide, narrow or medium beam)	300	2-lug	133.4	178.6	Clear front	

TUNGSTEN-HALOGEN LAMPS

	Watts	Cap	Length (mm)	Diameter (mm)	Light output (lumens)	Life
Tubular (standard voltage), 4,000 hours	100 (K16)	E27	105–110	28–31	1350	
	150 (K13)	E27	105–110	28–31	2100	
Linear	100 (K14)	R7s	78	78	1350	
	150 (K12)	R7s	78	78	2100	
	200 (K11)	R7s	118	118	3100	
	250 (K15)	R7s	78	78	4000	
	300 (K9)	R7s	118	118	5000	
	500 (K1)	R7s	118	118	2900	
Miniature low-voltage, single-ended						
6 volts	20 (M34)	G4	30	8.5	350	2,000 hours
12 volts	20 (M47)	G4	30	8.5	350	3,000 hours
	50 (M32)	GY6,35	44	11.5	850	3,000 hours
	100 (M28)	GY6,35	44	11.5	2400	2,000 hours
24 volts	250 (M36)	GY6,35	58	15	5750	2,000 hours

LAMP MANUFACTURERS AND DISTRIBUTORS

GTE Sylvania Ltd
Otley Rd
Charlestown, Shipley
W. Yorks
Tel: (0274) 595921

Lampways Ltd
Allenby House
Knowles Lane
Wakefield Rd
Bradford BD4 9AB
Tel: (0274) 686666

Mazda
29 rue de Lisbonne
75008 Paris
Tel: (1) 561 97 44
UK Office:
Thorn-EMI
(see below)

Moorlite Electrical Ltd
Burlington St
Ashton-under-Lyne
Lancashire OL7 0AX
Tel: (061) 330 6811

Osram-GEC
P.O. Box 17
East Lane, Wembley
London HA9 7PG
Tel: (01) 904 4321

Philips Lighting
P.O. Box 298
City House, London Rd
Croydon CR9 3QR
Tel: (01) 689 2166

Simplex Lighting Ltd
Groveland Rd, Tipton
West Midlands DY47XB
Tel: (021) 557 2828

Thorn-EMI Lighting Ltd
Victoria Trading Estate
Victoria Way, Charlton
London SE7 7PA
Tel: (01) 858 3281

Woton Lamps Ltd
Woton House
1 Gresham Way
Durnsford Rd
London SW19 8HO
Tel: (01) 947 1261

MANUFACTURERS OF FITTINGS

DENMARK

Abo-randers
Assentoft
8900 Randers
Tel: (45) 6 49 50 11

EIRE

Waterford Crystal Lighting Ltd
Butlerstown, Waterford
Tel: (Waterford) 73311

FINLAND

Lival
Pl 31
04131 Nikkilä
Tel: (90) 232 122

FRANCE

Academy
5 place de l'Odéon
75006 Paris
Tel: (1) 329 07 18

Bernard Carant Selection
41 Bd des Batignolles
75008 Paris
Tel: (1) 522 43 14

Disderot (Luminaires Pierre S.A.)
12 bis rue de Docteur-Roux
94600 Choisy le Roi
Tel: (1) 680 37 00

Ecart International
6 Rue Pavée
75004 Paris
Tel: (1) 272 47 77
UK distributor:
Crier, Cameron and Sons
Fourth Floor
13 Chelsea Wharf, Lots Rd
London SW10
Tel: (01) 351 6994

Gau (Lucien)
2 rue de la Roquette
75011 Paris
Tel: (1) 307 62 11

Holight
64680 Ogeu les Bains
Tel: (59) 39 32 11

Huit
26–28 rue des Clercs
57000 Metz
Tel: (8) 736 17 35

Lampes Drimmer
Z.I. B.P.8
12004 Rodez Cedex
Tel: (65) 67 00 21
UK distributor:
Drimmer UK Ltd
15A Manor Road
Caddington
Luton
Beds
Tel: (0582) 364 22

Le Dauphin (S.A.)
8 avenue de Romans
38160 Saint Marcellin
Tel: (76) 38 20 44

Lumen Center
18 rue de Verdun
13580 La Fare les Oliviers
Tel: (90) 42 53 69

Lumi Light
B.P. 9 Tavers
45190 Beaugency
Tel: (38) 44 82 95

Luminance
4 rue Sadi-Carnot
93170 Bagnolet
Tel: (1) 364 34 44

Megalit
B.P. 55
Z.I. du Breuil
18400 St Florent sur Cher
Tel: (48) 55 67 30

PRC
Division éclairage de Sorelia
51–53 rue Edouard-Vaillant
92704 Colombes Cedex
Tel: (1) 242 29 03

Philips
50 avenue Montaigne
75380 Paris
Tel: (1) 256 88 00
UK distributor:
Victor Mann & Co Ltd
85 Streatham Road
Mitcham
Surrey CR4 2AP
Tel: (01) 640 0107

Sedap S.A.
1 rue de Château
B.P. 166
44006 Nantes
Tel: (40) 47 19 04

Sélection Internationale
9 rue Edouard-Vaillant
93100 Montreuil
Tel: (1) 858 26 28

Sodium
147 bis rue d'Aguesseau
92100 Boulogne Billancourt
Tel: (1) 603 44 61

Swissex Music
90 rue Laharpe
33110 Le Bouscat
Tel: (56) 08 06 61

Verre Lumière
11 quai de Dion-Bouton
92800 Puteaux
Tel: (1) 772 00 63

ITALY

Arteluce
via Angelo Faini 2
25073 Bovezzo
Brescia
Tel: (030) 271 21 61
UK distributor:
Candell Lighting
Riverside Works
Broadmead Road
Woodford Green
Essex IG8 8PG
Tel: (01) 504 9501

Artemide (S.P.A.)
via Brughiera
20010 Pregnana Milanese
Tel: (02) 939 13 01
UK distributor:
Artemide
17 Neal St
London WC1
Tel: (01) 240 2346

Bianchi (S.R.L.)
via Salomone 41
20138 Milano
Tel: (02) 506 44 51

C.I.L.
via Prospero Santacroce 128
00167 Roma
Tel: (06) 623 16 22
UK distributor:
Victor Mann & Co Ltd
85 Streatham Road
Mitcham
Surrey CR4 2AP
Tel: (01) 640 0107

Controluce
Division Bruschi S.P.A.
via di Vacciano
50015 Grassina (FI)
Tel: (055) 64 14 94

Eleusi
via Verdi 7
22050 Lomagna
Como
Tel: (039) 54 20 16

Flos spa
via Moretto 58
25121 Brescia
Tel: (030) 280 281
UK distributor:
Flos Ltd
Heath Hall
Heath Rd
Wakefield WF1 5SL
Tel: (0924) 366446

i Guzzini Illuminazione spa
S.S. 77 Km
102.62019 Recanati
P.O. Box 39-59
Tel: (071) 980 582
UK distributor:
Victor Mann & Co Ltd
85 Streatham Road
Mitcham
Surrey CR4 2AP
Tel: (01) 640 0107

Leucos
via Treviso 63
30037 Scorze
Tel: 540 72 45

Luce Plan
via Bellinzona 48
20155 Milano
Tel: (02) 322 72 49

Luci
via Pelizza da Volpedo 50
Cinisello (MI)
Tel: (02) 612 66 51
UK distributor:
Candell Lighting
Riverside Works
Broadmead Road
Woodford Green
Essex IG8 8PG
Tel: (01) 504 9501

Martinelli Luce
via T Bandettini 145
55100 Lucca
Tel: (0583) 5883/5
UK distributor:
Atrium
113 St Peter's Street
St Albans
Hertfordshire AL1 3ET
Tel: (0727) 37356

Nuova Lamperti
via Milano 61
40026 Imola
Tel: (0542) 31665

Piuluce
via Bardella 8
36100 Vicenza
Tel: (444) 510 221

Sirrah
Via Molino Rosso 8
40026 Imola
Tel: (0542) 31665

Skipper
via Santo Spirito 14
20121 Milano
Tel: (02) 705 691

Stilnovo
via Borromini 12
20020 Lainate
Tel: (02) 93 74 471

Troncani (Enrico)
viale Cassala nr.55
20143 Milano
Tel: (02) 832 2097

Ve Ar Luce
via Moglianese 23
30037 Venezie-Scorze
Tel: (041) 445204

SPAIN

Metalarte
avenida de Barcelona 4
E, San Juan Despi
Barcelona
Tel: (93) 373 23 51

SWITZERLAND

Lumess (AG)
55 Baselstrasse
CH-4124 Schoenenbuch
Tel: (061) 63 00 66

Optelma Licht AG
Buemstrasse 91
CH-4500 Solothurn
Tel: (065) 22 59 52

UNITED KINGDOM

Allom Lighting Ltd
231/233 Winchester Road
Southampton SO9 1FW
Tel: (0703) 772471

Alumex Lighting
1–5 Tannoch Drive
West Lenziemill Industrial Estate
Cumbernauld G67 2SX
Tel: (02367) 22233

Anglepoise Lighting
Unit 51
Enfield Industrial Estate
Redditch B97 6DR
Tel: (0527) 63771

Associated Lighting Ltd
Gelderd Road
Leeds LS12 6NB
Tel: (0532) 632421

Beta Lighting Ltd
383–387 Leeds Road
Bradford BD3 9LZ
Tel: (0274) 721129

Best & Lloyd Ltd
William St West
Smethwick, Warley
Worcestershire B66 2NX
Tel: (021) 558 1191

Britannia Lighting Ltd
Luminaire House
York Street
Coventry CV1 3NB
Tel: (0203) 24992

British Electric Lamps Ltd
Spencer Hill Road
Wimbledon
London SW19 4EL
Tel: (01) 946 5035

C.A. Lighting Ltd
74–7 Magdalen Road
Oxford OX4 1RE
Tel: (0865) 243188

C.B. Lighting Co
8 Victoria Street
Bristol BS1 6BN
Tel: (0272) 22361

Chalham Lighting Ltd
Cross Lane Mills
St Horton
Bradford BD7 3JT
Tel: (0274) 501511

Concord Lighting Ltd
(showroom, literature, design service, after sales)
Concord House
241 City Road,
London EC1V 1JD
Tel: (01) 253 1200

Designplan Lighting Ltd
18 Grove Road
Sutton
Surrey SM1 1BW
Tel: (01) 643 2231

Emess Lighting (UK) Ltd
6 Anderson Road
Roding Lane South
Woodford Green
Essex IG8 8ET
Tel: (01) 551 4156

Erco Lighting Ltd
38 Dover Street
London W1X 3RB
Tel: (01) 408 0320

Exem (Lighting) Ltd
Cropmead Estate
Blacknell Lane
Crewkerne
Somerset TA18 7HG
Tel: (0460) 72024

Flexible Lamps Ltd
Rubbolite House
Centre Drive
Epping
Essex CM16 4JJ
Tel: (0378) 76181

Franklite Ltd
1 Bridgeturn Ave
Old Wolverton Road
Wolverton
Milton Keynes MK12 5QL
Tel: (0908) 316919

Hitech (UK Ltd)
Tower House
Lea Valley Trading Estate
Edmonton
London N18 3HQ
Tel: (01) 884 3333

Illuma Designs Ltd
Breakspear House
Bury Street
Ruislip HA4 7FB
Tel: (71) 37177

Light Ideas Ltd
Peartree Trading Estate
Upper Langford
Bristol
Avon BS18 7DW
Tel: (0934) 852929

Linolite Ltd
Malmesbury
Wiltshire SN16 0BN
Tel: (066) 62 2001

Lotus Water Gardens
260–300 Berkhamsted Rd

Chesham
Bucks HP5 3EY
Tel: (0494) 774451

Luxram Electric Ltd
9 Vine Lane
London SE1 2JQ
Tel: (01) 403 0590

M & P Fluorescent Fittings Ltd
Bridge Road Trading Estate
Haywards Heath
Sussex RH16 1UA
Tel: (0444) 412668

Marlin Lighting Ltd
Hanworth Trading Estate
Hampton Road West
Feltham
Middlesex TW13 6DR
Tel: (01) 894 5522

Millet Lighting Ltd
197 Baker Street
London NW1
Tel: (01) 935 7851

Moorlite Electrical Ltd
Burlington Street
Ashton-under-Lyne
Lancs OL7 0AX
Tel: (061) 330 6811

Paper Lantern Mfg Co Ltd
Peterjohn House
8-10 Trading Estate
off Park Royal Road
London NW10 7LX
Tel: (01) 961 2828

Philips Lighting
Lighting Division
P O Box 298, City House
London Road
Croydon CR9 3QR
Tel: (01) 689 2166

Prima Lighting
151 Deans Lane
Edgware
Middx HA8 9NY
Tel: (01) 959 0277

R J Chelsom & Co
Squires Gate Industrial Estate
Blackpool
Lancs FY4 3RN
Tel: (0253) 46324

Rotaflex Homelighting
Malmesbury
Wiltshire SN16 0BN
Tel: (066) 62 2001

Shiu Kay Kan
90 Belsize Lane
London NW3 5BE
Tel: (01) 431 0451

Simplex Lighting Ltd
Groveland Road
Tipton
West Midlands D74 7XB
Tel: (021) 557 2828

Stella Lamp Co Ltd
33-34 High Street
South Norwood
London SE25 6HF
Tel: (01) 771 3011

Thorn-EMI Lighting Ltd
Victoria Trading Estate
Victoria Way, Charlton
London SE7 7PA
Tel: (01) 858 3281

USA

Boyd Lighting Co
56 Twelfth Street
San Francisco
CA 94103
Tel: (415) 431 4300

George Kovacs Lighting Inc
24 West 40th Street
New York
NY 10018
Tel: (212) 683 5744

Koch & Lowy
21-24 39th Avenue
Long Island City
NY 11101
Tel: (212) 786 3520

WEST GERMANY

BEGA Gantenbrink-Leuchten OHG (Exterior Lights)
D-5750 Menden
Tel: (023 78) 811
UK distributor:
Concord Lighting Ltd
Concord House
241 City Road
London EC1V 1JD
Tel: (01) 253 1200

Brillantleuchten AG
Postfach 1109
2742 Gnarrenburg
Tel: (047 63) 890

Johann u Th Baulmann GmbH & Co
Werkstatten für Lichtgestaltung
D-5768 Sundern/Sauerland
P O Box 1149
Tel: (029 33) 3071

Erco Leuchten GmbH
Brockhauserweg 80-82
Postfach 2460
5880 Lüdenscheid
Tel: (023 51) 5511
UK distributor:
Erco Lighting Ltd
38 Dover Street
London W1X 3RB
Tel: (01) 408 0320

Staff GmbH & Co KG
Grevenmarsch 74-78
P O Box 760
4920 Lemgo
Tel: (052 61) 2121

RETAILERS OF LIGHT FITTINGS

The addresses below are of specialist lighting shops. A varied selection of fittings can be found in most major department stores and chain stores such as Habitat, most branches of British Home Stores and W.H. Smith's Bright Ideas.

BIRMINGHAM

Christopher Wray's Lighting Emporium
Bartholomew Row
Birmingham 5
Tel: (021) 233 3364

Lightolier Ltd
28-30 Bristol Street
Birmingham 5
Tel: (021) 622 4932/4096

West Midland Lighting Centre
10-12 York Road
Erdington
Birmingham B23 6TE
Tel: (021) 350 1999

BRISTOL

Bristol Lighting & Design
429 Wells Road
Bristol
Tel: (0272) 777 205

Uppingtons Exciting Lighting
113 Hotwell Road
Bristol
Tel: (0272) 25410

CARDIFF

City Lights
9 Royal Buildings
Penarth
Cardiff CF6 2ED
Tel: (0222) 707358

GLASGOW

Broadway
96 Gattowgate
Glasgow
Tel: (041) 552 7072

Nova Lighting
71 Candleriggs
Glasgow
Tel: (041) 552 7324

Pagazzi Interior Lighting
106 West George Street
Glasgow G2 1PS
Tel: (041) 333 0882

LIVERPOOL

Universal Lighting Services Ltd
Priory Street
Birkenhead
Tel: (051) 647 9472

LONDON

Artemide
17 Neal St
London WC1
Tel: (01) 240 2346

Christopher Wray's Lighting Emporium
600 Kings Road
London SW6
Tel: (01) 737 8434

E & F Lighting Co
656 Fulham Road
London SW6
Tel: (01) 736 2988

Equinox
64-72 New Oxford Street
London WC1
Tel: (01) 636 2345

Extralite Designs Ltd
26 Northways Parade
College Crescent
London NW3
Tel: (01) 722 7480

John Cullen Lighting Design
1 Woodfall Court
Smith St London SW3
Tel: (01) 730 8585

Lighting Design Service
205 Kentish Town Road
London NW5
Tel: (01) 267 9391

The Lighting Workshop
35-6 Floral Street
London WC2
Tel: (01) 241 0461

London Lighting Co. Ltd
135 Fulham Road
London SW3
Tel: (01) 589 3612

Marcatré
179 Shaftesbury Ave
London WC2
Tel: (01) 379 6865

Mr Light
307 Brompton Road
London SW3
Tel: (01) 581 3470

New Lites
7 Village Way E.
Rayners Lane
Harrow
London

MANCHESTER

Exchange Electrical Lighting Ltd
87 Gt Ancoats Street
Manchester 4
Tel: (061) 228 3071
48-52 Cheetham Hill Road
Manchester 4
Tel: (061) 834 4259

J.H. Miller & Son
Excelsior Works
Hulme Hall Road
Manchester 15
Tel: (061) 834 7569

NEWCASTLE

Electromode
1 Old Eldon Square
Newcastle 1
Tel: (0632) 321326

New Lighting Centre
62 Scotswood Road
Newcastle
Tel: (0632) 610141

LIGHTING CONSULTANTS

Designed Lighting
Goodge House
129 Station Road
Hayes
London
Tel: (01) 561 1193

Elegant Interiors
804 Wilmslow Road
Manchester 20
Tel: (061) 434 5268

Into Lighting
49 The High Street
Wimbledon Village
London SW19
Tel: (01) 946 8533

John Cullen Lighting Design
Albert Bridge House
Albert Bridge Road
London SW11
Tel: (01) 228 1212

Lighting Artists Ltd
Hillview
Vale of Health
London NW3
Tel: (01) 794 3948

Lighting Design Partnership
5 Northumberland Street
North West Lane
Edinburgh EH3 6JL
Tel: (031) 557 2244

The Lighting Workshop
35-36 Floral Street
London WC2
Tel: (01) 240 0461

Peter Burian Assoc.
Hillview, Vale of Health
London NW3
Tel: (01) 431 2345

OTHER USEFUL ADDRESSES

Chartered Institution of Building Services (Illuminating Engineering Society)
Delta House
222 Balham High Road
London SW12 9BS
Tel: (01) 675 5211

Consumers Association
14 Buckingham Street
London WC2
Tel: (01) 839 1222
In its monthly magazine *Which?*, the Association publishes reports on a wide range of goods including lamps and light fittings.

Decorative Lighting Association
Bryn House
Bryn, Bishop's Castle
Shropshire SY9 5LE
Tel: (059) 84658
Publications division
38 Charlotte St
London W1P 1HP
Tel: (01) 637 9792

The Design Council
28 Haymarket
London W1
Tel: (01) 839 8000
The Centre has changing exhibitions of electrical products, including light fittings, and an excellent bookshop.

The Electrical Contractors' Association
ESCA House
34 Palace Gate
London WC2 4H
Tel: (01) 229 1266

The Electrical Contractors' Association of Scotland
23 Heriot Row
Edinburgh EH3 6EW
Tel: (031) 225 7221

The Electricity Council
30 Millbank
London SW1P 4RD
Tel: (01) 834 2333

Institution of Electrical Engineers
Savoy Place
London WC2R 0B1
Tel: (01) 240 1871

The Lighting Industry Federation
Swan House
207 Balham High Road
London SW17 7BQ
Tel: (01) 675 5432
The LIF publishes a number of interesting booklets in their "Factfinder" series eg Lamp Guide (Factfinder 3)

National Inspection Council for Electrical Installation Contracting (NICEIC)
237 Kennington Lane
London SE11 5QJ
Tel: (01) 582 7746
The NICEIC will investigate complaints about defective electrical installations.

The Scottish Design Council
22 St Vincent Street
Glasgow
Scotland
Tel: (041) 221 6121

The Lighting Book cannot claim personal knowledge of all the companies and addresses given above. All information is correct at the time of going to press, but the editors cannot guarantee its continuing accuracy.

BIBLIOGRAPHY

Geoffrey Burdett, *Manual of Home Electrics*, David and Charles, Newton Abbot (Devon), 1984.

M.A. Cayless and A.M. Marsden (eds), *Lamps and Lighting*, Edward Arnold, London, 1983 (3rd edn).

CIBS Code for Interior Lighting, Chartered Institute of Building Services, London, 1984.

Jane Grosslight, *Light*, Prentice-hall, Inc., Englewood Cliffs (New Jersey), 1984.

J.B Harris, *Home Lighting*, David and Charles, Newton Abbot (Devon), 1984.

Stanley L. Lyons, *Domestic Lighting* (Question and Answer series), Newnes Technical Books, London, 1981.

Derek Phillips, *Planning Your Lighting*, Design Council, London, 1976.

Page numbers in **bold** refer to main entries. Page numbers in *italics* refer to illustrations.

A

"Abat-Jour" (Tronconi) 83
"Adonis" (Luci) 92
"Aerial" (One-Off) 94
"Aeroplane" (Sunset Ceramics) 94
Age, lighting and 103
"Ala" (Luci) 75
"Alola" (Skipper) 59
Alcove lighting 54, 79, 114, 128, 158
"Alesia" (Artemide) 63
"Alfiere" (Stilnovo) 85
"Alice" (Controluce) 44
"Alistro Morsetto" (Artemide) 82
Anglepoise 76, 82, 67, 77, 80
"Aquilone" (Eleusi) 62
Arad, Ron 94
Architects 124
  employing 182
"Arco" (Flos) 43
"Arcobalena" (Cil) 43
"Area" (Artemide) 63
Armstrong, Lord 22
Arnaldi 65, 72, 80, 81
Aroldi, D. and C. 81
Arteluce
  floor lights 93, 148
  pendants 63
  table lights 95
  wall lights 74
Asahara Sigheaki 93
"Aster" (Luci) 67
Asti, Sergio 92, 93, 95
Aulenti, Gae 65, 75

B

Background lighting 86, 104–105, 142
  from uplighters 86
Baffles 39, 48, 39
  on exterior lights 96
  on spotlights 54, 137
Barbieri, Raul 63, 84, 90, 91, 93
Barndoors 96, 112
Bathrooms 71, 138–41, 50, 51, 70, 138–41, 138, 170
  safety regulations 54,
Baulmann 44
Bayonet cap 24, 29
Bedrooms 30, 148–153, 93
Bedside lights 68, 105, 119, 124
  wiring for 180
Bega 164
Bellini, Mario 63
Beretta, R. 75
Best and Lloyd 81
"Bestlite" 81
"Bianca" (Tronconi) 44
"Bikini" (Tronconi) 47
"Bikoni" (Tronconi) 47
Bilumen
  pendants 43
  table lights 43
  task lights 80
"Bizzy" (Cil) 45
Blown-glass reflector lamps 30, 30
Boeri, Cini 83
Bofill, Ricardo 83
Bollard lights 97, 98
"Bollo" (Flos) 68, 73
"Bonbon" (Brillantleuchten) 94
Bonucci and Massacesi 95
Boyd Lighting Co.
  floor lights 86, 90
  wall lights 72, 73, 75
Brillantleuchten 46, 161
  exterior lights 96, 97, 98, 99
  floor lights 91, 93
  pendants 62, 64
  spotlights 44, 57, 84, 124
  table lights 84
  task lights 81
  wall lights 68, 72, 73, 94, 95
Brousse, B. 82
"Bugis" (i Guzzini) 84
Bulbs
  early manufacture of 24, 25
  types 28–33
Bulkhead lights 140, 68, 70
  exterior 96, 96
"Bullet Major" (Concord) 57
Bullet spotlights 55, 57, 152
Burian, Peter 166
"By the sea" (Koch and Lowy) 72

C

Cable 170, 172
  for exterior use 181
  for extending circuits 178, 178, 179
"Cabriolet" (Stilnovo) 74
"Calder" (Boyd) 82
"Callimaco" (Artemide) 93
"Campana" (Stilnovo) 62
Candle-type bulbs 58, 28, 30
Candlelight 12, 147
  in dining rooms 154–5, 154, 155, 156, 158, 159
  in history of lighting 22, 22
Carpani, D.S. 90
"Carrara" (Luci) 68
Carwardine, George 76
Cassia, A. Macchi 75
Castiglioni, Achille 46, 59, 43, 54, 58, 62, 85, 86, 93
Castiglioni, Livio 65
Castiglioni, Pier 75, 85, 86, 87
Ceiling roses 171, 176
Ceilings
  colour of 50, 148
  luminous 66, 134
  sloping 108
"Centro" (Ve Art Luce) 41
Ceramics, lighting 115
Chandeliers 11, 39, 59, 68, 106, 154, 62
Chelsom
  chandeliers 62
  exterior lights 99
  wall lights 68, 72
Childproof lights 160, 161
Children's rooms 106, 160–61, 124, 160, 161
Cibic Aldo 83
"Ciclope" (Tronconi) 93
Cil
  floor lights 43, 46
  pendants 45
"Circe" (Controluce) 41
Circolux (Wotan) 35
Circuit breakers 170
Circuits 170, 171
  extending 178
  exterior lights 178
Cleaning light fittings 157, 182
"Click" (Brillantleuchten) 57
"Cobra" (Martinelli Luce) 83
Collectibles, lighting 66, 112–13, 112, 113
Colour
  perception of 10–11
  walls and ceiling 14–15, 104, 120
  colour appearance 12, 28, 12
  colour rendering 12, 28, 14–15, 15
  picture lighting 112
  colour temperature 12–13, 29
Coloured bulbs 29
"Commercial Strip" (Eleusi) 92
"Composta" (Bilumen) 43
Concealed lighting 66, 104–105, 67, 104, 105, 145
  in bedrooms 150
  in dining rooms 158
  exterior lights 98
  in kitchens 134, 133, 134, 135
Concord 46
  downlighters 48, 49
  floodlights 55, 57
  floor lights 91
  spotlights 56, 57
"Condor" (Brillantleuchten)
Conduit (BESA) box 173, 179, 173
Cone shapes, in fittings 41
Contrast 88
  avoidance of 15, 16, 112, 128
Control gear **34**, 66
  reading and 103
Controluce
  pendants 41, 44, 59
  table lights 41
"Conus" (Orit Militscher) 75
Cool beam PAR lamps 117
Coolidge, William 24
Cord-pull switches 138
Cornice lighting 104, 108, 109
Coronelli, M. 74
Corridors 130, 50, 51, 128, 129, 130
Counterweights, in light fittings 42
"Crisol" (Arteluce) 64–5
Crown-silvered bulbs 30, 106, 30
"C.S." (Eleusi) 92
Cullen Lighting Design Inc., John 91
"Curve" (Bilumen) 43
Curved fittings 43

D

"Dardo" (Luci) 57
"Darklighter" (Concord) 48, 49
Davy, Humphry 22
Daylight
  changeability of 10
  colour temperature 13
  compared with artificial light 12
  illuminance of 16
  making allowances for in kitchens 132, 15, 120
De Pas, D'Urbino and Lomazzi 63, 85, 86, 92
"Deco Disc" (Boyd) 73
Decorative lighting 17, **106–107**, 106, 107
  in bedrooms 148, 149
"Delta" (Koch and Lowy)
Designers 47
Desk lights **76–82**, 102, 124, 150, 76–82, 94, 106, 162–3
Dichroic reflectors 56, 63, 76
Didone, Ezio 64
Diffused lighting 38, 39, 104, 38, 39, 104
Diffusers 38, 39, 44
  cone-shaped 41
  disc-shaped 41
Dimmers 47, **146**
  in children's rooms 160
  in dining rooms 154, 157
  in fluorescent fittings 56
  in uplighters 87
Dining areas **154–9**, 51, 135, 154–9
  with wall lights 71
"Dinos" (Megalit) 67, 156, 157, 156, 157
Direct lighting **39**, 39
Discharge lamps 25, 35
"Disco" (Brillantleuchten) 44
"Disco" (Stilnovo) 45
Discs, in light fittings 41
Display lighting **19**, **112–13**, 121, 13, 121
  with fluorescent lights 66
  with track-mounted spotlights 54
"Dogale" (Oluce) 81
"Donald" (Arteluce) 81
Double Life bulbs 29
Downlighters, ceiling-mounted **48–51**, 162, 48–51
  in bathrooms 51, 138, 139
  beam profiles 108, 121
  in bedrooms 148, 150, 153
  in dining rooms 155, 157
  exterior 97, 96
  installation 48, 173, 177
  in kitchens 21, 102
  in libraries and studies 163
  for picture lighting 112, 113
  pinhole 139, 48, 49
  track-mounted 108, 128
  wall-mounted 68
  wall washing 50, 108, 109
"Drachen"
"Dragonfly" (Tag) 74
Drimmer
  floor lights 42
  table lights 42
Du Pasquier, Nathalie 95

E

Earthing 170, 177
Edison, Thomas Alva **23–4**, 29, 23
Edison screw cap 24, 29
"Ediswan" 24
Electricians 182
Electricity
  household supply 170
  safety aspects 138, 171
Eleusi
  fluorescent fittings 67
  pendants 62
  table lights 67, 95
  wall lights 44, 84, 95
"Elle" (Stilnovo) 43, 75
Elysée Palace 90
Entrances **128–130**, 128–131
Exterior lights **96–7**, **164–7**, 7, 69, 96–7, 164–7
  psychological aspects 20
  wiring 181
Eyeball downlighters 48, 48, 49, 50, 51, 142
"Eyeball Major" (Concord) 48
Eyes, light and the **16–17**

F

Fabric in fittings 46
"Faccia" (Flos) 149
"Fante" (Stilnovo) 45, 76
Filaments 29, 29
  in early light bulbs 23–24, 23, 24
First-aid ideas **124–5**, 124–5
Fittings, light **36–97**
  categorization of 40
  design themes 41–6
  families 46, 46
  manufacturers 47
  upgrading 123
  see also under individual types, e.g. Downlighters
"Flemish-style" (Chelsom) 72
Flex 172
  concealing 124, 146
  as a design element 60,

76, 60, 64, 67, 68, 156
extending 174
"Flex" (Martinelli Luce) 80
Floodlamps 30
Floodlights 55, 57
exterior 96, 164, 98, 164
Floor lights **86–93**, 86–93
adjustable 46, 124
in bedrooms 124
in hallways 129
in living rooms 146, 147
in studies 162, 163
"Flopi" (Luci) 73
Flos 47
floor lights 43, 86, 87, 91, 93
pendants 42, 58
spotlights 54
table lights 70, 73
wall lights 69, 70, 73
Flowers, lighting **116–17**, 116–17
outdoors 97, 164, 97, 166
"Flu" (Luci) 67
Fluorescent lamps **33–5**, 182, 28, 33–5
atmosphere created by 20
circular 66, 67
colour appearance 66, 12
colour rendering 14, 29, 15
decorative use of 137
for display lighting 113, 114, 115
fittings for **66–7**, 177, 66–7, 74, 75, 82, 95, 144
invention of 25
in kitchens 134, 133, 135
miniature **34–5**, 66, 96, 150, 28, 34–5, 84, 92
and plant growth 117
portable 106
principles of 11, 34
for task lighting 76, 77, 102, 162, 77, 102
track systems 66
"Fold" (Raak) 83
Footcandles 12
Forcolini, Carolo 63
Form, light and **18–19**, 18–19

19, 118–19
Fuses
in fusebox 170
in plugs 174

G
Garden lighting **164–7**, 164–7
fittings for **96–7**, 96–7
Gecchelin, Bruno 74, 80, 81
Geissler, Heinrich 25
"Germana" (Luci) 63
"G.H." (Eleusi) 93
"Giardino" (Goccia) 99
"Giotto" (Ve Art Luce) 41
"Giovi" (Flos) 69
Gismondo, Ernesto 74, 82
Glare 16–17, 59, 144, 124, 16
background lighting and 104
in bedrooms 148
from exterior lights 96, 164
in seating areas 78–9
on staircases 130
with task lighting 102
with wall washing 108
Glass
bottomlighting 18, 114
candlelight and 154
non-reflective 112
reflections off 112, 16
"Glass form I" (Boyd) 73
Glove lights 18, 136, 162–3
for exterior use 129, 96–7
paper 58, 59, 60
wall lights 68
GLS lamps 30, 31, 31
"Gobbo" (Bilumen) 80
Goccia exterior lights 99
"Gomito" (Stilnovo) 70
Goose lights 111, 106
Gray, Eileen 144
Grolux tubes 117
"Guild House" (Eleusi) 93
exterior lights 84
table lights 84
wall lights 68
Guzzini, i 46
exterior lights 98
table lights 84

H
Halls **128–31**, 51, 128–31
"Halo Beam" (Brillantleuchten) 84
"Halo in the Air" (Shiu Kay Kan) 95
Hearth, pull of the 20, 20
Hemisphere, in light fittings 41
History of lighting **22–5**, 22–5

Hoffmann, Josef 152–3
Holme, Gregory 74
"Hot Dog" (Brillantleuchten) 124
House numbers, illuminated 96, 129, 128
"Horus" (Eleusi) 44

I
Illuminance 12, 16
Incandescent lighting 12, 13, 29
Indirect lighting 39, 104, 39, 153
fluorescent lights 66
task lights 78, 78, 151
uplighters 88
wall lights 71, 71, 151
"Ippogrifo" (Controluce) 59

J
Jewelry, spotlighting 114
"Jill" (Areluce) 87, 86, 87, 88, 149
"Jim" (Ve Art Luce) 41
"Jo-Jo" (Areluce) 64
Junction boxes 178
circuits 171
adding spurs from 175
multi-terminal 180

K
"Kandido" (Luci) 62
"Kea" (Leucos) 65
King, Perry 47, 65, 72, 80, 81
Kitchens **132–7**, 132–7
fluorescent lighting 14, 102, 102
task lighting 102, 102
Koch and Lowy
floor lights 90, 92
wall lights 72, 73
Kovacs
floor lights 91, 92
pendants 64
table lights 84

L
Lamp types **26–35**, 28–35
"Lampiata" (Stilnovo) 85
Landing lights 130, 130, 131
Langmuir, Irving 24
"Le Bagnanti" (Cil) 46
"Leggio" (Stilnovo) 92
Lehé, Albert 85
Lenses 39, 39
in downlighters 39, 163, 139
in spotlights 53

Leucos
pendants 65
table lights 83
"Libra" (Controluce) 41
Libraries 123, **162–3**, 110, 123, 162–3
"Lichtballon" (Brillantleuchten) 72
Licio, L. de 74
Light
measurement of **12**
nature of **10–11**
"Light Ball" (Flos) 42
Living rooms **144–7**, 144–7
Loop-in circuits 171, 178, 171, 178
"Lotto" (Luci) 98
Lotus fountain light 98, 99
"Lotus" (Boyd) 75
Louvers 39, 39
in downlighters 39, 48
in exterior lights 96
in fluorescent fittings 39, 66
in pendants 60
Low-energy light sources 35, 96
Low-voltage exterior lights 97, 167
Low-voltage halogen bulbs 32, 32
Low-voltage spotlamps 30
Luci
exterior 98
floor lights 43, 91, 92, 93
fluorescent fittings 66, 67
pendants 44, 62, 63
spotlights 57
table lights 83
wall lights 73, 75
"L'Una" (Ve Art Luce) 41
"Lytesphere" (Concord) 56

M
"Main Street Due" (Eleusi) 67
Maintenance 182
"Maniglia" (Stilnovo) 86
"Mantis" (Areluce) 80
Manufacturers 47
Manzu, P. 93
"Maria Theresa" (Chelsom) 62
Marianelli, Giorgio 63, 84, 90, 91, 93
Marlin
downlighters 49
exterior lights 96
Martinelli Luce
table lights 83, 85
task lights 80, 81
Maurer, Ingo 46, 111
Mazzucchelli and Fiorin 74
Megalit
table lights 95
task lights 67, 80, 82
"Megaron" (Artemide) 148
"Memphis" (Drimmer) 83
Memphis group 111
Mercatali, Davide 84
Mesh panels in fittings 44
Metal halide lamps 35, 91
"Mezzaluna" (Skipper) 76, 144
Militscher, Orit 75
Miniature fluorescent lamps **34–5**, 34–5
"Minibasket" (Eleusi) 84
"Minibox" (Stilnovo) 75
"Mini-Multigroove" (Concord) 49
Miranda, Santiago 47, 65, 72, 80, 81
Mirror lights 140, 73, 139
in bathrooms 140, 139, 141
in living rooms 144, 145
"Moni" (Flos) 62
"Monkey" (Areluce) 57
Montaguti, Gabriella 84
Montoya, Juan 122
Monumentalism 42, 118
Mood lighting 20, **143**
in bedrooms 148
in dining rooms 156
Morgan, David 81
"Multiplica" (Stilnovo) 58, 92

N
"Nastro" (Stilnovo) 94
Neon lighting 35, 140, 94, 106, 140
1970s vogue for 106
early 25
Nernst lamp 24, 25
Night lights 161
"Noa" (Luci) 83
Novelty lights 76, 161, 94–5
Nursery lights 160–61

O
Oil lamps 22, 143, 22
"Oluce task lights 81
"Omega" (Studio Editions) 43
One-Off Ltd 94
Opal bulbs 29
Optelma
table lights 42, 45
wall lights 46

P
"Pall" (Tronconi) 84
"Palma" (Stilnovo) 74
"Palomar" (Stilnovo) 86
Pamio, Roberto 83
"Papillona" (Flos) 91
PAR lamps **30**, 48, 54, 56, 166–7
cool beam 30, 117, 49
for exterior use 97
"Parentesi" (Flos) 54–5, 93
Paths, garden 164
Patios 164, 97, 99, 164, 165
Pearl bulbs 29
Pedrizzetti, Paolo 84
"Pellicano" (New Society) 42
Pelmet lighting 66, 105
Pendants **58–65**, 58–65, 73
in bedrooms 148, 150
central 59, 132, 148
defining space with 118, 118
fluorescent 66
in halls 129
industrial-style 135
installation 176, 173
in kitchens 132, 134, 133
over dining tables 156–7, 156, 159
repositioning 124–5, 125
rise and fall 162, 62, 63, 159
in seating areas 144, 118
shades for 39
in studies 162, 162–3
Penney-Bernstein Inc. 92
"Periscopio" (Stilnovo) 81, 86
"Perpetua" (Flos) 84
"Petite Fleur" (Brillantleuchten) 85
"Pfister" (Boyd) 72
"Pharo" (Stilnovo) 45
Philips
downlighters 48, 49
fluorescent fittings 67
PL lamp 34, 67
SL lamp 34
spotlights 54, 56
"Piatto" (Stilnovo) 63
Picture lights 72
Pictures
display lighting 48, **112–13**, 112–13, 128
table lights beneath 79
wall washing 108
"Pinco" (Tronconi) 65
"Pinhole" downlighter 139
"Pipeline" (Thorn EMI) 66
"Pitagora" (Martinelli Luce) 85
Piluce 99
PL miniature fluorescents 34, 67

Planning **120-23**, 120-23
Plants, lighting **116-17**, 154, 164-7
outdoors 97, 164-5, 97, 146, 174
Plug-in lights 120, 124, in bedrooms 150
spotlights 54
wiring 146, 174
Plugs 174
Pool lighting 166, 166-7
Porch lights 20, 128, 128
Porsche, F.A. 62
"Powerwasher" (Concord) 57
"Prestige" (Concord) 57
Profile spots see Framing projectors
"Psiche" (Brillantleuchten) 95
Psychology of lighting **20–21**, 20, 21

Q
"Quartet Major" (Concord) 57
"Quarto" (Flos) 70, 122, 154-5

R
Raak 83
Reading 103
Reading lights 71, **76-85**, 88, 162, 76-83, 84, 92
in bedrooms 150, 161
Reflectance 15, 39, 88, 104
Reflections
glare from 16, 16
in picture lighting 112
for revealing form and texture **18-19**, 18-19
in table tops 79
Reflector lamps 29, **30**, 124, 30
Reflectors
dichroic 30, 63
dimpled 38
disc-shaped 41
in downlighters 48
effect at finish 48
in light fittings 38
in floor lights 86
shape of 39
Refraction 39
Remote-control switches 47
Right angles in fittings 43
"Ring" (Arteluce) 80
"Rio" (Luci) 66, 67
Rise-and-fall pendants 58, 66, 58, 59, 61, 62, 63, 159
installing 177
Rizzato, Paolo 75
"Roof I" (Brillantleuchten) 99
Room size 15, 58, 104
Rotaflex spotlights 54

S
Safety
in children's rooms 160
exterior lighting 96
planning 120, 121
replacing 174
spurs from 175
Salvati and Tresoldi 73
"Samurai" (Stilnovo) 42, 93
Sapper, Richard 76
"Sarasar" (Leucos) 83
Sarfatti, Gino 62, 80, 81
"Scarpa" (Flos) 158
Scarpa, Tobia 73, 84, 91
Sculpture, lighting **19**, 114, 18-19
Seating areas 59-60, 78, 144, 118, 118
Security lights exterior 97, 128-9, interior 146
Sedap 42
Seris, Georges 62
Shades **39**, 39
conical 78
diffusers in 44
gas mantle 110, 72
glare and 17
for pendants 59, 60
stepped 45
for table lights 80-81
Tiffany 106, 110
for wall lights 71
Shadows patterns 148
in picture lighting 112
from plants 117, 117
1960s vogue for 111
lamps for 30, 30
in kitchens 133, 137
in halls 129
framing projectors 112
floor-standing 86, 55
exterior 164, 165, 96, 97, 165, 166
Shelf lighting **113-14**, 114
in studies and libraries 163, 162-3
and reflective surfaces 120
to reveal form 18, 19
for shelf lighting 114
wall-mounted 68
for wall washing 108, 107
"Shell" (Boyd) 90
Shiu Kay Kan
Sierakowski, Piotr 90
Sigheaki, Asahara 83
Silverware candlelight on 154
downlighters on 155
Sirrah pendants 59
table lights 85
wall lights 46
Skipper wall lights 74
Socket outlets 171, 173, 174
adding 175
planning 120, 121
replacing 174
spurs from 175
Sodium lighting 10, 13, 14, 63
"Solitaire" (Tronconi) 76, 63
Sonneman, Robert 91
Sottsass, Ettore 47, 93
Sources of light **26-35**, 26-35
Sparkle 17, 17
Spectrum, electromagnetic 10-11
Sphere motif in light fittings 42
"Splügen Bräu" 58
Sportes, Ronald 90
"Spot-on" (Thorn EMI) 56
Spotlamps **30**, 30
Spotlights **52-7**, **52-7**
in dining rooms 157
exterior 164, 165, 96, 97, 165, 166
floor-standing 86, 55
framing projectors 112
in halls 129
in kitchens 133, 137
lamps for 30, 30
1960s vogue for 111
from plants 117, 117
in picture lighting 112
patterns 148
decorative effects 52, 107
clip-on 124
in children's rooms 161
in bathrooms 141
two-way 179, 180, 181
with wall lights 71
on spotlights 54
remote-control 47
"Swan Line" 85
Swan, Joseph 23
Sunset Ceramics 94
"Suitcase" (Shiu Kay Kan) 85
Submersible lights 97, 166, 166
Style, creating **110-11**, 110, 111
Studio Tecnico 65
Studio lights 86
table lights 86
Studio Editions picture lights 72
Studies 102, **162-3**, 162, 163
tungsten strip lamps 30
for shelving 113-14, 134, 135, 136
in kitchens 134, 132-3
concealed 104-105, 104, 105, 128
Strip lighting in bathrooms 140
Storage units 134, 133, 94
wall lights 45, 70, 74, 75
Spurs, adding 171, 175, 178
Staff exterior lighting 98
Staircases 129-30
wiring for 181
Stairwells 60
Standard lamps 86
"Starter" (Concord) 56
Steps, exterior 164
"Stelo" (Tronconi) 90
Stern, Robert A.M. 123
Stilnovo 46
floor lights 86, 118, 86, 90, 92, 93
pendants 62, 63, 65
spotlights 45
"Sintesi Professionale" (Artemide) 74
spotlighting 114
"Sistema Gru" (Tronconi) 91
"600" (Arteluce) 80

T
Table lights **76-85**, 107, 76-85, 94, 95, 133, 149, 150-51
adjustable 46
for lighting objects 78-9, 113, 115
as symbol of welcome 20
"Taccia" (Flos) 85
Tag 75
"Tap Giardino" (Piuluce) 99
"Targa 50" (Concord) 56
"Targa" (Luci) **29-30**, 28, 30
Task lights 10, **76-85**, 76-85, 94
Tasks, light needed for 103
for shelf lighting 114
"Techlinea" (Boyd) 75
Television lighting for viewing 79, 144
"Tender" (Tronconi) 85
"Tenderone" (Tronconi) 164
Texture, light and 18-19, 18-19
Thorn EMI fluorescent track 66
spotlights 56
2D lamp 34, 35
Tiffany shades 106, 110
Time switches 97, 146
"Tizio" (Artemide) 76, 77, 78, 141, 148, 149
"Tobia" (Tronconi) 84
"Tokio" (Flos) 87, 86, 87
"Toltec" (Concord) 91
"Tomo" (Luci) 93
"Tomos" (Sirrah) 82
"Torre" (Stilnovo) 46
Toshiba Neoball 34
Toshiyuki Kita 57, 93
Toso, Renato 83
"Totem" (Drimmer) 85
Track lighting 110, 114, 121, 53, 128
traditional rooms 111
in studies and libraries 163, 163
switches for 47
Traditional-style lighting 110, 143
pendant fittings 60
in studies and libraries 163
colour of 124
exterior 96
highlighting **108-109**, 108, 109
washing with light 50, **108**, 157, 51, 75, 150, 151
"Trapezio" (Luci) 44
Transformers 30, 92 for exterior lighting 181
Trees 96, 97, **164**, 97, 164
Tronconi floor lights 47, 90, 91, 93
pendants 44, 47, 63, 65
table lights 47, 84, 85
wall lights 47, 83
"Tulipano" (Luci) 91
Tungsten-filament lamps **29-30**, 28, 30
colour rendering 14, 28, 133, 15
colour temperature 13, 29
history of **22-25**, 23, 24, 25
mood of 20
for plants 117
Tungsten-halogen lamps **32-3**, 32-3
colour characteristics 28
in downlighters 48
in floodlights (exterior) 164
in uplighters 86-7, 88

U
"Uno" (Eleusi) 95
Uplighters **86-93**, 104, 86-93
in bedrooms 150
in halls 129
for picture lighting 112
portable 91
in seating areas 144
in traditional rooms 111
vertical emphasis of 118
wall-mounted 68
for wall washing 108, 109

V
Ve Art Luce table lights 41
uplighters 41
wall lights 41
"Veronica" (Luci) 43

W
Wall lights **68-75**, 41, 45, 68-75, 95, 133
adjustable 46
exterior 96, 96, 97
matched to pendants 60
on mirror walls 139
spotlights 54
Walls colour of 124
exterior 96
highlighting **108-109**, 108, 109
washing with light 50, **108**, 157, 51, 75, 150, 151
Water exterior lighting 166
"Wedge" (Boyd) 74
Welcome lights 128, 20, 51, 128
Willson, David Winfield 64
Wiring for exterior lighting 96, 181
do-it-yourself **170-81**
new installations 124
planning 121

Z
"Ziggurat" (Stilnovo) 44
Zotta, Mario 80

Acknowledgments

Picture credits

The credits are listed in the following order: page number, position on page, source (photographer and/or agent in the case of photographs; source of reference material in the case of artwork). Pictures of light fittings were supplied by the manufacturers except where otherwise credited in this list.

Abbreviations
EWA Elizabeth Whiting Associates
MBI Mitchell Beazley International
l left r right b bottom t top
c centre

cover: Santi Caleca
half-title: Tronconi
title: Maison Francaise/Luc de Champris
p. 5: tl Eleusi, tr Brillantleuchten A.G., bl Boyd Lighting Co., br Luci
p. 7: Daniel Rozensztroch/Gilles de Chabaneix
p. 9: Santi Caleca
p. 11: David Parker/Science Photo Library
p. 12: t, cl, cr Marco de Valdivia, b Deidi von Schaewen
p. 14: John Cullen Lighting Design, r Tom Leighton/EWA
p. 15: Steve Tanner/MBI
p. 16: t Deidi von Schaewen/Ricardo Bofill
p. 17: Mark Ross/Tom Foerderer
p. 18: l Maison Francaise/Jacques Primois, r Carla de Benedetti
p. 19: Steve Tanner/MBI
p. 20: l Neil Lorimer/EWA, r Maison Francaise/Luc de Champris
p. 21: l Norman McGrath, r Andreas Einsiedel
p. 22: tl B.P.C.C./Aldus Archive, tr Michael Boys, bl Design Council, br B.P.C.C./Aldus Archive
p. 23: tl Mary Evans Picture Library, tr, b Ann Ronan Picture Library
p. 24: br Ann Ronan, all others Mary Evans Picture Library
p. 25: Mary Evans Picture Library
p. 27: Paul Brierley
p. 28: Strenger Color
p. 29: l Strenger Color, r GTE Sylvania Ltd.
p. 31: Chart based on information from Philips Lighting
p. 32: Chart based on information from Philips Lighting
p. 33: Diagrams based on information from GTE Sylvania Ltd.
p. 35: Artwork based on manufacturer's catalogue
p. 37: Arteluce
p. 38–47: Artwork based on manufacturers' catalogues

p. 50: tl, tr Brillantleuchten A.G., bl Emmett Bright, br Maison Francaise/Christian Gervais
p. 51: l Carla de Benedetti, r Emmett Bright
p. 53: Cutaway spotlight illustration based on information from Marlin, framing projector illustration from Concord
p. 54: t Norman McGrath, b Carla de Benedetti
p. 55: l Carla de Benedetti, r Richard Einzig/Arcaid
p. 58: bl Spike Powell/EWA, remainder supplied by manufacturers
p. 60: t, bl Camera Press, br Carla de Benedetti
p. 61: l Tim Saar/Arcaid, tr Camera Press, br Norman McGrath
p. 66: Carla de Benedetti
p. 67: tl and bl Carla de Benedetti, remainder supplied by manufacturers
p. 70: tl Stilnovo, bl Marco de Valdivia, tr Pascal Hinous/Agence Top/ Trigano, br Clive Helm/EWA
p. 71: t Carla de Benedetti, b Daniel Rozensztroch/Gilles de Chabaneix
p. 74: tc The Design Council, London, remainder supplied by manufacturers
p. 75: br The Design Council, London, remainder supplied by manufacturers
p. 78: t Maison Francaise/Jacques Primois, b Camera Press
p. 79: tl Maison Francaise/Christian Gervais, tr John Cullen Lighting Design, b Spike Powell/EWA
p. 80: bl, c (red light) The Design Council, London, remainder supplied by manufacturers
p. 81: tl, br, tr The Design Council, London, remainder supplied by manufacturers
p. 83: tl The Design Council, London, remainder supplied by manufacturers
p. 84: Pictures supplied by manufacturers and Camera Press
p. 88: t Deidi von Schaewen, b Maison Francaise/Christian Gervais
p. 89: t Maison Francaise/Christian Gervais, bl Maison Francaise/Arcadia, bc Deidi von Schaewen, br Abitare
p. 90: bl Deidi von Schaewen/Ronald Sportes, bc Richard Bryant/Arcaid, remainder supplied by manufacturers
p. 94: l Carla de Benedetti, c Design Council, London, remainder supplied by manufacturers
p. 95: tl Design Council, London,

p. 97: tr Camera Press, remainder supplied by manufacturers
p. 101: Concord Lighting Ltd.
p. 102: Peter Aaron/ESTO
p. 103: Camera Press
p. 104: Abitare
p. 105: Abitare
p. 106: l Mark Ross/Geoffrey Hassman, r Marco de Valdivia
p. 107: t Spike Powell/EWA, b Deidi von Schaewen, r Carla de Benedetti
p. 108: Spike Powell/EWA
p. 109: Marco de Valdivia
p. 110: l Andreas Einsiedel, r Marco de Valdivia
p. 111: Deidi von Schaewen
p. 112: Pascal Hinous/Agence Top
p. 113: l Andreas Einsiedel, r Frank Herholdt/EWA
p. 114: Deidi von Schaewen
p. 115: tl Andreas Einsiedel, tr Norman McGrath, b Carla de Benedetti
p. 116: l Carla de Benedetti, r Andrew Kolesnikow
p. 117: Joe Kelly
p. 118: Deidi von Schaewen
p. 119: tl Jillian Nieman/EWA, b Maison Francaise/Christian Gervais
p. 121: Deidi von Schaewen
p. 122: Norman McGrath, plan based on information from Juan Montoya Design Corp.
p. 123: Peter Aaron/ESTO, plan based on information from Robert A.M. Stern Architects
p. 124: l Deidi von Schaewen, r Brillantleuchten A.G.
p. 125: l Daniel Rozensztroch/Gilles de Chabaneix, r Camera Press
p. 127: Carla de Benedetti
p. 128: tl Marco de Valdivia, bl Camera Press, r Peter Aaron/ESTO
p. 129: Marco de Valdivia
p. 130: tl Andrew Kolesnikow, bl Maison Francaise/Christian Gervais, r Richard Bryant/Arcaid
p. 131: Peter Aaron/ESTO
p. 132: Richard Bryant/Arcaid
p. 133: Pascal Hinous/Agence Top/D. Kieffer
p. 134: l Abitare, r Carla de Benedetti
p. 135: l Michael Dunne/EWA, r Tim Street-Porter/EWA
p. 136: t Michael Boys, b Ron Sutherland/ EWA
p. 137: l Norman McGrath, r Maison Francaise/Christian Gervais
p. 138: l Maison Francaise/Christian Gervais, b Lucinda Lambton/ Arcaid
p. 139: Andrew Kolesnikow
p. 140: Carla de Benedetti
p. 141: tl Daniel Rozensztroch/Jan Staller, bl Camera Press, r Carla de Benedetti

p. 142: l Clive Helm/EWA, r Andreas Einsiedel
p. 143: t Andreas Einsiedel, b Camera Press
p. 144: t Norman McGrath, b Maison Francaise/Jean-Pierre Godeaut
p. 145: Mark Ross/Geoffrey Hassman
p. 146: Carla de Benedetti
p. 147: t Marco de Valdivia, b Camera Press
p. 148: Maison Francaise/Christian Gervais
p. 149: Carla de Benedetti
p. 150: t Maison Francaise/Christian Gervais, b Lucinda Lambton/ Arcaid
p. 151: Maison Francaise/Christian Gervais
p. 152: t Camera Press, r Carla de Benedetti
p. 153: Peter Aaron/ESTO
p. 154: Maison Francaise/Arcadia
p. 156: tl Emmett Bright, tr H. Dettling/ Suzanne Schwarz, b Deidi von Schaewen/Ricardo Bofill
p. 157: Carla de Benedetti
p. 158: t Marco de Valdivia, b Camera Press, r Norman McGrath
p. 159: W. Luthy/Suzanne Schwarz
p. 160: l Brillantleuchten A.G., b Jessica Strang
p. 161: Staff Leuchtenwerke GmbH
p. 162: t Carla de Benedetti, b Camera Press
p. 163: Andreas Einsiedel
p. 164: l Concord Lighting Ltd., r Norman McGrath
p. 165: t Tim Street-Porter/EWA, b Staff Leuchtenwerke GmbH
p. 166: tl Stapeley Water Gardens, tr Peter Burian Associates, b Richard Einzig/Arcaid
p. 167: Peter Aaron/ESTO

Other credits

The author and publishers would like to thank the following for their generous help in the making of this book: The Lighting Workshop (London) for checking the addresses list, glossary and lamp chart and for general help and encouragement; Thorn EMI Lighting Ltd (and in particular J. Kenney) for checking technical information in the text; Philips Lighting (and in particular A.F. Heathcote) for advice about tungsten-halogen lamps; Peter Burian for advice on garden lighting and on employing designers and consultants.

Fittings used as artwork references were kindly lent by the Lighting Workshop and Anglepoise Lighting. The chair photographed for page 15 was lent by Harrods.